Reading Ideas in Victorian Literature

Edinburgh Critical Studies in Victorian Culture
Series Editor: Julian Wolfreys

Recent books in the series:
Rudyard Kipling's Fiction: Mapping Psychic Spaces
Lizzy Welby

The Decadent Image: The Poetry of Wilde, Symons and Dowson
Kostas Boyiopoulos

British India and Victorian Literary Culture
Máire ní Fhlathúin

Anthony Trollope's Late Style: Victorian Liberalism and Literary Form
Frederik Van Dam

Dark Paradise: Pacific Islands in the Nineteenth-Century British Imagination
Jenn Fuller

Twentieth-Century Victorian: Arthur Conan Doyle and the Strand Magazine, 1891–1930
Jonathan Cranfield

The Lyric Poem and Aestheticism: Forms of Modernity
Marion Thain

Gender, Technology and the New Woman
Lena Wånggren

Self-Harm in New Woman Writing
Alexandra Gray

Suffragist Artists in Partnership: Gender, Word and Image
Lucy Ella Rose

Victorian Liberalism and Material Culture: Synergies of Thought and Place
Kevin A. Morrison

The Victorian Male Body
Joanne-Ella Parsons and Ruth Heholt

Nineteenth-Century Settler Emigration in British Literature and Art
Fariha Shaikh

The Pre-Raphaelites and Orientalism
Eleonora Sasso

The Late-Victorian Little Magazine
Koenraad Claes

Coastal Cultures of the Long Nineteenth Century
Matthew Ingleby and Matt P. M. Kerr

Dickens and Demolition: Literary Afterlives and Mid-Nineteenth-Century Urban Development
Joanna Hofer-Robinson

Artful Experiments: Ways of Knowing in Victorian Literature and Science
Philipp Erchinger

Victorian Poetry and the Poetics of the Literary Periodical
Caley Ehnes

The Victorian Actress in the Novel and on the Stage
Renata Kobetts Miller

Dickens's Clowns: Charles Dickens, Joseph Grimaldi and the Pantomime of Life
Jonathan Buckmaster

Italian Politics and Nineteenth-Century British Literature and Culture
Patricia Cove

Cultural Encounters with the Arabian Nights in Nineteenth-Century Britain
Melissa Dickson

Novel Institutions: Anachronism, Irish Novels and Nineteenth-Century Realism
Mary L. Mullen

The Fin-de-Siècle Scottish Revival: Romance, Decadence and Celtic Identity
Michael Shaw

Contested Liberalisms: Martineau, Dickens and the Victorian Press
Iain Crawford

Plotting Disability in the Nineteenth-Century Novel
Clare Walker Gore

The Aesthetics of Space in Nineteenth-Century British Literature, 1843–1907
Giles Whiteley

The Persian Presence in Victorian Poetry
Reza Taher-Kermani

Rereading Orphanhood: Texts, Inheritance, Kin
Diane Warren and Laura Peters

Plotting the News in the Victorian Novel
Jessica R. Valdez

Reading Ideas in Victorian Literature: Literary Content as Artistic Experience
Patrick Fessenbecker

Forthcoming volumes:
Her Father's Name: Gender, Theatricality and Spiritualism in Florence Marryat's Fiction
Tatiana Kontou

The Sculptural Body in Victorian Literature: Encrypted Sexualities
Patricia Pulham

Olive Schreiner and the Politics of Print Culture, 1883–1920
Clare Gill

Victorian Auto/Biography: Problems in Genre and Subject
Amber Regis

Gissing, Shakespeare and the Life of Writing
Thomas Ue

Women's Mobility in Henry James
Anna Despotopoulou

Michael Field's Revisionary Poetics
Jill Ehnenn

The Americanisation of W.T. Stead
Helena Goodwyn

Literary Illusions: Performance Magic and Victorian Literature
Christopher Pittard

Pastoral in Early-Victorian Fiction: Environment and Modernity
Mark Frost

Edmund Yates and Victorian Periodicals: Gossip, Celebrity, and Gendered Spaces
Kathryn Ledbetter

Literature, Architecture and Perversion: Building Sexual Culture in Europe, 1850–1930
Aina Marti

Oscar Wilde and the Radical Politics of the Fin de Siècle
Deaglán Ó Donghaile

Home and Identity in Nineteenth-Century Literary London
Lisa Robertson

Manufacturing Female Beauty in British Literature and Periodicals, 1850–1914
Michelle Smith

New Media and the Rise of the Popular Woman Writer, 1820–60
Alexis Easley

For a complete list of titles published visit the Edinburgh Critical Studies in Victorian Culture web page at www.edinburghuniversitypress.com/series/ECVC

Also Available:
Victoriographies – A Journal of Nineteenth-Century Writing, 1790–1914, edited by Diane Piccitto and Patricia Pulham
ISSN: 2044-2416
www.eupjournals.com/vic

Reading Ideas in Victorian Literature

Literary Content as Artistic Experience

Patrick Fessenbecker

Edinburgh University Press is one of the leading university presses in the UK. We publish academic books and journals in our selected subject areas across the humanities and social sciences, combining cutting-edge scholarship with high editorial and production values to produce academic works of lasting importance. For more information visit our website: edinburghuniversitypress.com

© Patrick Fessenbecker, 2020, 2022

First published in hardback by Edinburgh University Press 2020

Edinburgh University Press Ltd
The Tun – Holyrood Road, 12(2f) Jackson's Entry, Edinburgh EH8 8PJ

Typeset in 11/13 Adobe Sabon by
IDSUK (DataConnection) Ltd

A CIP record for this book is available from the British Library

ISBN 978 1 4744 6060 6 (hardback)
ISBN 978 1 4744 6061 3 (paperback)
ISBN 978 1 4744 6062 0 (webready PDF)
ISBN 978 1 4744 6063 7 (epub)

The right of Patrick Fessenbecker to be identifiedastheauthorofthisworkhasbeen asserted in accordance with the Copyright, Designs and Patents Act 1988, and the Copyright and Related Rights Regulations 2003 (SI No. 2498).

Contents

Series Editor's Preface	vi
Acknowledgements	viii
List of Abbreviations	xi
Introduction: In Defence of Paraphrase	1
1. Content and Form	39
2. Anthony Trollope on Akrasia, Self-Deception and Ethical Confusion	76
3. Justifying Anachronism	108
4. The Scourge of the Unwilling: George Eliot on the Sources of Normativity	140
5. Everyday Aesthetics and the Experience of the Profound	173
6. Robert Browning, Augusta Webster and the Role of Morality	203
Epilogue: Between Immersion and Critique – Thoughtful Reading	232
Index	238

Series Editor's Preface

'Victorian' is a term, at once indicative of a strongly determined concept and an often notoriously vague notion, emptied of all meaningful content by the many journalistic misconceptions that persist about the inhabitants and cultures of the British Isles and Victoria's Empire in the nineteenth century. As such, it has become a by-word for the assumption of various, often contradictory habits of thought, belief, behaviour and perceptions. Victorian studies and studies in nineteenth-century literature and culture have, from their institutional inception, questioned narrowness of presumption, pushed at the limits of the nominal definition, and have sought to question the very grounds on which the unreflective perception of the so-called Victorian has been built; and so they continue to do. Victorian and nineteenth-century studies of literature and culture maintain a breadth and diversity of interest, of focus and inquiry, in an interrogative and intellectually open-minded and challenging manner, which are equal to the exploration and inquisitiveness of its subjects. Many of the questions asked by scholars and researchers of the innumerable productions of nineteenth-century society actively put into suspension the clichés and stereotypes of 'Victorianism', whether the approach has been sustained by historical, scientific, philosophical, empirical, ideological or theoretical concerns; indeed, it would be incorrect to assume that each of these approaches to the idea of the Victorian has been, or has remained, in the main exclusive, sealed off from the interests and engagements of other approaches. A vital interdisciplinarity has been pursued and embraced, for the most part, even as there has been contest and debate amongst Victorianists, pursued with as much fervour as the affirmative exploration between different disciplines and differing epistemologies put to work in the service of reading the nineteenth century.

Edinburgh Critical Studies in Victorian Culture aims to take up both the debates and the inventive approaches and departures from convention that studies in the nineteenth century have witnessed for the last half century at least. Aiming to maintain a 'Victorian' (in the most positive sense of that motif) spirit of inquiry, the series' purpose is to continue and augment the cross-fertilisation of interdisciplinary approaches, and to offer, in addition, a number of timely and untimely revisions of Victorian literature, culture, history and identity. At the same time, the series will ask questions concerning what has been missed or improperly received, misread, or not read at all, in order to present a multifaceted and heterogeneous kaleidoscope of representations. Drawing on the most provocative, thoughtful and original research, the series will seek to prod at the notion of the 'Victorian', and in so doing, principally through theoretically and epistemologically sophisticated close readings of the historicity of literature and culture in the nineteenth century, to offer the reader provocative insights into a world that is at once overly familiar, and irreducibly different, other and strange. Working from original sources, primary documents and recent interdisciplinary theoretical models, Edinburgh Critical Studies in Victorian Culture seeks not simply to push at the boundaries of research in the nineteenth century, but also to inaugurate the persistent erasure and provisional, strategic redrawing of those borders.

Julian Wolfreys

Acknowledgements

Perhaps more so than is usually the case, the origins of this book lie in a single moment. Meeting with me after reading another interminable dissertation chapter, my advisor Amanda Anderson told me, with just a hint of asperity, 'You can't treat novels like they just say things!' Although I had been thinking about the relationship between philosophy and literature for years, Amanda articulated in that moment the real question I was asking: why don't we treat literary works as if they say things, and what would an interpretive practice and artistic theory based on valuing them for what they said look like? My first thanks go to her for that question, and for supervising the beginnings of this book with patience and rigour; I hope her concerns have been at least to some extent addressed. And I am grateful to everyone who made Johns Hopkins into an enormously rich environment for interdisciplinary work in the humanities. Seminars from Amanda, Sharon Cameron, Yi-Ping Ong and Mark Jenkins introduced me to many of the works and thinkers described in these pages, and I'm grateful too for conversations with my fellow students – Maggie Vinter, Kara Wedekind, Robert Day, Nick Bujak, Doug Tye, Rob Higney and others. Matthew Flaherty and Roger Maioli deserve special mention: I'm humbled by the way they have acknowledged my work in the development of their own thinking and am delighted to be able to return the favour.

In the Program for Cultures, Civilizations, and Ideas at Bilkent I've been extremely fortunate in my colleagues, who combine polyglot capacities with humility in ways that I certainly would not. Thanks especially to Cory Stockwell, Daniel Leonard, Will Coker, Nathan Leidholm, Buffy Turner, Dragan Ilic, Costa Costantini, Victor Lenthe and not least Mustafa al-Nakeeb, who hired me. Several faculty members outside CCI are helping to invigorate anglophone literary studies at Bilkent and have graciously made time to read and listen to my work in doing so: let me thank Patrick Hart, Tara

Needham, Timothy Wright, Jonathan Williams and Stein Haugom Olsen for their valuable comments. Sandrine Berges is a model of academic charity; her invitations to present my work to the philosophy department at Bilkent are greatly appreciated.

My two-year fellowship at the Centre for Uses of Literature at the University of Southern Denmark was a magnificent opportunity to reframe the project after a wrong turn. The Centre modelled for me what it means to be genuinely supportive of fellow scholars: this book would be much, much worse than it is without the chance I had to work there. Peter Simonsen, Anne-Mari Mai, Klaus Petersen, Anita Wohlmann, Emily Hogg, Sophy Kohler, Mathies Græsborg, Marie Elisabeth-Holm, Anne-Marie Søndergaard Christensen and Alastair Morrison all read and commented on various aspects of the project. The Welfare State studies group was open-minded enough to read and think through a version of Chapter 3: Pieter Vanhuysse, Peter Starke and Paul Marx in particular engaged it carefully. My office-mate, collaborator and friend Bryan Yazell deserves special notice: it's been a pleasure writing with him. My thanks to all.

No academic has done as much to support this book as Rita Felski. In the midst of carrying out her own sophisticated rethinking of method in literary criticism, she has found ways to make possible methodological reflections on the part of many other scholars, and I have been lucky to have benefited from her efforts. My relationship with Rita began in the summer of 2012, when on one of the more exciting days of my life I got an email informing me that my essay 'In Defense of Paraphrase' had won the Ralph W. Cohen Prize and would appear in *New Literary History*. In talking with Rita since then, first at an NLH seminar on post-critical methods in Charlottesville and then more substantially in Denmark, I have been amazed at the breadth of her knowledge and the depth of her energy for scholarship. I can only aspire to it.

Academic work is made possible by many people, though, who too often go unnoticed; let me not continue the practice. I've been lucky to work with a number of kind and helpful academic administrators: Karen Tiefenwerth and Nicole Goode at Johns Hopkins, Süheyla Yılmaz at Bilkent, and especially Pernille Hasselsteen at SDU have made a number of aspects of my work easier. Portions of this book have appeared previously in *New Literary History* and *Victorian Studies*; my gratitude is due to both journals and their staffs for permission to republish. Michelle Houston at Edinburgh University Press is a prompt, sympathetic and thoughtful correspondent, who was always willing to find time for me and my work; we should all be sending our best stuff to Michelle. And Hira Noor helped me with the final manuscript preparation at a crucial moment.

But the last thanks must go to my wife Wilhelmina, who has sacrificed more for this project than anyone else. Being married to a junior scholar in literary studies in the twenty-first century is not an easy thing: she would certainly be happy going back to St Louis, but has moved internationally three times because she knew it was the only way I could continue my work. And while growing increasingly disillusioned with the state of the academic humanities – in words I cannot quite print – she has never stopped believing in me. I write these lines in the wake of the birth of our second child; Edwin Ruel joins his sister Anna Sophia in being born a Fessenbecker in Ankara, and I can't imagine a better partner for building a family with than Willie. Books and babies, in my opinion, go best together.

Abbreviations

BBA   Robert Browning, 'Bishop Blougram's Apology', in Thomas Collins and Vivienne Rundle (eds), *The Broadview Anthology of Victorian Poetry and Poetic Theory* (Peterborough, ON: Broadview, 2000), pp. 263–77.

C   Augusta Webster, 'A Castaway', in *Augusta Webster: Portraits and Other Poems*, ed. Christine Sutphin (Peterborough, ON: Broadview, 2000), pp. 192–213.

CY   Anthony Trollope, *Can You Forgive Her?* (New York: Penguin, 1972).

DD   George Eliot, *Daniel Deronda*, ed. Terence Cave (New York: Penguin, 2003).

DM   Charles Darwin, *The Descent of Man, and Selection in Relation to Sex* (Princeton: Princeton University Press, 1981).

ED   Anthony Trollope, *The Eustace Diamonds* (New York: Penguin, 1969).

FH   George Eliot, *Felix Holt*, ed. Lynda Mugglestone (New York: Penguin, 1995).

ID   Augusta Webster, *In A Day* (London: Kegan et al., 1882). Electronic copy made available via the Hathi Trust.

LR   K. K. Collins, 'G. H. Lewes Revisited: George Eliot and the Moral Sense', *Victorian Studies* 21.4 (1978), pp. 463–92.

LTL   Richard Gaskin, *Language, Truth and Literature* (Oxford: Oxford University Press, 2013).

MU   Quentin Skinner, 'Meaning and Understanding in the History of Ideas', *History and Theory* 8.1 (1969), pp. 3–53.

ME   Henry Sidgwick, *The Methods of Ethics* (Indianapolis: Hackett, 1981).

P   Augusta Webster, 'Pilate', in *Augusta Webster: Portraits and Other Poems*, ed. Christine Sutphin (Peterborough, ON: Broadview, 2000), pp. 149–60.

PF   Anthony Trollope, *Phineas Finn: The Irish Member* (New York: Oxford University Press, 1999).

SC   Christine Korsgaard, *Self-Constitution: Agency, Identity, and Integrity* (New York: Oxford University Press, 2009).
TDC   Anthony Trollope, *The Duke's Children* (New York: Oxford University Press, 1999).
TFL   Peter Lamarque and Stein Haugom Olsen, *Truth, Fiction, and Literature: A Philosophical Perspective* (Oxford: Clarendon Press, 1994).

Introduction: In Defence of Paraphrase

Teachers of Literature are apt to think up such problems as 'What is the author's purpose?' or still worse, 'What is the guy trying to say?'

Vladimir Nabokov

Whatever it may have been in the past, the idea of content is today mainly a hindrance, a nuisance, a subtle or not so subtle philistinism.

Susan Sontag

Ideas in poetry are usually stale and false, and no one older than sixteen would find it worth his while to read poetry merely for what it says.

George Boas

Near the end of *Distant Reading*, a collection of his influential essays on literary methodology, Franco Moretti writes that 'formal analysis is the great accomplishment of literary study', and that any alternative to it must show that it is somehow superior or at least equal.[1] The claim is presented as if it is more or less obvious; what is necessary in Moretti's mind is not to justify formalism, but instead to show that his variation on formalism can offer new insights. But that phrase – 'the great accomplishment' – should give one pause. Why, exactly, is formalism the most significant achievement of literary criticism, and what conception of literature lies behind this claim?

Caroline Levine's award-winning book *Forms* shares the same basic sense of the nature of literary criticism. 'One of the great achievements of formalism', she tells us, 'has been the development of rich vocabularies and highly refined skills for differentiating among forms.'[2] Indeed reading for form is 'what literary critics have traditionally done best'.³ Susan Wolfson, in the book that initiated the 'New Formalism', similarly holds up formalism as the element of literary criticism that is worth preserving.⁴ She is 'struck by how tenacious the subject has proven'; quoting Geoffrey Hartman approvingly, she notes how hard – and by hard she means impossible – it is to move beyond formalism.⁵ Levine's version of formalism and her justification for it differs significantly from Moretti's – and Wolfson's differs from both – but all three writers share the same basic sense that the greatest thing literary studies has done is to think about form.

The fact that each of these writers explains the value and purpose of literary criticism differently while landing on the same feature of the literary text as the thing worth studying should surprise literary critics more than it does. If a commitment to formalism can and does survive disagreement about most of the other elements of literary texts, this suggests that at least some of the work of Levine, Moretti and the other formalists is *ex post facto* reasoning: the arguments offered are not the real source of the commitment to formalism, but rather rationalisations given to justify the pre-existing commitment. And as Marjorie Levinson has noted, 'the shared commitment' to form without consensus about what it is suggests that what is really going on here is a buried commitment to the aesthetic.⁶ The situation thus calls for a genealogy, one that explains where and when the commitment to form in contemporary literary criticism originated, why it was originally adopted and subsequently maintained, and what alternatives it was developed against.

The need for a genealogy is all the move obvious because of how inadequate formalism is as a description of the varieties of reading practice and literary aesthetics. Jonathan Kramnick and Anahid Nersessian have recently and approvingly noted the tendency of criticism to redefine 'form' at the beginning of an essay and let the argument flow from there, but I want to ask what ways of reading this model of literary analysis leaves out.⁷ By definition, it would seem, formalism will have trouble explaining any attachment a reader might have to the content of a literary work. The unloved and maligned second child of literary history, content has never received the same kind of attention as her big sister form: at best, she can hope only that a writer will dissolve the distinction, and grant content equal status to form on the grounds that ultimately it is impossible to distinguish coherently between the two.⁸ Yet surely a primary interest in a text's content is an ordinary and easily understood kind of reading experience. Readers who come away from *Pride and Prejudice* with an affection for Elizabeth and Mr Darcy, who leave Ayn Rand with a new set of thoughts about the individual and property rights (or Upton Sinclair with a different set of thoughts about the same topics), or who leave *Hamlet* thinking that perhaps suicide is a more complicated question than they had realised do not seem crazy or mistaken. How, then, did such an ordinary kind of reading experience become so anathema to the practice of literary criticism, such that 'reading for the message' could become a label that critics would hasten to escape?[9] The answer lies in the history of literary theory in the twentieth century, and the commitment through a broad succession of theoretical approaches to an essentially similar account of the nature of the literary text.

This is a book that tries to move beyond that account, that offers a new description of literature and the reading experience, and that offers an alternative to formalism. The commitment to formalism in literary studies is deep and pervasive, and it turns up in all sorts of surprising places: one finds it at the highest level, in the theoretical accounts of the nature of literature and aesthetic experience, and at the lowest level, in the practice of literary criticism and the everyday decisions that critics make about which elements of texts require explanation. Correspondingly, an emphasis on content proves surprisingly difficult to maintain: my account here will move back and forth between engaging overt and reflective defences of formalism and drawing out the unreflective and instinctive formalist gestures in specific pieces of criticism in order to counter both in developing its alternative. The problem is complicated by the fact that content is by its nature messy; although I do my best to define the term in Chapter 1, I don't see a way to give 'content' the simple and straightforward definition that form has received from its many defenders. Correspondingly, I will limit my defence here to intellectual content, to the ideas in texts, and to a related experience of reading that one might call reading-as-thinking or thoughtful reading. Scepticism about this practice is central to the rise of formalism, but it has not disappeared – far from it. I suspect that it cannot disappear, because it is a central part of what readers enjoy about books. But to bring thoughtful reading into the light, it is necessary to understand how it was hidden in the first place.

What Happened to the Novel of Ideas? The Long Tail of Aestheticism

As with any genealogy, it is not easy to pick a point of origin for formalism in literary criticism. But the end of the nineteenth century in England stands out for several reasons. First, it is in a literal and institutional sense the origin for a good deal of the discourse of contemporary literary studies. The subsequent work of I. A. Richards, F. R. Leavis and the first generation of academic literary critics in the universities shows their inheritance of problems in late nineteenth-century aesthetics. And additionally, as Mary McCarthy observed a generation ago, the high realist novel of the period from approximately 1850 to 1890 married intellectual content with all the rest of its elements and effects. It is telling, she argues, that there was not a separate category for the 'novels of ideas': all the high realist novels were saturated with ideas, with theoretical observation and analysis.[10] So the implication of the phrase 'novels of ideas' – that some novels might not be novels of ideas, might not have intellectual content, and that thoughtful reading might be a practice applied only to certain books – seemed foreign. By the end of the century, however, that conjunction between intellectual content and other aesthetic effects was coming apart. So if one wants to know what happened to literary content, we can perhaps begin there.

In *The Anthology and the Rise of the Novel*, Leah Price points out that the practice of extracting propositional knowledge, in the form of aphorisms, was a popular way of understanding George Eliot's fiction in particular.[11] Eliot, according to Price, was of two minds about this sort of adulation. On the one hand, Eliot compliments one anthologist's attentiveness: 'you know what I mean, and care the most for those elements in my writing which I myself care the most for'.[12] On the other hand, Eliot had deep reservations about the violations of her narrative form, complaining of readers who 'cut' *Daniel Deronda* 'into scraps [. . .] I meant everything in the book to be related to everything else there.'[13] This implies both an ending and a beginning: just as Eliot gave the novel the moral and theoretical sophistication that Victorian anthologists required, making narrative extraction possible, she also articulated a worry about the importance of narrative form as an aesthetic element – which, properly attended to, made extracting impossible.

Price goes on to contend that the sort of extractable 'didactic digressions' characteristic of Eliot became associated in the English fiction of the 1890s 'with a feminine moralism opposed at once to the narrative pleasure of masculine romance like Stevenson's or Kipling's and to the avant-garde doctrine of art for art's sake'.[14] Certainly, the link between extractable digressions and moralism is central to Oscar Wilde's argument for an alternative aesthetics; for Wilde, the rejection of the ethical evaluation of art came part and parcel with a broader rejection of interpretation based on any assessment of a text's intellectual content. Wilde stresses at a number of moments his refusal of ethical criteria in aesthetic analysis, perhaps most famously in the claim that 'there is no such thing as a moral or immoral book. Books are well written, or badly written. That is all.'[15] But this went alongside an insistence that the presence of an extractable message in a work of art did not matter for, and perhaps actively interfered with, its aesthetic quality. As Ernest puts it in 'The Critic as Artist', 'the aesthetic critic rejects those obvious modes of art that have but one message to deliver', preferring instead 'modes as suggest reverie and mood' that 'by their imaginative beauty make all interpretation true and no interpretation final'.[16] For a text to have an extractable content, a 'message', was thus to group it with the uninteresting 'obvious modes of art'.

But there is room here for an important distinction. The worry about extraction represents at least three versions of a claim in aesthetics. First, as Eliot's reservations suggest, it is simply a worry about dismissing narrative complexity. Second, as Wilde's reservations suggest, it is a worry about a reliance on moralistic evaluation and the tendency to reduce the analysis of a text's content to moral approval or disapproval. But third, it is a worry about the independence of aesthetic criteria and the distinctiveness of art as such; as Price notes, one of Eliot's reviewers asserted that 'a novel ceases to be a novel when it aims at philosophical teaching. It is not the vehicle for conveying knowledge. Its business is to amuse.'[17]

Now, this represents an importantly different worry than those about complexity and moralism: it instead objects to the notion that literary narratives make assertions worthy of genuine consideration. In the process of ensuring that the critic did not extract pieces of narratives unjustifiably or treat narratives moralistically, a powerful strain of literary criticism over the course of the next two generations – one that culminated in the New Criticism – came widely to adopt what philosophers of art call anti-cognitivism, or the claim that literary texts do not make knowledge claims, and thus accepted the validity of the third objection.[18] What I want to suggest is that there was a missed opportunity here, insofar as a style of interpretation that avoided unsophisticated extraction and condemnatory moralism but allowed for the possibility that literature could convey sophisticated ideas was eliminated almost by accident.

Henry James's work on the theory of the novel is a central step in this process, developed in part as a criticism of Eliot. As he writes in 'Daniel Deronda: A Conversation', 'What can be drearier than a novel where the function of the hero [. . .] is to give didactic advice?'[19] The problem, James notes, is that such didacticism disrupts the 'current' of the story and renders it into a series of fragments.[20] The idea here, which emphasises the importance of aesthetic coherence, would form a central part of *The Art of Fiction*, where James writes: 'the idea, the starting-point, of the novel' is the only feature that can be thought of as 'something different from its organic whole [. . .] in proportion as the work is successful, the idea permeates and penetrates it, informs and animates it, so that every word and every punctuation-point contribute directly to the expression'.[21] James thus emphasises the necessity of a singular coherence for the 'organic whole' of the aesthetic object.[22] And what the Jamesian novelist does is attempt to render every element of the story in harmony with that 'idea', so that it 'permeates and penetrates' all the parts of the novel in such a way that everything contributes to the idea's expression. James has in mind something very much like aesthetic unity – the creation of a clear pattern that governs the elements in the novel. And crucially, it is attending to and explaining this unity that constitutes proper engagement with a novel on the part of the literary critic.[23]

Other critics developed versions of James's central insight – most importantly Virginia Woolf, who remarks in an essay on George Meredith that

> when philosophy is not consumed in a novel, when we can underline this phrase with a pencil, and cut out that exhortation with a pair of scissors and paste the whole into a system, it is safe to say that there is something wrong with the philosophy or with the novel or with both. Above all, his teaching is too insistent [. . .] characters in fiction resent [nothing] more. If, they seem to argue, we have been called into existence merely to express Mr. Meredith's views upon the universe, we would rather not exist at all. Thereupon they die; and a novel that is full of dead characters, even though it is also full of profound wisdom and exalted teaching, is not achieving its aim as a novel.[24]

Woolf expresses here, even more clearly than James, the importance of rendering philosophical ideas as organic parts of the work of fiction: when a message can be 'cut out', as the Victorians did with Eliot, there is 'something wrong with the philosophy or the novel or both'. And we see in the second half of the passage an anti-cognitivist theory of narrative emerging. When the novelist allows the expression of her ideas to dominate the structure of the work, the characters – who are thus merely means to express the author's view – in some fashion 'die', and the novel fails 'as a novel'. Woolf does not quite say that it is inappropriate to read a novel for its wisdom, or that such wisdom is irrelevant to a work's virtues, but the impression is nevertheless clear that such things are incidental to the text's status as literary art.

This is not to say that the movement towards anti-cognitivism was quite complete. For one thing, James himself seemed to acknowledge that literature might have epistemological virtues. This is part of his critique of Anthony Trollope: noting Trollope's claim that he was only engaged in 'make believe', James remarks that this is a 'betrayal of a sacred office', insofar as 'it implies that the novelist is less occupied in looking for the truth [. . .] than the historian'.[25] Even if James thinks the ideas within a novel can only be properly understood in relation to each other and as part of an overall structure, there is no reason to think that this structure – once understood – will be cognitively empty. The 'sacred office' of the Jamesian novelist, in fact, is to ensure that the novel will *not* be empty in this way.

But the movement towards anti-cognitivism would eventually triumph in the Anglo-American academy. In *The Craft of Fiction*, his 1921 interpretation of James's prefaces, Percy Lubbock developed a version of the Jamesian account that was much more hostile to a notion of the novel as a vehicle for propositional content. Lubbock famously distinguishes between 'showing' and 'telling'; in his words, 'the art of fiction does not begin until the novelist thinks of his story as a matter to be *shown*, to be so exhibited that it will tell itself'.[26] Now, as Dorothy Hale has suggested, this is still not quite incompatible with a cognitivist theory – in her gloss, 'when Lubbock insists that the novelist show rather than tell, he only means that the novelist should represent her judgements *indirectly* rather than expressly'.[27] But it is nevertheless eager to prevent the separation of such judgements from the aesthetic experience itself, insofar as ideal novelistic form requires that the author not overtly communicate anything to the reader; in Hale's gloss, 'If anyone is to speak for himself in the Lubbockian novel, it must be a character, whose partiality is subordinated to the objective and coherent whole of the "piece".'[28] The world of the work of art is separate from the real world and the world of the reader, and characters and authors must not abrogate the gap between them, for doing so betrays the artistic nature of the text. Put more casually, Lubbock requires that the work of art not embody the artist's ideas too obviously, and that no one communicate them too straightforwardly.

The anti-cognitivist way of thinking about narrative appeared most dramatically in the New Criticism, which scholars generally recognise as a development from the 'art for art's sake views' of the

British aesthetes.[29] In his foundational text *The Well-Wrought Urn* (1947), Cleanth Brooks argued that it is in terms of 'structure' that 'one must describe poetry', where this is

> a structure of meanings, evaluations, and interpretations; and the principle of unity which informs it seems to be one of balancing and harmonising qualifications [. . .] The unity is not a unity of the sort to be achieved by the reduction and simplification appropriate to an algebraic formula. It is a positive unity, not a negative; it represents not a residue, but an achieved harmony.[30]

This is akin to James's notion about the way a novelist's 'idea' must permeate every element of a novel. For Brooks, interpreting a poem means understanding its 'harmony' – the way its various elements, which include but are not limited to its metre, rhyme and other standard poetic devices, cohere in some fashion.

On this view, while a poem might involve some propositional ideas or theoretical content, it is crucially mistaken to think that an understanding of these is an understanding of the poem. Brooks acknowledges that 'the dimension in which the poems moves is not one which excludes ideas', but goes on to say that

> any proposition asserted in a poem is not to be taken in abstraction but is justified, in terms of the poem, not by virtue of its [. . .] truth, but [. . .] in terms of a principle analogous to that of dramatic propriety. Thus, the proposition that 'Beauty is truth, truth beauty' is given its precise meaning and significance by its relation to the total context of the poem.[31]

This is to say that, while poems certainly do engage in ideas, one cannot treat them as simple expositions of a set of propositions.

The techniques of narrative interpretation that stem from this way of thinking about literature are especially apparent in *Understanding Fiction*, a textbook composed by Brooks and Robert Penn Warren. The opening essay of the book, a 'Letter to the Teacher', indicates that it 'is their first article of faith that the structure of a piece of fiction, in so far as that piece of fiction is successful, must involve a vital and functional relationship between the idea and the other elements in that structure'.[32] In other words, although thematic content matters, it is essentially important primarily insofar as it creates an aesthetic structure. Brooks and Warren allow that it is better when the ideas are profound ones: 'a piece of fiction must involve an idea of some real significance for mature and thoughtful human beings'.[33] But they stress that the idea does not matter as an idea: 'The mere presence in a piece of fiction of an idea which is held to be important [. . .] does not necessarily indicate anything about the importance of the piece of fiction. One might almost as well commend a piece of fiction for exemplifying good grammar.'[34] This passage stresses the secondary and contingent nature of literary cognitive content in the New Critical approach to fiction – no matter how profound, ideas are ultimately only as important a part of literary art as grammar.

One finds the anti-cognitivist impulse equally in the 1942 textbook *Theory of Literature*, by René Wellek and Austin Warren. Writing of psychology in literature, they indicate that even if an author's portrayal is accurate, 'we may well raise the question whether such "truth" is an artistic value'.[35] Making the formalism clear, they go on to say that 'psychological truth is an artistic value only if it enhances coherence and complexity'.[36] In a section aptly titled 'Literature and Ideas', they ask rhetorically, 'Must we not rather conclude that "philosophical truth" as such has no artistic value just as we argued that psychological or social truth has no artistic value as such?' and conclude, 'Poetry of ideas is like other poetry, not to be judged by the value of the material but by its degree of integration and artistic intensity.'[37] The idea that intellectual content might contribute to a text's artistic value, and moreover that one might appreciate the text primarily by engaging with that content, is on this view deeply mistaken; even if present, the only way such elements can matter is insofar as they contribute to the 'complexity' of a poem.

As historians of English as a discipline have noted, the New Criticism spread quickly; this way of thinking about literature became the dominant methodology in academic literary criticism by the late 1950s.[38] It has had a tumultuous history since; though it would be largely supplanted in literature departments, first by the rise of structuralist and (almost immediately afterwards) post-structuralist thought, and subsequently by the hermeneutics of suspicion and ideology critique, it remains a central touchstone in most critical anthologies. Moreover, the anti-cognitivist impulse would prove durable, to the point that one literary critic could proclaim confidently, 'Novels and poems – to repeat the trustworthy commonplace – aren't made out of ideas.'[39] And it continues to appear, even in texts that are in some sense predicated on denying it: in *George Eliot's Intellectual Life*, Avrom Fleishman dismisses the interpreter who claims 'here is an idea in a novel or poem, and the author must have believed it' as practising a mere 'extractive approach', and champions instead a 'functional approach', which examines 'how an idea works in the course of a novel'.[40] In this preference for aesthetic structure over intellectual content – explained quickly and almost in passing, an instinctive formalism more than anything else – the dominance of the kind of criticism that Woolf alluded to and that Brooks and Warren practised is clear.

What is more, for all the ways in which structuralist and post-structuralist models of literary interpretation resisted the theoretical commitments of New Criticism, they nevertheless largely agreed that literary texts did not make assertions that interpretations might usefully summarise. This was an overt position in the first great rise of structuralist narratology, developed by figures such as Tzvetan Todorov, Roland Barthes and Gerard Genette.[41] As Todorov explains in his essay 'Structural Analysis of Narrative':

> [S]tructural analysis coincides (in its basic tenets) with theory, with the poetics of literature. Its object is the literary discourse rather than works of literature, literature that is virtual rather than real. Such analysis seeks no longer to articulate a paraphrase, a rational resume of the concrete work, but to propose a theory of the structure and operation of the literary discourse, to present a spectrum of literary possibilities, in such a manner that the existing works of literature appear as particular instances that have been realised.[42]

This is to say that for the structuralists, the point of literary analysis is not to generate an interpretation of a specific work, but rather to understand the way general linguistic laws function in generating specific texts. As Todorov puts it, the goal is to understand the nature of 'literary discourse' generally, and individual works of literature are relevant mainly as 'particular instances' or realisations of that discourse.

Similarly, the post-structuralist criticism of narrative, by figures such as Jacques Derrida, Paul de Man and J. Hillis Miller, ultimately shared key New Critical assumptions. As Gene Bell-Viada puts it, 'deconstruction and its kin qualify as latter-day elaborations of the Western tradition of Art for Art's sake'; such critics see the belief that literature might 'help us see the truth' as just the 'pre-Derridean preserve of naïve readers'.[43] In a brief reflection on literary criticism in the 1980s, Jane Gallop suggested something similar: while 'those against theory fought hard to defend the heritage of New Criticism', she remarks, 'many of those on the other side were practicing, often under the name of deconstruction, a form of close reading of literary texts not in fact so radically different from New Criticism'.[44] She goes on: 'Looking back now at that period, I would emphasize not the debate about theory but the close-reading practice appearing on both sides of the divide.'⁴⁵

One way in which the two practices of close reading coincided was their mutual insistence that literary texts did not convey theoretical content. As Derrida explains, to read a literary text as a straightforward expression of ideas would be to engage in 'transcendent reading', which he seeks to 'put in question'.⁴⁶ To 'transcend' in this regard means 'going beyond interest for the signifier, the form, the language [. . .] in the direction of the meaning or referent'; as an alternative, Derrida defends interpretive techniques that analyse 'the functioning of language' and thus note the problematics of reference and assertion.⁴⁷ On this view, '"good" literary criticism' – indeed, 'the only worthwhile kind' – tries not to offer a coherent summary or analysis of a literary text, but instead 'never lets itself be "completely objectified"'.⁴⁸

The practical dismissal of literary assertions is particularly apparent in Derrida's analysis of Franz Kafka's parable 'Before the Law'. Derrida might have understood the parable as asserting a very deconstructive insight: the story describes a man who tries to gain admission to 'the law', but is barred by a doorkeeper; he waits for many years, only to learn just before his death that no one ever gains access to the law. In this way, the story could offer an allegory for the fruitless pursuit of a clear referential foundation for language.⁴⁹ However, this would be to read the story transcendently. Derrida thus instead suggests:

> The story *Before the Law* does not tell or describe anything but itself as text. It does only this or does also this. Not within an assured specular reflection of self-referential transparency [. . .] but in the unreadability of the text, if one understands by this the impossibility of acceding to its proper significance and its possibly inconsistent content, which it jealously keeps back. The text guards itself, maintains itself – like the law, speaking only of itself, that is to say, of its non-identity with itself.⁵⁰

This is to say that the Kafka parable is interesting for Derrida not because its allegorical content is philosophically persuasive, nor even because it is about itself in a way that demonstrates its awareness of its textual nature, but rather because its elements function together in such a way as to make the text 'unreadable', by which I take Derrida to mean impossible to paraphrase – as he puts it later, 'ultimately ungraspable, incomprehensible'.⁵¹ It thus guards itself, preventing access to its 'content'.

And finally, the dismissal of the text's 'overt' or 'superficial' ideas is an essential part of the process of 'symptomatic reading' and the broader 'hermeneutics of suspicion'. The classic statement of this sort of reading is Fredric Jameson's 1981 text *The Political Unconscious*, which asserts that 'interpretation proper' or 'strong rewriting' depends upon 'some mechanism of mystification or repression in terms of which it would make sense [. . .] to rewrite the surface categories of a text in the stronger language of a more fundamental interpretive code'.[52] Moreover, responding to an interlocutor who claims that 'the text means just what it says', he writes:

> Unfortunately, no society has ever been quite so mystified in quite so many ways as our own, saturated as it is with messages and information, the very vehicles of mystification [. . .] If everything were transparent, then no ideology would be possible, and no domination either: evidently that is not our case.[53]

The point here is that, as with the previous three models, attention to the text's straightforward assertions misunderstands the right way to approach cultural products; one ought instead to look for what the text does not or, as Jameson points out elsewhere, cannot say.[54] This lets the critic penetrate the cover of ideological mystification and reveal the way in which the text is a symptom of some more fundamental process.

Although Jameson prefers an emphasis on political processes, his reference to the possibility of multiple versions of fundamental codes alludes to the notion that critics using a number of different theoretical frames could deploy this tactic of reading.[55] And much of the literary criticism since 1981 has indeed taken Jameson's provocative argument as an interpretive guide, to the extent that Eve Sedgwick – who herself developed a powerful symptomatic reading in *The Epistemology of the Closet* – remarked in 2003 that 'in the context of recent U.S. literary theory', 'to apply a hermeneutics of suspicion is [. . .] widely understood as a mandatory injunction rather than a possibility among other possibilities'.[56] Rita Felski summarises this attitude by remarking that current approaches 'share the conviction that the most rigorous reading is one that is performed against the grain, that the primary rationale for reading a text is to critique it by underscoring what it does not know and cannot understand'.[57] Felski makes clear that Jameson's suggestion has been thoroughly followed, as a variety of theoretical frameworks have been deployed as fundamental 'codes' used to identify some feature of the world that the literary text 'does not know and cannot understand'.

What is important here is the fact that Derrida, Jameson and their compatriots and followers dismiss literary assertions in the same way that the New Critics and the structuralists did. Admittedly, in Derrida's analysis, the ideas in Kafka's parable matter insofar as they produce 'unreadability', whereas in Jameson's analysis, the ideas matter insofar as they produce an ideological cover; both differ from the New Critical emphasis on their subsumption to form and the structuralist reference to them as evidence of linguistic laws.[58] But there is nevertheless an implicit agreement among all these ways of approaching a text that the ideas are not worthy of analysis in themselves, and that the literary critic must in some sense look past them.[59]

The Ethical Turn's Suspicion of Moral Philosophy

I have suggested that the commitment to formalism is deep and broad, and that it is as much an instinct as it is a reflective position. One area of scholarship where this is clear is the criticism in the movement that scholars have come to call the 'ethical turn'. In an area where it would seem natural to work out the nature of thoughtful reading and of interpretive practices that emphasise content, what one finds in fact is that an emphasis on content became a mark of shame, and that reading for the content, when that was construed as treating a literary text as if it had asserted an ethical or philosophical claim, was for virtually all critics something to be avoided.

To see this, let me briefly survey the broad movements in the ethical turn, which involved the confluence of several trends in late twentieth-century thought.[60] The first trend, which one might call the 'Aristotelian' thread and where the major figure was Martha Nussbaum, arose out of Anglo-American analytic moral philosophy and drew on works of literature – particularly the great Greek tragedies – to develop a neo-Aristotelian challenge to the dominant utilitarian and Kantian positions.[61] The second trend, which one might call the 'Hegelian' thread and where the major figures are Richard Rorty and Charles Taylor, involved challenges to dominant 'scientistic' epistemological and ontological models, arguing that 'facts' are constituted by consciousness just in the same way 'values' are, and that it is a mistake to be any more sceptical of the latter than of the former.[62] Seeing the self and the world this way made literary texts a natural ally; as Michael Eskin notes, Rorty called in part for a 'turn away from theory and towards narrative'.[63] A third trend, best thought of as a 'Post-Structuralist' thread, depended on the rethinking of ethics in the late works of Jacques Derrida and Michel Foucault.[64] This trend, perhaps because of the deep influence post-structuralism has had on contemporary literary criticism, was the first to generate book-length reconsiderations of the relationship between ethics and literature from within the literary academy.[65] But of course, there had always been a few critics and philosophers who resisted the trends of their fields, working on autochthonous projects along these lines.[66]

And since these initial arguments, there has been a flood of ethical criticism of all kinds.[67] Though it is perhaps obvious, it is worth stressing the diversity of thought that falls under this rubric: neo-Aristotelian moral philosophers, Levinasian post-structuralists and followers of Stanley Cavell perhaps form the core, but the 'ethical turn' has grown large enough to incorporate thinkers from many traditions and backgrounds. As such, it would be a mistake to see the 'ethical turn' as resulting from a shared research programme; rather, there was a confluence between several relatively independent intellectual movements. Despite these differences, there was a key claim on which the canonical interpretations in the ethical turn depend. Eskin describes it well: what 'is at stake in "ethics" and literature', he writes, is 'the singular encounter' between the reader and the text.[68] In other words, ethical criticism has generally assumed that if there is something especially *ethically* interesting about literature, it is because there is something peculiar about the nature of literature, a peculiarity that creates a relationship with the reader that is fundamentally different from the relationship readers have with non-literary texts.

A classic and in many ways representative example of this kind of argument occurs in J. Hillis Miller's influential *The Ethics of Reading*. In his analysis of *Adam Bede*, he claims that even though the novel is committed in its 'overt affirmations' to 'realism as exact reproduction', its 'covert argument is for a use of figurative language'.[69] The tension between these two impulses is not an accident, but is rather the necessary result of the 'law of reading', which involves the way the text makes present its own unreadability.[70] What makes the novel ethical, then, is not its overt treatment of moral dilemmas and problems in practical reasoning; instead, it is the way that presentation is necessarily undermined – and the experience of that necessity in reading *Adam Bede* is an experience of a law like the Kantian categorical imperative. Thus, the ideas in the book are not interesting as such; they are only interesting as elements in the unstable pattern of the novel as a whole.

This basic claim about the distinctiveness of literature merits interrogation.⁷¹ It depends on a sense of the strangeness of literary experience, eliding the potential insights that literary texts might offer in more ordinary terms. But the notion that literature is peculiar in this way is neither obvious nor self-evident. The claim reflects the influence, though critics in the ethical turn rarely explained this, of the long anti-cognitivist tradition in literary criticism and the century-long championing of aesthetic form. And to posit the peculiarities of the encounter with the literary text as central in this way misses the ways in which literature is a kind of ethical thinking recognisably valuable in the same way as any interesting philosophical or theoretical text. The dismissal of this thinking emerges particularly clearly in the dispute between Wayne Booth and Adam Zachary Newton.

For Wayne Booth, the ethical value of a literary text depends on its implication of an author, whose values the work under interpretation shares with the reader. The metaphor Booth lands on for this theory of reading is 'friendship': the reader encounters the text and its implied author in the way we might meet a friend. As he puts it, 'For our purposes, all stories [. . .] can be viewed not as puzzles or even as games but as companions, friends – or [. . .] as *gifts* from would-be friends.'⁷² On this view, then, the reader engages in a process of communal evaluation that Booth calls 'coduction'.⁷³ He offers an example of this process in an extended reading of *Huckleberry Finn*, a book he initially admires. However, upon drawing out the 'fixed norms' of the implied author, which include the belief that 'Black people are [. . .] so naturally good that the effects of slavery will not be discernible once slavery is removed' – his coduction ultimately finds the text problematic.⁷⁴

Adam Zachary Newton departs from Booth's claim that the moral value of fiction lies in the sharing of values by arguing that if fiction is ethically compelling, it is precisely because it is not transparently available to readers:

> By purposeful contrast, my proposal of a narrative ethics implies simply narrative *as* ethics: the ethical consequences of narrating story and fictionalizing person, and the reciprocal claims binding teller, listener, witness, and reader in that process. [Thus] the difference lies between readings which allegorize the [text's] events to a second-order story of translated meaning and those I will develop in ensuing chapters which attend exclusively to the shape, the drama, and the circumstances of the [text's] own story, its strictly narrative details, since that story already reads, or allegorizes, itself.⁷⁵

Newton's point here is that previous critics have thought of the relationship between ethics and fiction as consisting in a two-step process: first, one interprets the text and establishes a meaning; second, one evaluates it according to the basis of some criteria. Though they might disagree about what these criteria should be, they share a conception about how ethical criticism ought to proceed. Newton contrasts this with his own way of reading, which will forgo the evaluative step in favour of a closer, more intimate reading. As he goes on to put it, 'It is the difference, to put it another way, between a deontology and a phenomenology [. . .] One faces a text as one might face a person, having to confront the claims raised by that very immediacy, an immediacy of contact, not of meaning.'[76]

Newton argues in particular that Booth's model of 'friendship' depends on a view of reading as receiving a message from the author, which fails to sufficiently consider the way the reader is involved *prior* to the clear construction of the message. In his words, 'acts of assent, surrender, seduction, coercion and bestowal all occur inside fictional texts; we must be a party to these, before we construe literary texts as messages sent from authors to readers'.[77] And this is a version of a critique of philosophical ethical criticism made elsewhere: Simon Haines argues, for instance, that 'even the most alert and well-intentioned of philosophers still read poems or novels as if they were containers or vehicles with separable concepts inside them, or as if they were examples of re-formulable ideas'; while David Parker suggests that 'the ethical interest of imaginative literature is not then, as often implied, in ethical propositions that can be gleaned from it'.[78]

This criticism requires two responses. The first is that this kind of critique is not quite fair: if Booth, Nussbaum and other philosophical literary critics arguably in practice do construe texts as expressing a message of 'ethical propositions', this is not at any rate how they understand themselves. While Booth certainly holds that texts have values with some sort of content, he does not conceive of this simply as a message the text conveys to the reader – indeed, part of what makes friendship with a text so interesting is the way the text and the reader interact in producing the reading experience.

And to the extent that Booth does not in fact offer a view that reads literary texts for their 're-formulable ideas', it indicates a gap in the field. Thus, my second response would be that there is a place for an un-selfconscious version of the kind of criticism that Newton dismisses. Precisely because they do not wish to see narratives as just carrying a message, Booth and Nussbaum (another common target of this criticism) do not work out what it would mean for literary texts to do so. Although they appeal to ideas in narratives at various moments, these appeals are subsumed in the broader approach; the comprehension of ideas in reading a literary text matters only as an element in an experience that cannot be understood in purely intellectual terms. Thus, although Booth recognises that literary texts can have 'profound intellectual import', he contends that the critic must understand these aspects as part of a text's 'miraculous unity'.[79] Similarly, although Nussbaum suggests that Henry James's novels present 'the best account I know' of moral perception, she insists that her approach does not turn literary texts into 'systematic treatises, ignoring in the process their formal features and their mysterious, various, and complex content'.[80] Both of these approaches thus preserve a sense of the special features of literary experience. And to the extent that they remain committed to the formal uniqueness of literary texts and the readerly experience of them, the analysis of what it means for a literary text to express ideas goes under-developed.

Joshua Landy's response to the ethical turn in his 2012 book *How to Do Things With Fictions* ironically ends up duplicating this same pattern. Early on in the book, Landy speaks of the need to 'rescue' literary criticism from the 'meaning-mongers' who constantly read for 'the message' of literary texts – thus reiterating the process of accusing one's rivals of reading for the message in order to lend support to one's own, supposedly more formally sensitive, theory of criticism.[81] But Landy doesn't offer a specific example of a contemporary critic who is a meaning-monger: his example in a footnote, tellingly, is Jennifer Lopez's discussion of the movie *Crash* in her speech at the 2006 Academy Awards, and he speaks broadly and generally of this approach to literature as one 'currently being taught in high schools' and 'evaluated in the public domain'.[82] As my argument so far would suggest, Landy's inability to find a specific 'meaning-monger' is not surprising: at least at the level of literary theory, form-fetishists are much more common.

Why does this pattern keep recurring, whereby one writer insists that another is simply reading for the message, while himself distinguishing his own view from a straightforward reading for the message? Why did Landy have to bring Jennifer Lopez into this? Not, I submit, because these critics share a theory about the essential importance of literary form of which Lopez was unpardonably unaware. As the review of literary theory in the twentieth century above suggested, a commitment to form has been able to survive vast disagreement about why it was important. Rather, talking about the importance of 'form' has become a way of marking one's sophistication as a critic. Correspondingly, an instinctive sense of the complexity and peculiarity of literary texts, and a view of criticism as the tracing of this complexity, undergirds all these arguments. But that instinct has become so prominent and widespread in literary theory that no one is open about rejecting it, and so disputants and interlocutors must be found elsewhere.

Yet for all that, Landy is not wrong to think that reading for the meaning is indeed a common practice, and that meaning-mongers really do exist. They just don't exist – at least not any more – at the level of literary theory; one must move out into the world of ordinary, garden-variety literary criticism. Here it is possible, and in fact not difficult, to find instances of meaning-mongers, when that is construed as a critical emphasis on literary content. And there is moreover a sort of repressed or at any rate marginalised tradition of this sort of thoughtful reading: all the while that theorists were insisting on the importance of form over content, practising literary critics have long demonstrated a continuing interest in the content of the works they engage. This tradition reflects an insight that literary theory would do well to acknowledge; as Julie Orlemanski writes, 'I am inclined to give more credence to *what we do* in our discipline than to what we say about what we do.'[83] To put it another way, we might take the recurrence of this kind of reading – the omnipresent but quiet meaning-mongering – as a guide to an alternate theory of the literary text. To start that process, let me highlight a few moments in the history of reading for the content.

A Buried History of Reading for the Content

Cleanth Brooks's *The Well-Wrought Urn*, perhaps the quintessential articulation of anti-cognitivist literary aesthetics, appeared in 1947. The very first mentions of the book naturally appeared in bibliographies of recent scholarship; what is telling about such lists is how much of the criticism published in the heyday of New Criticism was not, in fact, new criticism. To pick one salient example, *Modern Philology*'s list of criticism on Victorian literature for 1947, which contains a citation for *The Well-Wrought Urn*, also includes a book called *Human Dignity and the Great Victorians* by Bernard Schilling.[84] This book appears to have faded from the critical consciousness – it has been cited eight times in the last thirty years. Yet it makes for surprisingly interesting reading. Schilling is interested in the way free market capitalism in Victorian England, both as practised and as theorised, undermined the human capacity for dignity; he traces how various nineteenth-century writers, from Coleridge through Matthew Arnold to William Morris, sought to criticise market-based social structures and reaffirm the fundamental dignity of the person.[85] This is to say that Schilling insists on the importance of the authors he considers as thinkers, a point that was obvious to the book's reviewers: George Boas's brief review of the book concludes by noting, 'there will be no longer any excuse for seeing nothing but the "aesthetic" in these poets and novelists. Professor Schilling has made that impossible.'[86]

Among the first articles to use the expression the 'heresy of paraphrase' in print was an essay by Peter Viereck called 'My Kind of Poetry' in an August 1949 issue of a now-defunct magazine called *The Saturday Review*.[87] Viereck is sceptical of the new approach; as he writes, 'The "heresy of paraphrase," as it is called, is supposedly an insult to the intelligence of the reader. I wish more poets would "heretically" heap insults on my intelligence by paraphrasing their "double-crostics".'[88] Admittedly, Viereck is perhaps not entirely fair; Brooks is happy to concede Viereck's contention that paraphrases are an essential tool in coming to understand a poem, and Viereck admits that paraphrase is inadequate by itself.[89] Nevertheless Viereck was right to see to himself as opposed to the New Criticism; he writes that his own poetry violates the new dicta for poetics because he has 'content – something to say about the profane world they scorn – and not only form'.[90] Viereck was writing in part because he had a message to convey, and as he puts it here, engaging his poetry means understanding that message. In this sense, the dispute about paraphrase connects to a broader disagreement about what literature is and what meaningful engagement with it looks like.

And a glance through the back issues of *PMLA*, for more than a century a central organ in Anglo-American professional literary criticism, offers a wide variety of essays that emphasise the content of the works they engage. To pick one example contemporaneous with Brooks's work, in September 1949 Margaret Church published 'Thomas Wolfe: Dark Time'.[91] The essay is an attempt to understand Wolfe's philosophy of time, as compared to the theory of time in Henri Bergson and Marcel Proust; it is not troubled by the fact that Wolfe's theory is expressed in fiction, beyond noting, 'Wolfe did not write pages explaining his metaphysical solutions of the time question: he applied them'.[92]

Moving outside the academy also complicates the history of criticism. Percy Lubbock's contemporary H. L. Mencken combined admiration for formalist aesthetics with the celebration of the capacity to convey ideas.[93] He commends Balzac and Zola as figures who 'deal seriously and honestly with the larger problems of life', and complains of much American literature that 'the flow of words is completely purged of ideas'.[94] Mencken is hardly a 'meaning-monger', if that phrase denotes criticism ignorant of aesthetic evaluation or sensitivity, but he does not take that sensitivity as forbidding praising literary texts for conveying ideas worth taking seriously.

Bernard Schilling, Peter Viereck, Margaret Church and H. L. Mencken are, of course, not alone. Rather, they are a few examples of the tradition of thousands of critics whose practice resisted the dominant thrust of literary theory, and who were happy to read for the content and to treat literary authors as thinkers whose ideas had intellectual weight and which were worthy of sustained attention in the face of literary theory indicating that this was a mistake. Recovering the history of this tradition is daunting, in part because of its size, but more importantly because it has never conceived of itself as a tradition. Nevertheless it is one, and one that relies on an implicit theory of the literary text worth taking seriously.

Part of the need for recovering this tradition and theorising this approach appears moreover in the sometimes tortured justifications that critics give for emphasising literary content. Consider a few more recent essays in *PMLA*.

> At the same time, Gay renders London unlike any place that exists today. His representation of street surfacing tests our ability to see the rise of eighteenth-century London through the eyes and words of one of its citizens. Listening to this account can help us grasp two related concepts: a historical idea of the city as a gloriously broken object of upkeep and a chronologically delimited infrastructuralism able to make meaning of civic enterprises in earlier ages. (Alff)[95]

> I argue that the rational elephant can help us read early modern speciesism against itself and distinguish early modernity from modernity in ways that historicise – and denaturalise – their different speciesism. Remembering this creature from a bygone paradigm, one that was more capable of recognising rationality across differences in physical form, enables us to understand the past more closely in its own terms. It also provides a historically grounded vantage point from which we can question modern assumptions about the special status of nonhuman as well as human primates. (Alkemeyer)[96]

> Ultimately, a reaccounting of the historicity of Blake's poetic text yields a heroine and a reading population struggling to view themselves as at the centre of a reflexive system that governs and exploits the mutual relation of natural and social surroundings but that also is governed and exploited by the same biopolitical apparatus. (Hadley)[97]

What all these arguments have in common is an overt link between a historical goal and a philosophical goal. Alff wants to reveal the way a previous century viewed a city and a new way to think about cities in general; Alkemeyer wants to uncover a previous way of conceiving the difference between humans and non-humans and to question the distinction as it is currently used; and Hadley wants both to clarify a debate about an allusion in Blake and to critique a nostalgic version of environmentalism that believes mere transformations in consciousness (without changes in underlying power relations) would be sufficient.

Those goals are roughly compatible, but after a little reflection it is easy to see that they can come apart quickly. Arguments supporting the philosophical goal would be out of place in the historical account, and detail clarifying the historical account can seem unnecessary and distracting if the goal is to get to a philosophical claim. If, for instance, Alkemeyer means to question the distinction between humans and non-humans, it is not immediately obvious why that is the sort of thing that requires or even benefits from 'a historically grounded vantage point'. And Alff's conclusion brings out the dual goals clearly: 'Gay's poetic street view adumbrates a prehistory of – *and alternative to* – the top-down taxonomic structures we use to render urban experience legible today.'[98] His phrasing hides the tension, but it should be clear that the best argument for a view as an alternative is not necessarily the view that uncovers its history. Concerns such as these highlight the somewhat odd nature of this particular rhetorical structure, and make one wonder where precisely it comes from.[99] The insistence on historicity as a way to get to philosophy – one comes at Blake's theory of the environment only by way of recovering a historical feature of the text – suggests that the historical claims are really of secondary importance, of service mostly in justifying attention to the content of the text.

Compare this, for instance, with Rachel Hollander's argument in *Narrative Hospitality in Late Victorian Fiction*, which contends that political changes had a transformative effect on Victorian ethics:

> As colonial conflicts, nationalist anxiety, and the intensification of the woman question become dominant cultural concerns in the 1870s and '80s, the problem of self and other, known and unknown, begins to saturate the representation of home in the English novel. In the wake of an erosion of confidence in the ability to understand that which is unlike the self, I argue, a moral code founded on sympathy gives way to an ethics of hospitality.[100]

What one sees here is a redescription of reading for the content as a kind of historical analysis, one that turns literary criticism into an account of the impact of political and social events. But this transformation of the claim into a historical contention also renders it into an argument that literary criticism by itself is not capable of supporting. Surely, after all, the 1870s were not the first time English writers were forced to confront the problem of 'self and other', and so it is difficult to see shifts in ethical thinking in fiction as evidence of a unique event. The sort of link between ethical reflection and political situation would require a much more extensive and comparative history; at least, one would need to move systematically through the thinking about ethics in the fiction of preceding eras. But it is also not necessary to justify the kind of analysis Hollander subsequently does; whether late Victorian fiction reflects in important ways on the tensions between an ethics of hospitality and an ethics of sympathy is an interesting question, I submit, in and of itself.

Somewhat ironically, one also sees this sort of strained justification of reading for the content in literary criticism that avoids the historicist prong and simply claims that its primary goal is philosophical. Here I should admit that I'm knocking down a glass house. In my 2011 essay 'Jane Austen on Love and Pedagogical Power', I sought to call attention to the fact that Jane Austen's depictions of pedagogical dynamics in loving relationships – in other words, teachers falling in love with students, and vice versa – were often attentive to the power structures in such relationships, a dynamic that I used ideas from G. W. F. Hegel and Michel Foucault to describe.[101] However, I phrased the interpretation as if I were engaging in a philosophical dispute with Hegel while using Austen as an ally, writing: 'to a certain extent, we can read this as Austen asking, "What happens if the Lord's attempt to control the Bondsman fails?"'[102] This way of putting it implies that the argument was really philosophical – a dispute involving an unexplored problem in Hegel's thought – in which case the reading of *Pride and Prejudice* that the essay offers would simply be distracting, a sidetrack on the road to an interpretation of *The Phenomenology of Spirit*. If the question at hand really were what happens in the conflict between the Lord and the Bondsman – as opposed to how best to understand *Pride and Prejudice*, which was actually the point of my essay – then the extensive literary criticism would largely be confusing. Why bother with the details of Austen's novel if it is really a starting point for a different kind of argument altogether?

This is to say that there is often a gap between the justification given for the argument and the actual argument that follows. That gap is indicative of a missing theory, one that would explain and defend the reasons a reader might have for caring primarily about the ideas in a literary text. In the absence of that theory, critics offer historical and philosophical gestures as justifications for their criticism, but these often do not survive sceptical examination. Rather than merely pointing out their inadequacy, however, one should go further and ask where the gap between justification and actual critical practice comes from. For this is another instance of the lip service that criticism must pay to formalism: rather than overtly admitting that they are reading for the content, critics seek out other, disparate reasons why an emphasis on content is justified in a particular instance. The notion that reading for the ideas in a book might be a reasonable practice entirely on its own (and reading for form on its own has been a distinguished form of criticism for a century) is never openly invoked, but the fact that it is the real explanation for what is going on appears in the often gestural justifications that are actually given. But critical practice can be wiser than we know: what is in fact going on here results from a different kind of reading experience and a differing understanding of the literary text. Alff, Alkemeyer, Hadley and Hollander are working with the ideas in the texts they consider, and we should take seriously an account of the literary text that values its ability to create such an experience.

Where might we turn for such an account? Well, it's worth recalling the modernist roots of the formalist assumptions in literary studies described earlier; the near-instinctive insistence on the importance of literary form has a fairly specific origin point for its rise to prominence in method and literary criticism. Toril Moi puts the point well:

> Most academic defences of literature rest on one particular aesthetic norm, one particular definition of literature, namely that of late modernism [. . .] Such definitions are variations on the usual formalist definition of 'literariness', as if attention to form were the key feature of all literature, or at least of all valuable literature.[103]

And if we are looking for alternative methods, we might look first at the approach to literature that modernist assumptions replaced. It is worth recalling in this light that John Ruskin, the great art critic of the mid-Victorian era, was reluctant to designate the mental faculty at work in the experience of art the 'aesthetic'; as he writes in the second volume of *Modern Painters*, he prefers to think of the recognition of intrinsic value, entities 'desirable or admirable in themselves and for their own sake', as the product of the 'theoretic' faculty.[104]

Similarly, he insisted on portraying imagination not as a faculty for unrestrained creativity, but as a means of grasping the truth: 'Let it be understood once for all, that imagination never designs to touch anything but truth.'[105] And even more than the overt claim of its philosophers of art, one can look to the artistic practice in Victorian narrative to see a much different way of thinking about the value and purpose of literature – one in which innovations in literary form were often secondary considerations, placed beneath the primary goal of saying something true and interesting about an important topic. Famously, of course, this was Dickens's defence of *Oliver Twist*: however one might object to the morality of Nancy the prostitute, Dickens is content to fall back on the claim that 'IT IS TRUE' as a defence of its value for aesthetic representation.[106]

Victorian narrative is, of course, not the only place one might turn to as an aesthetic practice in which form was only of secondary importance. As Roger Maioli has recently brought out, the question of truth in art was essential to eighteenth-century debates about the English novel; novelists sought to defend themselves against charges of frivolity while simultaneously differentiating themselves from biographers and historians by expanding on the nature of truth, in such a way that a text might simultaneously be fictional and truthful.[107] Similarly, one might think of David Foster Wallace's diagnosis and recommendation of the 'New Sincerity' in contemporary fiction as a return to the capacity for truth-telling after a century of formal experimentation.[108] In a very different tone and register, one might see Heather Love's argument for a 'descriptive' turn and an emphasis on literature as a description of the world as another iteration of this tradition.[109] And of course, it's really a very old way of thinking about art: against Plato's diagnosis of poetry as an elaborate form of lying, one might recall Aristotle's contention that poetry was an expression of the universal.[110] As we saw earlier, critics have read literary texts for their ideas about time, urban life and the environment, and to move somewhat further afield, Michael Clune has recently pointed out that H. G. Wells's invention of the notion of time travel offers an obvious example of an exciting idea in a literary text.[111] In other words, it could have been otherwise; I want to stress that I do not take the ideas in Victorian narrative to be the only kind of interesting content literature can offer.

But if the Victorian era was not the only point at which the true mattered as much as the beautiful in art, it was certainly one such. What Henry James called the 'loose baggy monsters' of nineteenth-century fiction did not lack aesthetic merit or an artistic essence, as he suggested; rather, they reflected a different sense of what value in art might be, one in which being true was just as important and essential to artistic status and merit as being beautiful.[112] Moreover, the content of the Victorian novel and in particular its moral thought has the attraction of what social scientists call the 'least likely case', as the quintessential example of a kind of content without artistic value. After all, when the British modernists claimed that they were not interested in what the work of art could say, it was exactly the Victorian tendency to offer moral claims that they were worried about. Show that even this content is interesting, therefore, and ideas in many other areas will be justified by default. Thus the specific examples I will consider are from a relatively narrow time period, roughly Victorian fiction and narrative poetry from 1850 to 1880.

But the ethics in Victorian literature are particularly interesting for the way the scholarship on the topic follows the broad critical patterns I have identified. Long the subject of severe critique, it has received renewed attention in recent scholarship in the work of critics such as George Levine, Amanda Anderson and especially Andrew Miller and Jesse Rosenthal, but such criticism is strikingly formalist in nature – indeed it is becoming more so.[113] At the same time, there is a long tradition, one mostly undisturbed by shifts in the methods advocated by literary theory, of considering the ethical thought in Victorian literature at a more thematic level; recent books from Valerie Wainwright and Constance Fulmer indicate the general continuation of that trend.[114] The opposition between the two traditions is not necessarily fundamental: Levine's remark that it is a mistake to 'condescend to the Victorians' and to assume that 'we have got past their questions', and Miller's suggestion that it is an interest in 'moral psychology' that 'distinguishes nineteenth-century British literature' could be taken as justifications for why the second tradition should exist.[115] But the emphasis on explanatory structure is different, and the contrast between the two traditions reveals both the formalist attitude of the first tradition and the implicit alternative model of criticism in the second. Roughly, then, while I am sympathetic to both traditions, my goal here is to explore and defend the method of the second camp, and consider what its method and aesthetic theory might look like if brought into the light.

Content Versus Surface

Of course, there have been several powerful interrogations of the standard assumptions of the methodology of literary criticism in recent years, stemming in large part from a broader movement that questioned the hermeneutics of suspicion. In the words of one critic, such alternatives seek to read 'with', as opposing to reading 'against', the 'grain' of the text, and the approach to content I am arguing for responds to the same concerns.[116] Perhaps the most prominent of these interventions was the introduction of the concept of 'surface' reading in an essay by Stephen Best and Sharon Marcus, and, by way of conclusion, it is worth distinguishing my emphasis on content from the idea of surface reading.[117]

At a broad level, the two approaches are clearly congruent: Best and Marcus describe their approach as in part taking texts 'at face value', and emphasising the 'literal meaning' of a work.[118] Moreover, the relationship between philosophy and literature in my approach aligns with Best and Marcus's sense that theory 'is already present' in texts, and that a criticism that restrains itself to tracing 'what the text says about itself' need not be a criticism that dismisses theoretical questions. And an emphasis on content fits perhaps even more closely with Marcus's specific approach (said to be an instance of 'surface reading'), a method she calls 'just' reading. She writes:

> Just reading attends to what Jameson, in his pursuit of hidden master codes, dismisses as 'the inert givens and materials of a particular text' [. . .] I invoke the word 'just' in its many senses. Just reading strives to be adequate to a text conceived as complex and ample rather than as diminished by, or reduced to, what it had to repress. Just reading accounts for what it is in the text without construing presence as absence or affirmation as negation.[119]

There is a good deal here to admire. The approach I am recommending sees literary narratives as complex expressions of sophisticated ideas and tries to understand their elements as components of such expressions. This, I think, is a version of Marcus's conception of texts as 'complex and ample', and moreover fits with her decision to account for what is 'in the text' as opposed to looking for evidence of absence.

Nevertheless, my own approach will not use their terms beyond this point. The approach I am defending is a content aesthetics – a theory that literary content can form part of a text's aesthetic value and that it is possible to develop interpretive methods attuned to that value. But Best and Marcus are suspicious of a renewed aesthetics; distinguishing their approach from the 'New Formalists', they contend that such formalists believe that the artwork possesses 'autonomy from ideology', mistakenly ignoring the fact that what 'freedom' the artwork has lies in its 'struggles with its historical conditions and limits'.[120] It is not obvious why this matters: I don't know why caring about a text's surfaces requires a proper account of what 'freedom' it has or doesn't have. One might object to the claim that artworks have autonomy from ideology on several grounds, in other words, but it's tough to see how surface reading as such leads to this objection.

Still, it seems clear that what Best and Marcus have in mind and want to avoid is a sort of dehistoricised aesthetic evaluation. By calling attention to the way the creation of a work of art is always caught up in historically instantiated material processes, they avoid attributing to the surface reader the naive belief in aesthetic autonomy. But the aesthetic cannot be dealt away quite so easily, if for no other reason than without some version of aesthetic evaluation, it is difficult to see why artworks are worth caring about. The point is even more salient because Best and Marcus strip the surface reader of a belief in the use of cultural criticism to effect political or social change. As they state rather bluntly, 'literary criticism alone is not sufficient to effect change'.[121] If artworks aren't worth caring about because they're aesthetically valuable, and they're not worth caring about because they're sources of political change, then why should critics bother describing their surfaces?

As best as I can tell, Best and Marcus don't think this question needs answering. Best explained in a subsequent essay that he and Marcus sought to borrow from Bruno Latour's critique of critique, along with Latour's broader contention that scholars should undo the Kantian turn and return to sensitive descriptions of their objects of study, instead of obsessive investigation of their conditions of possibility.[122] Latour's argument is that one should deny that only the study of 'matters of fact' merits the title of 'realism'.[123] What is needed, Latour argues, is a study of the way 'matters of concern', formed of human desires and motivations, coalesce in the objects that we call 'matters of fact', but a study that in so engaging such objects maintains a sense of their 'thinginess', of their reality.[124] Whatever one might say about this practice in science studies – Latour's own field – it should be clear that to bring it into literary studies wholesale ducks one of the most important questions: namely, which objects merit the close analysis that comes with unpacking the 'matters of concern' behind a 'matter of fact'. The decision to interpret an Anthony Trollope novel instead of a newspaper column or a piece of wallpaper, after all, is not neutral. Symptomatic reading and deconstruction are more than just interpretive techniques: they are theories about why the objects of literary study are worth studying, and their techniques are fitted to the properties of the objects that justify their analysis.[125] In that sense, to dispute either approach merely on the level of interpretive technique is to miss a key feature of the motivations behind the respective positions.

Second, the 'surface/depth' metaphor is in several important ways misleading. Perhaps no element of the essay, which has sparked an incredible amount of response, has drawn as much attention as the vexed question of understanding what exactly the 'surface' of a text is.[126] As Ellen Rooney writes, it is not clear that the metaphor is consistent with what Best and Marcus are trying to do: 'that what the text is "saying about itself" (assuming such a saying exists) would be more visible on its surface than at some depth – why should every text eschew the possibility of a double game? – is a point that isn't argued'.[127] Presumably Best and Marcus would concede the point that texts can and often do play a 'double game', but this is much harder to account for without redefining 'surface' to include at least some of what would seem to be 'depth'.

To give the most obvious example, if I grasp that a text is using irony, is that a reading that works on the surface or the depth of the text? It almost doesn't matter how Best and Marcus would answer. If they say 'yes', then it would seem that 'surface' can be broadened to include a recognition that the literal meaning of a text is not its true meaning, which would make 'surface' a much more capacious and unclear category than it would at first seem to be. If they say 'no', then it would seem that surface reading cannot capture many of the most significant techniques that literary texts use. It is for reasons such as this that even those critics otherwise sympathetic to the project of surface reading find the metaphor unhelpful. For example, Rita Felski writes in *The Limits of Critique* that while she shares Best and Marcus's 'commitment to "looking at" rather than "seeing through"', she is not sure 'that the metaphor of the surface is the best way of capturing the merits of the new direction they canvass'.[128]

The content/form distinction, of course, has its own problems. As the next chapter will suggest, giving precise definitions to either term is hardly straightforward. But 'content formalism' has two advantages as way of characterising an alternate methodological approach. First, it avoids the metaphors that have become so common in this debate – aside from 'surface' and 'just', recent critics have proposed 'distant' reading, 'hyper' reading, 'reparative' reading and 'choratic' reading, among others.[129] Metaphorical labels can be useful and enabling, insofar as they can group disparate alternatives and distil them into a simple but suggestive phrase, but there is a point at which the lack of clarity inherent in the gesture is more confusing than helpful. When a phrase is meant to capture a variety of disparate approaches not obviously compatible with each other, then the lack of a precise definition to the term appears to be a way of avoiding troubling methodological questions. But second and more importantly, a phrase such as 'content formalism' concedes one of the most important objections to a method based on reading for the message: there is no way to read for the content without also reading for (what critics generally designate as) form. The point is instead one of emphasis: content formalism refuses to reduce content to explanatory material for understanding the form, instead viewing form as a means of expression while insisting that much of what goes under the banner 'form' is, in fact, content.

* * *

Let me briefly explain how the argument will proceed. I take formalist practice in literary criticism to have three main argumentative supports, each of which assembles a variety of intuitions about what a literary text is. First, there is a basic sense that what distinguishes literature from other kinds of things in the world is, essentially, something about its form, and thus that literary analysis as literary analysis must be an engagement with form. Second and correspondingly, there is a general agreement that what it means to be historically responsive to the conditions surrounding a text's composition is to be aware of its place in the history of form, and particularly of moments of change in that history. And a final broad intuition is that if literature can offer something like aesthetic experience or even other opportunities for pleasure, then this too must be a property of its form. In what follows, Chapters 1, 3 and 5 take on each of these ideas respectively, offering objections to the key supports and suggesting alternatives. Chapters 2, 4 and 6 then seek to exemplify those alternatives, with each chapter emphasising its differences from the version of formalist criticism explained in the theoretical chapter preceding it. But the examples and theoretical arguments are complementary: each of the exemplifying chapters in fact demonstrates the use of the alternate method taken as a whole, so that it is possible to look back on Chapter 2 – the example for a new way of thinking about form and content – and see both its use of a different kind of historical method and its invocation of a different form of aesthetic experience. With this map in place, then, let us turn to a consideration of the crucial form/content distinction.

Notes

1. Franco Moretti, *Distant Reading* (New York: Verso, 2013), p. 204.
2. Caroline Levine, *Forms: Whole, Rhythm, Hierarchy, Network* (Princeton: Princeton University Press, 2015), p. 4.
3. Levine, *Forms*, p. 23.
4. Susan Wolfson, *Formal Changes: The Shaping of Poetry in British Romanticism* (Palo Alto: Stanford University Press, 1999); see also 'Reading for Form', *MLQ* 61.1 (2000), pp. 1–16, her introduction to an influential special issue on form. See Marjorie Levinson, 'What is New Formalism?', *PMLA* 122.2 (2007), pp. 558–69, and Fredric Bogel, *New Formalist Criticism: Theory and Practice* (New York: Palgrave Macmillan, 2013) for descriptions of the movement.
5. Geoffrey Hartman, *The Fate of Reading and Other Essays*, p. vii, quoted in Wolfson, *Formal Changes*, p. 2.
6. Levinson, 'What is New Formalism?', p. 562. Bogel agrees that this is true of at least some versions of New Formalism, which are 'engaged in a recovery of the aesthetic from the commandeerings of literary texts performed by various modes of political, theoretical, historical, and ideological criticism' (*New Formalist Criticism*, p. 79).
7. Jonathan Kramnick and Anahid Nersessian, 'Form and Explanation', *Critical Inquiry* 43 (2017), pp. 650–69 (p. 661).
8. This is, for instance, how Geoffrey Hartman begins his defence of formalism in 'Beyond Formalism', *MLN* 81.5 (1966), pp. 542–56.
9. See, for instance, Jeanne-Marie Jackson's lamenting of the tendency of the 'law and literature movement' to 'read for the message'. 'Reading Around the Law: Sentimental Construct and *Cry, The Beloved Country*', *Peer English* 6 (2011), pp. 65–78 (p. 75).
10. Mary McCarthy, *Ideas and the Novel* (New York: Littlehampton, 1981).
11. This is exemplified most clearly by Alexander Main's volume *Wise, Witty, and Tender Sayings in Prose and Verse Selected from the Works of George Eliot*. See Leah Price, *The Anthology and the Rise of the Novel* (New York: Cambridge University Press, 2000), p. 106.
12. Price, *The Anthology and the Rise of the Novel*, p. 134.
13. Price, *The Anthology and the Rise of the Novel*, p. 131.
14. Price, *The Anthology and the Rise of the Novel*, p. 151.
15. Oscar Wilde, *The Picture of Dorian Gray*, ed. Michael Patrick Gillespie (New York: Norton, 2007), p. 3.
16. Oscar Wilde, *The Major Works*, ed. Isobel Murray (Oxford: Oxford University Press, 2000), p. 266.
17. Price, *The Anthology and the Rise of the Novel*, p. 151.
18. See, for instance, Gordon Graham, 'Aesthetic Cognitivism and the Literary Arts', *Journal of Aesthetic Education* 30.1 (1996), pp. 1–17.
19. Henry James, 'Daniel Deronda: A Conversation', *Atlantic Monthly* (December 1876). Cited in Price, *The Anthology and the Rise of the Novel*, p. 146.

20. James, 'Daniel Deronda: A Conversation', p. 105.
21. Henry James and Walter Besant, *The Art of Fiction* (Boston: Cupples, 1885), p. 76.
22. There is admittedly a certain irony in claiming that this passage alludes to an important moment in the dismissal of textual ideas from literary criticism. But as will soon become clear, the Jamesian 'idea' has little to do with propositional content.
23. This is discernible in both positive and negative reactions to James's aesthetics in the next generation of writers. E. M. Forster, in *Aspects of the Novel*, claims that 'there is no philosophy in the novels', and that in James everything serves 'the interests of the pattern. The longer James worked, the more convinced he grew that a novel should be a whole [. . .] A pattern must emerge, and anything that emerged from the pattern must be pruned off as wanton distraction' (*Aspects of the Novel* [New York: Rosetta Books, 2010], p. 110). T. S. Eliot, in a much more admiring tone, states that 'James's critical genius comes out most tellingly in his mastery over, his baffling escape from, Ideas'. The term 'idea' is no less complex in Eliot's usage than it is James's own, but the point seems to be that James does not traffic in anything so straightforward as simple propositions. This famous passage is from Eliot's 'In Memory', *Little Review* 5.4 (August 1918), pp. 44–7. I am guided here by several sources, including most prominently McCarthy's *Ideas and the Novel*.
24. Virginia Woolf, 'George Meredith', in *The Common Reader*, Second Series (New York: Mariner, 2003), p. 226.
25. James and Besant, *The Art of Fiction*, p. 56.
26. Percy Lubbock, *The Craft of Fiction* (New York: Scribner's and Sons, 1921), p. 62. Emphasis in original.
27. Dorothy Hale, *Social Formalism: The Novel in Theory from Henry James to the Present* (Palo Alto: Stanford University Press, 1998), p. 55.
28. James and Besant, *The Art of Fiction*, p. 56.
29. Gene Bell-Viada, *Art for Art's Sake and Literary Life: How Politics and Markets Helped Shape the Ideology and Culture of Aestheticism, 1790–1990* (Lincoln: University of Nebraska Press, 1996).
30. Cleanth Brooks, *The Well-Wrought Urn* (New York: Mariner, 1956), p. 195.
31. Brooks, *The Well-Wrought Urn*, p. 205.
32. Cleanth Brooks and Robert Penn Warren, *Understanding Fiction* (New York: Prentice Hall, 1943), p. xv.
33. Brooks and Warren, *Understanding Fiction*, p. xvii.
34. Brooks and Warren, *Understanding Fiction*, pp. xvii–xviii.
35. René Wellek and Austin Warren, *Theory of Literature* (New York: Harcourt, 1942), p. 92.
36. Wellek and Warren, *Theory of Literature*, p. 93.
37. Wellek and Warren, *Theory of Literature*, p. 124. In a recent essay, Heather Keenleyside has brought out how Wellek and Warren and the New Critics more generally were working to distinguish themselves

from the 'History of Ideas' approach of A. O. Lovejoy; see 'Matter, Form, Idea: What Lovejoy's History of Ideas Might Have to Do with Literature', *ELH* 84.1 (2017), pp. 223–57.
38. This claim is probably too familiar to need citation, but see, for instance, Vincent B. Leitch, 'Introduction to Theory and Criticism', in *The Norton Anthology of Theory and Criticism*, ed. Vincent B. Leitch et al. (New York: Norton, 2001), pp. 3–4; John Guillory, *Cultural Capital* (Chicago: University of Chicago Press, 1995), pp. 134–41; and Bell-Viada, *Art for Art's Sake*, pp. 186–90.
39. Duke Maskell, 'Locke and Sterne; or, Can Philosophy Influence Literature?', *Essays in Criticism: A Quarterly Journal of Literary Criticism* 23 (1973), pp. 22–40 (p. 36). I am grateful to Roger Maioli for directing me to this essay.
40. Avrom Fleishman, *George Eliot's Intellectual Life* (New York: Cambridge University Press, 2010), p. x. I touch on this issue as well in my review of Fleishman's book, *Review 19*, available at <http://www.review19.org/view_doc.php?index=120> (last accessed 16 January 2020).
41. I am guided in my understanding of the history of narratology by David Herman's many useful discussions of the field, particularly the entry on 'Structuralism' in the *Routledge Encyclopedia of Narrative Theory* (New York: Routledge, 2005) and his introductory essay to *Narratologies* (Columbus: Ohio State University Press, 1999).
42. Tzvetan Todorov and Arnold Weinstein, 'Structural Analysis of Narrative', *NOVEL: A Forum on Fiction* 3.1 (1969), pp. 70–6 (pp. 70–1). In fact, Todorov faults the New Critics for producing only a 'paraphrase of the work, which is supposed to reveal the meaning better than the work itself' (p. 70). In this sense, the structuralists take themselves to be even more critical of interpretations that generate paraphrases than the New Critics, who would by no means have described themselves as engaged in 'paraphrase'.
43. Bell-Viada, *Art for Art's Sake*, pp. 196, 271.
44. Jane Gallop, 'The Historicization of Literary Studies and the Fate of Close Reading', *Profession* (2007), pp. 181–6 (p. 182).
45. Gallop, 'The Historicization of Literary Studies', p. 182.
46. Jacques Derrida, '"This Strange Institution Called Literature": An Interview with Jacques Derrida', in *Acts of Literature*, ed. Derek Attridge (New York: Routledge, 1992), pp. 33–75 (p. 43).
47. Derrida, 'This Strange Institution', p. 45.
48. Derrida, 'This Strange Institution', p. 52. The critic should offer 'an inventive experience of language, *in* language, an inscription of the act of reading in the field of the text that is read' (p. 52).
49. Jacques Derrida, 'Before the Law', in *Acts of Literature*, pp. 181–220 (pp. 196–7).
50. Derrida, 'This Strange Institution', pp. 210–11.
51. Derrida, 'This Strange Institution', p. 211.

52. Fredric Jameson, *The Political Unconscious: Narrative as a Socially Symbolic Act* (New York: Routledge, 2002), pp. 45–6.
53. Jameson, *The Political Unconscious*, p. 46.
54. For an effective discussion of Jameson on this point, see Jeremy Tambling, *Allegory* (London: Routledge, 2009), p. 156.
55. Jameson, *The Political Unconscious*, p. 46. Jameson overtly suggests this, noting that psychoanalysis has long served as a similar fundamental code for a number of critics, and is in some sense 'the most influential and elaborate interpretive system of recent times' (*The Political Unconscious*, p. 61).
56. Eve Sedgwick, 'Paranoid Reading and Reparative Reading, or, You're so Paranoid, You Probably Think this Essay is about You', in *Touching Feeling: Affect, Pedagogy, Performativity* (Durham, NC: Duke University Press, 2003), p. 125.
57. Rita Felski, 'Suspicious Minds', *Poetics Today* 32.2 (2011), pp. 215–34 (p. 217).
58. My point here is in sympathy with Toril Moi, who writes, 'When it comes to aesthetic strategies, then, formalism and culturalism are not as different as they seem. In fact, they are barely different at all. For how long are formalists and culturalists going to go on [. . .] losing themselves in the contemplation of the linguistic beyond?' *Henrik Ibsen and the Birth of Modernism* (Oxford: Oxford University Press, 2006), p. 22.
59. I do not mean to deny that there have been dissident voices recommending something similar to the approach I defend here. Gerald Graff has defended the notion that literary texts can make 'truth claims'; see especially the 'Literature as Propositions' section in *Literature Against Itself: Literary Ideas in Modern Society* (Chicago: University of Chicago Press, 1979). Frederick Crews's satires of a number of theoretical approaches, most recently in *Postmodern Pooh* (New York: Farrar, Straus, and Giroux, 2001), perhaps also ultimately support reading for the content. And there is also a much larger tradition of silent dissent, of which more in a moment.
60. The account I offer here of the history of the ethical turn largely parallels the standard interpretations. See Michael Eskin, 'The Double "Turn" to Ethics and Literature?', *Poetics Today* 25.4 (2004), pp. 557–72; and David Parker, *Ethics, Theory, and the Novel* (Cambridge: Cambridge University Press, 1994), pp. 1–43.
61. See, most prominently, Martha Nussbaum, *The Fragility of Goodness: Luck and Ethics in Greek Tragedy and Philosophy* (New York: Cambridge University Press, 1986). See also Bernard Williams, *Shame and Necessity* (Berkeley: University of California Press, 1993), and Alasdair Macintyre, *After Virtue: A Study in Moral Theory* (South Bend, IN: University of Notre Dame Press, 1981).
62. See especially Richard Rorty, *Philosophy and the Mirror of Nature* (Princeton: Princeton University Press, 1979), and Charles Taylor,

Sources of the Self: The Making of Modern Identity (Cambridge, MA: Harvard University Press, 1992).
63. Eskin, 'The Double "Turn" to Ethics and Literature?', p. 558.
64. Jacques Derrida, *The Gift of Death* (Chicago: University of Chicago Press, 1996); *The Politics of Friendship* (New York: Verso, 1997). For Foucault, see *The Use of Pleasure*, trans. Robert Hurley (New York: Vintage, 1990) and *The Hermeneutics of the Subject*, trans. Graham Burchell (New York: Picador, 2001). Simon Critchley, in *The Ethics of Deconstruction: Derrida and Levinas* (New York: Blackwell, 1992), is generally recognised as being among the first critics to describe the shift in deconstructive thought as a shift. See David Parker's concise and informed summary in 'The Turn to Ethics in the 1990s', *The Critical Review* 33 (1993), pp. 3–15.
65. J. Hillis Miller's *The Ethics of Reading* was perhaps the first treatment in this regard; Adam Zachary Newton's *Narrative Ethics* developed Derrida's Levinasian insights a decade later. J. Hillis Miller, *The Ethics of Reading* (New York: Columbia University Press, 1987); Adam Zachary Newton, *Narrative Ethics* (Cambridge, MA: Harvard University Press, 1997).
66. In particular, Wayne Booth, in literary studies – whose 1988 monograph *The Company We Keep* is a central text in ethical criticism – had long been working on the rhetorical force of fiction; similarly, Stanley Cavell, in philosophy, had been thinking about the interrelationship between normativity and literature along Wittgensteinian lines; finally, Iris Murdoch – as both a moral philosopher and a novelist – crossed the boundaries between the fields for her entire life. See Wayne C. Booth, *The Rhetoric of Fiction* (Chicago: University of Chicago Press, 1961); Stanley Cavell, *Must We Mean What We Say?* (New York: Cambridge University Press, 1969); and, for a nuanced discussion of Murdoch's thought, Maria Antonaccio, *Picturing the Human: The Moral Thought of Iris Murdoch* (New York: Oxford University Press, 2000).
67. Lawrence Buell noted in 2000 that some fourteen hundred essays in 'ethics-related literature scholarship' were published between 1981 and 1997, and the number has only increased since.
68. Eskin, 'The Double "Turn" to Ethics and Literature?', p. 560.
69. Miller, *The Ethics of Reading*, p. 75.
70. Miller, *The Ethics of Reading*, p. 122.
71. This is in one sense broadly in line with those critics who have resisted the notion that aesthetic experience is ethically transformative. See Joshua Landy, 'A Nation of Madame Bovarys: On the Possibility and Desirability of Moral Improvement through Fiction', in Gary Hagberg (ed.), *Art and Ethical Criticism* (New York: Wiley-Blackwell, 2008), pp. 63–94; and especially Suzanne Keen, *Empathy and the Novel* (New York: Oxford University Press, 2007).
72. Wayne C. Booth, *The Company We Keep: An Ethics of Fiction* (Berkeley: University of California Press, 1988), p. 175.

73. Booth, *The Company We Keep*, p. 70.
74. Booth, *The Company We Keep*, p. 476.
75. Newton, *Narrative Ethics*, p. 11.
76. Newton, *Narrative Ethics*, pp. 10–11.
77. Newton, *Narrative Ethics*, p. 65.
78. Simon Haines, 'Deepening the Self: The Language of Ethics and the Language of Literature', in Jane Adamson et al. (eds), *Renegotiating Ethics in Literature, Philosophy, and Theory* (New York: Cambridge University Press, 1998), pp. 21–38 (p. 24); Parker, 'The Turn to Ethics', p. 17.
79. Booth, *The Rhetoric of Fiction*, p. 112. Booth's example is Dostoevsky: 'In *Crime and Punishment* we experience a wide variety of intellectual appeals. We are curious about the philosophical and religious and political battle between nihilism and relativism on the one hand and salvation on the other' (p. 134). However, Booth then goes on to link these 'intellectual appeals' to our 'qualitative and practical' interests as well – in the form of formal beauty and character identification.
80. Martha Nussbaum, *Love's Knowledge: Essays on Philosophy and Literature* (New York: Oxford University Press, 1992), pp. 148, 29. Nussbaum explains further: 'It is, in fact, just this that we wish to preserve and to bring into philosophy. The very qualities that make the novels so unlike dogmatic abstract treatises are, for us, the source of their *philosophical* interest' (p. 29).
81. Joshua Landy, *How to Do Things with Fictions* (New York: Oxford University Press, 2012), p. 8. I have touched on these issues in my review of Landy's book; see 'Why Books Can Be Good for You', *Journal of Literary Theory Online*, March 2013, available at <http://nbn-resolving.de/urn:nbn:de:0222-002427> (last accessed 18 December 2019).
82. Landy, *How to Do Things with Fictions*, pp. 153, 8.
83. Julie Orlemanski, 'Scales of Reading', *Exemplaria: Medieval, Early Modern, Theory* 26.2–3 (2014), pp. 215–33 (p. 227).
84. Austin Wright, 'Victorian Bibliography for 1947', *Modern Philology* 45.4 (1948), pp. 246–69.
85. Bernard Schilling, *Human Dignity and the Great Victorians* (New York: Columbia University Press, 1946).
86. George Boas, 'Review', *The Journal of Aesthetics and Art Criticism* 6.1 (1947), pp. 73–5 (p. 74).
87. Peter Viereck, 'My Kind of Poetry', *The Saturday Review* 51 (August 1949), pp. 7–8, 34–6. As an editor's note explains, Viereck's essay was the third in a series of essays debating the New Criticism and the current state of poetry. The debate was quite intense: the editor writes, 'As Mr. Viereck has pointed out, he "was serving against Fascism as an American sergeant in the Italian campaign at the very time when Ezra Pound was comfortably broadcasting his Fascism and treason from Mussolini's Ministry of Propaganda"' (p. 7).

88. Viereck, 'My Kind of Poetry', p. 36.
89. Viereck, 'My Kind of Poetry', p. 35.
90. Viereck, 'My Kind of Poetry', p. 7.
91. Margaret Church, 'Thomas Wolfe: Dark Time', *PMLA* 64.4 (1949), pp. 629–38.
92. Church, 'Thomas Wolfe: Dark Time', p. 630.
93. Percy Lubbock, *A Book of Prefaces* (New York: Knopf, 1917), p. 199.
94. Lubbock, *A Book of Prefaces*, pp. 202, 219.
95. David Alff, 'Before Infrastructure: The Poetics of Paving in John Gay's Trivia', *PMLA* 132.5 (2017), p. 1136.
96. Bryan Alkemeyer, 'Remembering the Elephant: Animal Reason before the Eighteenth Century', *PMLA* 132.5 (2017), p. 1149.
97. Karen Hadley, 'Blake's Visions of the Daughters of Albion and the Biopolitical Unconscious', *PMLA* 133.2 (2018), p. 316.
98. Alff, 'Before Infrastructure', p. 1146, emphasis mine.
99. I shall have much more to say about the relationship between historical reconstruction and philosophical argument in a moment.
100. Rachel Hollander, *Narrative Hospitality in Late Victorian Fiction* (New York: Routledge, 2012), p. 3.
101. Patrick Fessenbecker, 'Jane Austen on Love and Pedagogical Power', *SEL* 51.4 (2011), pp. 747–63.
102. Fessenbecker, 'Jane Austen on Love', p. 758.
103. Toril Moi, *Revolution of the Ordinary: Literary Studies after Wittgenstein, Austin, and Cavell* (Chicago: University of Chicago Press, 2017), p. 214.
104. John Ruskin, *Modern Painters*, vol. II (New York: The National Library Association, 1905), Section I, Chapter I, § 8. Available at www.gutenberg.org. I don't want to overstate the value of this model, however; Ruskin's is a fairly clear example what Toril Moi calls 'idealist' aesthetics, in seeing a religiously inflected union of the true, the good and the beautiful (*Ibsen*, p. 74). I mean more simply to note that there are ways of regarding the capacity of art to tell the truth as important.
105. Ruskin, *Modern Painters*, Section II, Chapter II, § 22. In a recent essay, Andrea Selleri has brought out what he calls the related 'authorialist' assumptions of Victorian literary criticism, among which is the idea that a work of literature is something the author has said. 'Oscar Wilde on the Theory of the Author', *Philosophy and Literature* 42.1 (2018), p. 52.
106. Charles Dickens, *Oliver Twist*, ed. Fred Kaplan (New York: Norton, 1993), p. 6.
107. Roger Maioli, *Empiricism and the Early Theory of the Novel* (New York: Palgrave Macmillan, 2016). See especially the discussion of the role that truth played in the 'rise of the novel' debate in his introduction (pp. 1–38).

108. See David Foster Wallace, 'E Unibus Pluram: Television and US Fiction', *Review of Contemporary Fiction* 13.2 (1993), pp. 151–94.
109. See Heather Love, 'Close but Not Deep: Literary Ethics and the Descriptive Turn', *New Literary History* 41.2 (2010), pp. 371–91. The essay presents itself as a challenge to traditional humanist forms of interpretation, but read charitably I think it can be seen as a renewal of one of that tradition's oldest premises.
110. *Poetics*, trans. S. H. Butcher (New York: Macmillan, 1895), ch. IX.
111. See Michael Clune, 'Formalism as the Fear of Ideas', *PMLA* 132.5 (2017), p. 1194. Rita Felski's *The Uses of Literature* (New York: Blackwell, 2011) offers as an example of the knowledge literature can offer the insights that Edith Wharton has into interpersonal dynamics.
112. See Henry James, 'Preface' to *The Tragic Muse* (New York: Penguin, 1995), p. 4.
113. See George Levine, *Dying to Know: Scientific Epistemology and Narrative in Victorian England* (Chicago: University of Chicago Press, 2002), and *Realism, Ethics, and Secularism* (New York: Cambridge University Press, 2008); Amanda Anderson, *The Powers of Distance: Cosmopolitanism and the Cultivation of Detachment* (Princeton: Princeton University Press, 2001); Andrew H. Miller, *The Burdens of Perfection* (Ithaca: Cornell University Press, 2008); and Jesse Rosenthal, *Good Form: The Ethical Experience of the Victorian Novel* (Princeton: Princeton University Press, 2017). For a survey of this recent movement, I am indebted to Hao Li, 'Deploying "Ethics" in Victorian England', *Literature Compass* 7.3 (2010), pp. 226–42 (p. 227).
114. See Valerie Wainwright, *Ethics and the English Novel from Austen to Forster* (Burlington, VT: Ashgate, 2007), and Constance Fulmer, *George Eliot's Moral Aesthetic* (New York: Routledge, 2018). For a slightly older example, see Jil Larson, *Ethics and Narrative in the English Novel, 1880–1914* (New York: Cambridge University Press, 2001).
115. Levine, *Realism, Ethics, and Secularism*, p. 53; Miller, *The Burdens of Perfection*, p. xi.
116. This is Tim Bewes's phrase, though I am not sure that I am using it quite the way he does. Tim Bewes, 'Reading with the Grain: A New World in Literary Criticism', *Differences* 21.3 (2010), pp. 1–33.
117. Stephen Best and Sharon Marcus, 'Surface Reading: An Introduction', *Representations* 108.1 (2009), pp. 1–21.
118. Best and Marcus, 'Surface Reading', p. 12.
119. Sharon Marcus, *Between Women: Friendship, Marriage, and Desire in Victorian England* (Princeton: Princeton University Press, 2007), p. 75.
120. Best and Marcus, 'Surface Reading', p. 14. Best and Marcus are following in this regard Levinson, 'What is New Formalism?'
121. Best and Marcus, 'Surface Reading', p. 2.
122. Stephen Best, 'Well, that was obvious', response to *Representations* 125 (2014), special issue 'Technically, Denotatively, Literally',

available at <https://www.representations.org/two-responses-to-denotatively-technically-literally/> (last accessed 14 January 2020). This is present in the original essay as well, which ends by invoking Latour's contention that 'the question was never to get *away* from facts but *closer* to them' ('Surface Reading', p. 19; the quotation is from Bruno Latour, 'Why Has Critique Run Out of Steam?', *Critical Inquiry* 30 [winter 2004], pp. 225–48 [p. 231]).
123. Latour, 'Critique', p. 231.
124. See Latour, 'Critique', p. 237: 'Why can we never describe the same stubbornness, the same solid realism by bringing out the obviously webby, "thingy" qualities of matters of concern?'
125. It seems to me that this problem remains and is if anything exacerbated in their subsequent work on the issue. In 'Building A Better Description', Best and Marcus – along with Heather Love – explain that they are interested in recuperating and defending description as such, as opposed to the more penetrative act of interpretation. Maybe, but the question of exactly what one should describe remains unanswered. Stephen Best and Sharon Marcus, 'Building A Better Description', *Representations* 135.1 (2016), pp. 1–21.
126. In addition to Felski and Rooney, described below, see Nathan Hensley, 'Figures of Reading', *Criticism* 54.2 (2012), pp. 329–40, and E. H. Anderson, 'Why We Do (Or Don't) Argue About the Way We Read', *The Eighteenth Century* 54.1 (2013), pp. 125–8.
127. Ellen Rooney, 'Live Free or Describe: The Reading Effect and the Persistence of Form', *differences* 21.3 (2010), pp. 112–39 (p. 124).
128. Rita Felski, *The Limits of Critique* (Chicago: University of Chicago Press, 2015), p. 55.
129. See Moretti, *Distant Reading*; N. Katherine Hayles, *How We Think: Digital Media and Contemporary Technogenesis* (Chicago: University of Chicago Press, 2012); Sedgwick, 'Paranoid Reading and Reparative Reading'; Rebekah Sheldon, 'Form/Matter/Chora: Object-Oriented Ontology and Feminist New Materialism', in Richard Grusin (ed.), *The Nonhuman Turn* (Minneapolis: University of Minnesota Press, 2015), pp. 193–222.

Chapter 1

Content and Form

What is the content of a literary text? The extent to which literary criticism has thought this question trivial and unimportant is conveyed well by the *Routledge Dictionary of Literary Terms*, which offers a seven-paragraph definition for 'form' but contains no entry for 'content', going directly from 'consonance' to 'context' (it is perhaps worth noting that the dictionary does find space for 'cybercriticism', 'eurocentrism', and a six-paragraph definition of 'rhizome'). Yet the dictionary also, if only accidentally, conveys a sense of the necessity of the concept. Aside from the use of the term 'content' in dozens of definitions of other terms, the dictionary's definition of 'paraphrase' ends with this line: 'See also CONTENT, FORM, STYLE, TEXTURE'.[1] So at some point it appears that the authors recognised the need for a definition of content, but in the face of the competing need to devote adequate attention to Deleuze and Guattari they ultimately decided it wasn't worth it.[2]

To its credit, the *Oxford Dictionary of Literary Terms* at least includes the word, defining it thus:

> CONTENT: The term commonly used to refer to what is said in a literary work, as opposed to how it is said (that is, to the form or style). Distinctions between form and content are necessarily abstractions made for the sake of analysis, since in any actual work there can be no content that has not in some way been formed, and no purely empty form. The indivisibility of form and content, though, is something of a critical truism which often obscures the degree to which a work's matter can survive changes in its manner (in revisions, translations, and paraphrase) and it is only by positing some other manner in which this matter can be presented that one is able in analysis to isolate the specific form of a given work.[3]

What is striking about this attempt to define the word is the way it reverses itself. The definition starts with what has been one common way of defining content and explicating the content/form distinction: it's the what-is-said by the text, versus the how-it-is-said of form.

But the dictionary then quickly undermines this distinction, explaining that form and content are not really different and cannot exist independently of each other; the reader will not be surprised to learn that no such qualification is included in the dictionary's definition for 'form'.[4] Having thus qualified the term, it then reverses itself again, claiming that the indivisibility of form and content is just a critical truism, and that actually a text's 'matter' (and the silent slippage from 'what is said' to 'matter' is worth noting) can and does survive changes in the text's 'manner'. And the argument for this claim turns to something readers can do with a text: namely, they can present its matter in a different way. But the definition ends with an odd return to the importance of form, contending (somewhat dubiously) that it is only by imagining an alternative presentation of the text's content that it is possible for critics to talk about its form.

The problem, it is worth stressing, is not with the dictionary's author. The confusions here are representative of the field's broader approach, which generally regards content as uninteresting while continuing to rely on a vague and ill-defined notion of the concept. But the definition does at least offer a starting point: a text's content is either 'what it says' or its 'matter'. Moreover, the final portion of the definition contains an important insight: the notion that a text has a content is in some peculiar way tied up with an interpretive activity – namely, paraphrasing, revising and translating. To recognise a literary text's content is part and parcel of a decision of what to do with it, how one wants to experience it.

This feature is not unique to content. The decision to designate part of a text as its 'form' is, I will argue, already to choose to experience it in a certain way. This is an element of the versions of formalism in contemporary literary criticism, which generally avoid aesthetic justifications for the interpretation of literature, that has tended to disappear. But pressing on the basic definition of content and thus of form reveals how an implicit ranking of the various ways of reading the text underlies the basic distinction between form and content in the first place. If, however, we undo that implicit ranking, then we can develop both a clearer definition of content and form and explain more clearly what it means to read for one or the other.

The Work as Form, the Work as Content

The implicit privileging of one kind of reading inherent in the designation that a particular element of a text constitutes its form is perhaps clearest in the works of those critics who try to do away with the content half of the form/content dyad entirely, using what I will call the 'shape/matter' version of the form/content distinction. As Angela Leighton notes, 'form' can be and has been thought of as one half of three different dyads: form/content, form/matter, or 'form/formlessness'.[5] And as we saw in the definition from the *Oxford Dictionary*, the definitions have a tendency to slip into each other – content is turned into matter, which enables the view that it is fundamentally randomness and bare substance, brought into definite existence by form. A more self-conscious version of this transformation occurs, for instance, in Noël Carroll's *Philosophy of Art: A Contemporary Introduction*. Noting that not all art has representational content, and that therefore an attempt to define form as the opposite of content will be unable to account for some instances of artistic form, he suggests instead that one conceive of a work of art as made up of 'parts', and form as the 'webs of relations' between the various parts.[6]

Such definitions are especially appealing when one is looking for what literature has in common with the other arts, as in what Daniel Albright calls 'panaesthetics', or indeed with other substances.[7] But when they are applied to literature, they implicitly presuppose a certain way of reading. Take, for instance, this group of definitions:

> Because form is precisely the repeatable element of literature: what remains fundamentally unchanged over many cases and many years. This, then, is what formalism can do for literary history: teach it to smile at the colorful anecdote [. . .] and to recognise instead the regularity of the literary field.[8]

> I want to say three things along these lines: 'No formalism without ontology'; 'No genre without form'; and form as nothing more – and nothing less – than the shape matter (whether a poem or a tree) takes.[9]

> 'Form' always indicates an arrangement of elements – an ordering, patterning, or shaping [. . .] Form, for our purposes, will mean all shapes and configurations, all ordering principles, all patterns of repetition and difference.[10]

> Form repeated in English the complications of its Latin development, of which two are principally relevant: (i) a visible or outward shape, with a strong sense of the physical body [. . .] an essential shaping principle, making indeterminate material into a determinate or specific being or thing.[11]

These are not definitions that care very much about content. Even in their basic articulation of the distinction between form and content, one gets a sense of which term really matters. Nevertheless a family resemblance between the definitions emerges. According to this line of thought, literary content is the matter, material or element of the text; it is vague and ill-defined by itself, but it is given determinacy, shape or pattern by the fact of form.

Clearly this way of understanding the form/content distinction has a good deal of intuitive appeal, but in terms of literature it contains a deep mistake. Most elements of a literary text can be plausibly thought of as either part of the ordering principle/shaping pattern or as the matter/material that is ordered/shaped. Whether one regards it as form or content does not reflect some fact about the text but instead the attitude one brings to the experience of reading. Correspondingly, the designation of certain elements as 'formal' and therefore worthy of study depends on an implicit privileging of one distinctive kind of aesthetic experience.

To show this, let me turn to a justly famous paper in the philosophy of art, Kendall Walton's 1970 essay 'Categories of Art', which contains the following thought experiment:

> Imagine a society which does not have an established medium of painting, but does produce a kind of work of art called guernicas. Guernicas are like versions of Picasso's 'Guernica' done in various bas-relief dimensions. All of them are surfaces with the colors and shapes of Picasso's 'Guernica', but the surfaces are molded to protrude from the wall like relief maps of different kinds of terrain. Some guernicas have rolling surfaces, others are sharp and jagged, still others contain several relatively flat planes at various angles to each other, and so forth. Picasso's 'Guernica' would be counted as a guernica in this society – a perfectly flat one – rather than as a painting.[12]

The point Walton draws from this thought experiment is that the way we experience Picasso's work depends on the category of art we place it in, and thus upon the expectations that we bring to the work. To us, *Guernica* is violent, disturbing and disorganised – a representation of the chaos of war. But to a society with guernicas, Picasso's *Guernica* would probably feel entirely different – its flatness conveying stillness or perhaps lifelessness, when experienced against the background of its more dramatic and differently shaped brethren.

Let me take this thought experiment a step further, in a direction Walton doesn't go. To us, *Guernica* is a representation of war; the screaming horse at the centre of the painting forms a focal point for the broken bodies scattered around it, and dramatically conveys chaotic violence. There is a clear content here; the painting represents horses, swords, human bodies, spears, fire and other discrete objects, and depends for its effect on our recognition of these facts. But in a society with guernicas, it is not at all obvious that the painting would continue to represent these things (How would one convey the chaos of war in a world with guernicas? Certainly not with *Guernica*.) In other words, the representational elements would pass into a status of constitutive features of this particular category of art. I want to suggest that they would pass from being contents to being forms, at least under the shape/matter version of the form/content distinction. Picasso's horse, for instance, would cease to be an element given shape by the rest of the painting, and become part of the pattern giving shape to other features.

This might seem somewhat far-fetched, of interest only to philosophers. But genre history offers a surprisingly close analogy. Consider one of Franco Moretti's examples of a formal feature – the clue in a mystery novel. As he explains, the clues in a mystery novel are 'a formal device', because 'their narrative function (the encrypted reference to the criminal) remains constant, although their concrete embodiment changes from story to story'.[13] What Moretti hypothesises is that clues have a more or less discrete moment of invention as a formal feature in Arthur Conan Doyle's Sherlock Holmes stories. Then, this feature propagates into the twentieth century, as those mystery writers who do not use clues are ignored and forgotten. What the comparison to Walton's guernicas thought experiment highlights is how much the recognition of the formal dimension of clues depends on the later tradition of mystery fiction. In other words, clues were not formal features to begin with. As Moretti notes, even Conan Doyle didn't figure out how to really structure a story around clues; that took Agatha Christie.[14] Clues, instead, were elements of the content – things shaped by other narrative features, not the thing doing the shaping.[15]

Can a feature go the other way – from form into content? I'm not aware of any genre studies that look at literary history in this way, but it doesn't seem too difficult to imagine. Any time authors draw on a formal tradition that has disappeared, and which is no longer active as a standard expectation underlying the experience of their readers, they reintroduce as content a feature that an earlier audience would have understood as form. To stay with genre fiction for a moment, J. R. R. Tolkien's decision to use tropes from the tradition of Germanic mythology – a broken sword, a magic ring, and perhaps above all a mythic style, with its songs and archetypal, larger-than-life characters – affect contemporary audiences much differently than they did the listeners of medieval Germany.[16]

And more immediately and importantly, this is what happens the first time a reader encounters a particular formal tradition. Going back to Moretti's example of detective fiction, the genre's widely used formal pattern of initial crisis–misleading clue–false suspect–revealing clue–real suspect is essentially and importantly not a pattern at all when it is read from the perspective of the reader reading a mystery for the first time.[17] Indeed the idea that such a reader could ever find or care about a pattern or shape in the book begins to seem a little strange. How can one know what is part of the pattern and what is not if there is only one object in question? Shapes emerge, after all, via comparison.

Moreover, to emphasise their formal dimension is misleading insofar as it fails to capture the appeal of such features of the text. To the reader first encountering detective fiction, a crucial condition for the effect of the so-called 'formal' elements is precisely the fact that they are surprising. The possibility that there might not be a pattern to the story – that the first suspect might actually be guilty, and that anything might happen – is essential to the aesthetic experience of the first-time reader. That's true even if the story is in fact a deeply generic example of the literary tradition: the reader experiences as content what the author and more informed readers would see as form. And we should resist the idea that some elements are inherently more formal than others; as Walton's example of a tradition of guernicas brings out, no feature of the text is inherently more 'repeatable' – Moretti's word – than any other. Which features are repeated and which aren't depends on the contingencies of literary history.

If this argument is persuasive, then what it leads to is the conclusion that the shape/matter version of the form/content distinction does capture something important about reading a literary text, but what it captures is less about the text and more about the experience of reading. 'Form' and 'content' are not really distinct elements of the text, but names for different attitudes readers might take towards the same elements. The assumption that an element is one or the other presupposes a certain experience, and there is no immediately obvious reason why we should prefer one or the other as more inherently accurate. This doesn't mean that one could do away with the word 'form' entirely, but it does imply a limitation of its scope to the open and overt experience of repetition and pattern, as in poetic effects such as rhyme, and dismissing the idea that the form is a structuring principle.

Let me illustrate this contention with a brief example. Consider Robert Frost's 'Desert Places':

> Snow falling and night falling fast, oh, fast
> In a field I looked into going past,
> And the ground almost covered smooth in snow,
> But a few weeds and stubble showing last.
>
> The woods around it have it – it is theirs.
> All animals are smothered in their lairs.
> I am too absent-spirited to count;
> The loneliness includes me unawares.
>
> And lonely as it is, that loneliness
> Will be more lonely ere it will be less –
> A blanker whiteness of benighted snow
> With no expression, nothing to express.
>
> They cannot scare me with their empty spaces
> Between stars-on stars where no human race is.
> I have it in me so much nearer home
> To scare myself with my own desert places.

In what sense is it true that this poem has a rhyme scheme – an AABA CCDC EEBE FFGF pattern – and in what sense does that scheme 'structure' the poem? For rhyme here is certainly an effect discernible by the first-time reader, and insofar as rhyme involves the recognition of a repetition, it has a strong case to make that it is a formal element and not part of the content. But to say that it 'structures' the poem is already to presuppose a certain experience of reading. The rhymes do not form a schematic to the reader the first time through, and surely the fact that the schematic is unknown and the rhymes come as a surprise creates part of the effect. In a famous essay, Eve Sedgwick critiques the hermeneutics of suspicion as committed to a paranoid style, a critical approach committed to vigilant anticipation: 'the aversion to surprise seems to be what cements the intimacy between paranoia and knowledge'.[18] Although the hermeneutics of suspicion are often regarded as a rejection of traditional formalism, here is another area in which they concur: formalism is a technique for managing surprise, for finding pattern and predictability amid contingency.

To come at it from another way, the idea that aural effects of rhyme are somehow more fundamental and structural to the poem than the sequence of ideas presupposes the basic background of expectations that Walton has shown us are mutable. We trained readers approach the poem with the knowledge of the term 'poetry', and know that many poems do use rhyme schemes, while rather fewer use an extended visual metaphor to describe the experience of depression. But this is certainly historically contingent. It is possible to imagine a world in which a genre called *desert places* exist – where all the instances have a specific sequence of images describing a snowy field and end with a psychological meditation. And the variation or matter of the text in that world might well be the rhyme schemes, with different *desert places* rhyming in different ways. More humbly, it's not hard to imagine someone hearing this poem without knowing what poetry is or what rhyme schemes are. Such a reader would certainly still hear the rhyme and thus in some sense perceive it as a pattern, but the more elaborate claims about form as shape or structure would be difficult to reconcile with this reader's experience.

My argument here is thus democratic in a small-d sense. One way to put my challenge would be to insist that every time it is claimed that a given element of a text is a form, a sceptical interlocutor should ask the following: to which reader and in which reading experience does the form appear, and why is that reader's experience authoritative for determining the nature of the text? Are there reading experiences in which the element does not appear as a form, and why are such experiences irrelevant to the analysis? Mine is thus a version of Stanley Fish's argument about interpretive communities, as one way to see the background of expectations that Walton describes as a community that helps determine the meaning of the work of art.[19] And Fish could presumably agree with the relativistic point that whether an element of the text is form or content depends on the nature of the reader. But it is worth stressing that we have not yet got to the idea of the text as having a meaning: I have instead focused on the experience of the work of art. Then, too, formalism is not best thought of as a community: it is rather an attitude.

The Formalist Attitude

As Marjorie Levinson notes, one of the surprising features of the new formalism in literary studies is that it does not share a view of what form is; indeed, it hasn't really retheorised form at all.[20] But this fits and indeed is what one would expect if it is primarily attitudinal, a preference for certain ways of experiencing literary texts, rather than a shared philosophical view and research programme. That attitude above all involves the positioning of oneself as well informed and sophisticated. Formalists grasp the work's relationship to other works, its exemplification of and variation upon the patterns and shapes it has inherited, and they keenly perceive which elements of the text are fundamental and which are merely superficial. Literary form is rarely simple, according to the formalist, and certainly never when it's interesting. Susan Wolfson accurately if perhaps unintentionally conveys this attitudinal coherence in her essay 'Reading for Form'; the essay, which introduced a number of formalist essays in a special issue of the journal *Modern Language Quarterly*, explained that they fitted together because

> All share a sense that the reductive critique of formalism, in publication and pedagogy, has had unfortunate results, not the least a dulling of critical instruments and a loss of sensitivity to the complexity of literary form: its various and surprising work, its complex relation to traditions, and its interaction with extraliterary culture.[21]

The adjectives here are striking: Wolfson reiterates that literary form is complex, while the critique of formalism is 'reductive'. As opposed to the dull and insensitive non-formalist reader, the formalist will bring sharp 'critical instruments' to bear. Even in Wolfson's charitable summary, the writers don't agree on a theory so much as they share a set of investments and a critical stance.

We should pause further over that word 'sensitive', for the idea of a distinctive sensitivity is also a key component of the formalist attitude. The idea of the formalist as someone alive to details of human life that the vast majority of us ignore has seduced a variety of contemporary critics; Caroline Levine's 'canny formalists' can see the interlocking patterns in political and social life, while Martha Nussbaum's readers of Henry James can see the tiny details that make nuanced ethical responses possible.[22] Nathan Hensley's formalism can see the impacts of political reality, even those realities that try to stay hidden, while John Gibson's formalist is 'alive to those patterns of value, significance, and meaning, that are woven into the aspects of the world we otherwise merely know'.[23] It would be easy to extend this list much further: the sensitivities of the formalist are myriad and diverse, and moreover are attested to by critics – such as Levine and Hensley – who are sceptical of ethical criticism and motivated by more overtly political concerns.

One such sensitivity that recurs often, however, is the formalist's distinct kind of pleasure. Acknowledging the varieties of artistic pleasure introduces a complex and important issue that merits its own turn at the centre of attention, especially since many contemporary formalists explicitly disavow justifications for formalism that depend on aesthetic pleasure; I'll come back to this more substantively in Chapter 5. It is worth noting briefly here, however, because of the link between formalist pleasure and the formalist attitude; an essential element of formalist enjoyment, when it is appealed to, is the formalist's own sense of the distinctiveness and sophistication of his or her appreciation of the work of art. As Toril Moi puts it in a discussion of Charles Altieri, 'such readers are likely to admire themselves for being capable of self-conscious admiring'.[24] In a scathing review of Marjorie Garber's *The Use and Abuse of Literature*, William Deresiewicz makes a similar point, diagnosing her refusal to evaluate literary art in terms of its 'outcomes, impact and application' as ultimately the reflection of her commitment to the kind of reading specific to English professors – the discernment of 'endless interpretability, the never-ending multiplication of meanings'.[25]

Another way to come at this point is via Derek Attridge's recent explanation of the 'inventiveness' and 'singularity' of the literary text. He contends – to my mind rightly – that something about the experience of reading a good book makes it 'come across as different from any other work we know, even though its materials – the various components of the techne that the artist deployed in creating it – may be familiar'.[26] To enjoy a literary text involves saturating it and its production with agency, seeing its elements not as the inevitable result of a pattern but as the contingent and surprising product of the author's decisions. But Attridge's implicit reliance on formalist aesthetics emerges in his premise that a text can only have this element insofar as it carries the mark of the author's own inventiveness, her own improvements of the literary tradition – in his words, 'we're aware that the words we're reading bear the impress of a creative act [. . .] and we take pleasure in reliving that act'.[27] The idea that readers might experience inventiveness in a book that is not surprising to its author – that we might be surprised and intrigued by a well-executed detective novel from an experienced author of crime fiction – does not seem important to Attridge; his view seems to be that the reader can only be surprised if the author is doing something new.[28] But very few of us are as well read as Derek Attridge, and one need not make the condition for a text's capacity to surprise generally be the capacity to surprise him.

It would be easier to let these dimensions of the formalist attitude pass unmentioned if it were not for a final element – the deep contempt that formalists tend to have for readers who read literary texts by paraphrasing their contents. Attridge insists that this approach ignores its aesthetic dimensions: 'simply to consume a novel for its content' – the paraphraser apparently swallows a book's ideas like a philosophical potato – 'with no enjoyment of its form, no sense of an author, no pleasure in the handling of language, is to read it as a text'.[29] Gordon Williams is even more blunt: 'One of the least sensible procedures in criticism and interpretation of poetry is to make a prose paraphrase of a general statement or a moral concept and then inquire into its truth or otherwise.'[30] And Ellen Rooney is perhaps even more contemptuous: 'to read past or through this formal work is not to misread but to dismiss reading as such'.[31]

The knives are certainly out in a debate in literary theory when it is claimed that one side is dismissing 'reading as such'. Yet although I'm tempted to push back against Rooney's worry in particular (if paraphrasers aren't reading, what exactly are we doing?), these are ultimately fairly ordinary reiterations of the formalist attitude. What is striking instead is their hyperbole and contemptuous affect. It isn't sufficient just to say that paraphrasing isn't as effective an interpretive method as some alternative; it has to be one of the 'least sensible' things a reader can do. Another moment in Rooney's essay gives a hint as to the source of this rhetoric: she writes, 'Reading and textuality, as terms of art in literary studies, refer to a range of quite specific theoretical practices [. . .] but none of them provides a warrant to credit the bare paraphrasing of the content of a document as a "reading".' Rooney takes this to be a significant objection to reading for the content; all sorts of readers are paraphrasing, but no one in literary theory actually thinks this counts as reading; ergo, readers should stop doing it and study literary form.[32] What it actually reveals is how wide the gap is between reading practice and literary theory: if there is a widely common reading habit that no literary theorists think actually counts as reading, it takes serious self-confidence to claim that this situation is actually the fault of ordinary readers. That is to say that the rhetoric is made possible because no one in Rooney's discursive sphere disagrees with it. The judgemental tone in favour of formalism can always increase, because it reflects and reinforces the widely shared formalist attitude in literary criticism.

A subtler but more pervasive symptom of this element of the formalist attitude appears in those moments when literary critics do find themselves writing about the contents of literary works; often, the literary critic structures her argument in such a way that a concern with content appears necessary to explain the text's form. This assumption about argumentative structure is particularly striking when one compares scholarship on literary texts that have been read by both philosophers and literary critics. For instance, there is an immensely deep and diverse body of work on Herman Melville's short story 'Bartleby, the Scrivener', which includes sophisticated philosophical responses from Giorgio Agamben, Gilles Deleuze and Jacques Ranciére, alongside recent and equally sophisticated literary critical treatments from Nancy Ruttenberg, Branka Arsić, Barbara Foley, Wendy Anne Lee and others.[33] Ruttenberg has characterised this body of scholarship as divided by a tension between content and context: 'theoretical readings have cut closer to the bone in disclosing the metaphysical import of Bartleby's aberrance, while Americanist scholarship has targeted those cultural-historical specificities of context which identify the aberration as such'.[34] Certainly it is true that literary critics have been more interested in historicist reading than philosophers, but it isn't as if literary critics (including Ruttenberg herself) have not been interested in Bartleby's 'metaphysical import'. However, when they do take such an interest, they view philosophical ideas as an explanatory tool in an account of the text's form.

So, for instance, Agamben's account reads Bartleby as a figure for contingency – the possibility that something might not be – and in his hands the story becomes something like a parable about whether potentiality, a figure that can both be and not be, can actually exist as such. Ruttenberg's objection to (or perhaps development of) this argument is a formal one: she argues for a 'specifically Melvillean employment of suspense and tautology in narrative which, in crediting the power of the still centre, does not therefore deny the enveloping storm'.[35] Similarly, Wendy Anne Lee's reading takes Bartleby's passivity or insistent potentiality to be saying something about the way narrative form relies on a starting point of non-responsiveness. Indeed she is quite clear about the specifically literary dimension of her objection: 'these philosophical abstractions [. . .] precisely concern the origins of narrative itself'.[36] What is important is not just that Ruttenberg and Lee are formally attentive readers – although they are – or that they are saying that philosophers such as Agamben tend to ignore the story's form – although they do – but that the structure and conclusion of their reading differs as a result of these objections, moving from an explication of the story as a parable into an analysis of it as an instance of literary form. It is tempting to say that this is as it should be, that it is natural for philosophers to write about the ideas in a text when they are philosophically useful and that literary critics should write about those ideas when they matter for the text's form. But to fall back on this intuition is precisely to fall back into the formalist attitude and to concede the formalist's definition of literature. The notion that a literary text's ideas are somehow less essential to it or less definitive of its status as a work of art, and that therefore they are not the purview of critics, is exactly the assumption that needs to be critically examined.

The various elements of the formalist attitude – sophistication and knowledge, the self-consciously distinctive aesthetic pleasure, and the contempt for reading as paraphrase – were more clearly and overtly linked in older versions of formalism, such as the famous accounts of A. C. Bradley and Cleanth Brooks. As Peter Kivy points out, both Brooks and Bradley thought of paraphrase as an inadequate approach to the literary text because paraphrase could never duplicate its effect; in particular, a paraphrase could never capture the poem's unique marriage of form and content. As Bradley puts it,

> When poetry answers to its idea and is purely or almost purely poetic, we find the identity of form and content; and the degree of purity attained may be tested by the degree in which we feel it hopeless to convey the *effect* of a poem or passage in any form but its own.[37]

Brooks agrees: if we try to say what a poem says entirely accurately, we will find ourselves compelled to 'resort to the methods of the poem – analogy, metaphor, symbol' in our paraphrase to even approximate it, since form and content are so intimately linked. But as Kivy notes, there is a problematic circularity that comes with defining poetry (much less literature) as the unity of form and content, insofar as it assumes that a particular experience is the only distinctively literary experience, and then uses that experience to define certain texts as literature – namely, those that provide the experience.[38] Kivy writes: 'How do we know when we are properly experiencing a poem? Why, when we are experiencing form and content as fused. And why should we think that this is the only proper way of experiencing the poem? [. . .] Because the form-content identity thesis is true.'[39] Kivy is having none of it: 'Poetry and fiction are not special conduits to the font of wisdom. They are ways some wise folks (and some not so wise) have tried to express some of the things they have found out or others have found out.'[40]

Let me expand on Kivy's point a little. Bradley's phrasing is more accurate than Brooks's about what the claim really is; while Brooks occasionally refers to the 'total meaning' or the 'real core of meaning' of the poem, Bradley speaks of its 'effect'.[41] The gap between the two is precisely what matters: one can concede that the 'effect' of a poem cannot be conveyed, but maintain that its meaning can be.[42] According to Brooks's example, the statement 'Beauty is truth, truth beauty' can only be given 'its precise meaning and significance by its relation to the total context of the poem', but we ought not to concede the terms so quickly.[43] Keats's statement has a propositional content that we can paraphrase; of course, the tools for conveying that content might be clumsier than the original text, and of course they will not have the same elegance of the original line. But an explanation of the core idea is hardly impossible. We see here how Brooks and Bradley's insistence on the inseparability of form and content depended on an implicit aesthetic evaluation, or more precisely a preference for certain aesthetic experiences. The parts of a poem's value that depend on its paraphrasable content are dismissed as irrelevant to its literary nature, while the essential 'effect' or 'meaning' of a poem stems from those elements that a paraphrase cannot capture. If we do not accept this evaluation, however, then there is no reason to deny that form and content can be separated.[44]

I am not convinced, moreover, that contemporary formalists have overcome this circle. Peter Lamarque and Stein Haugom Olsen's *Truth, Fiction, and Literature* is an impressive and influential recent attempt to develop a philosophical aesthetics of literature.[45] Yet they ultimately fall back into a version of the Bradley/Brooks problem: responses to a text's content are deemed illegitimate because they do not respond to the distinctive literary features of the text, but this relies on a narrow and tendentious definition of what literature is. Initially, they define literature as a particular kind of practice, with a particular set of 'conventions and concepts which both regulate and *define* the actions and products involved in that practice'; the most salient practice is that the literary author gives 'artistic unity and coherence' to the materials of daily life via thematic organisation (*TFL*, pp. 256, 455). And when it comes time to consider whether the reader who primarily reads texts for their ideas is making a mistake, Lamarque and Olsen rely on their definition. Explaining that 'the question is whether assessment of their truth enters into the reader's appreciation of a literary work as a literary work', they answer no: 'there is no accepted place for debate about the truth or falsity of general statements about human life or the human condition' in literary criticism (*TFL*, p. 332). Here again, a reaction that emphasises a text's content is deemed illegitimate because it is not sufficiently responsive to the specifically literary qualities of the text. And again, the rejection does not follow if one does not accept their distinctive and evaluative definition of literature in the first place.

But there's an important difference between the earlier formalists such as Brooks and Bradley and their late twentieth-century philosophical heirs such as Lamarque and Olsen. These more recent philosophers demonstrate a different attitude, one more amenable to the idea of reading for the content. The work in this line of thought is just as formalist as its counterpart in literary theory; analytic philosophical formalists (to coin an ugly phrase) are if anything even more willing to speak overtly about the aesthetic value of literary form as a justification for their work. But the attitude is different: even when they end with formalist conclusions, analytic philosophers of literature tend to agree that paraphrasing a literary text for its ideas is an understandable approach that readers might reasonably adopt. And part of their sympathetic reconstruction of that stance is a more persuasive account of the form/content distinction than the shape/matter version, one that develops the intuition behind the what-it-says/how-it-says-it version.

The Possibilities of Paraphrase: The Analytic Philosophy of Literature

The philosophy of literature in the analytic tradition has, roughly speaking, two main sources. The first grows out of that tradition's founding interest in the nature of language and meaning, which led to a somewhat reluctant investigation of the strangeness of literary language (the uses of which Gottlob Frege tried to organise in a single group under the heading of 'tone') and in particular the peculiar truth conditions of fictional sentences. It is true, for instance, that Captain Ahab commanded a ship called the *Pequod*, but it's difficult at first blush to explain what makes this true, since neither Captain Ahab nor the *Pequod* ever existed.[46] The second source of the discourse of contemporary philosophy of literature comes later in the analytic tradition, and is further from the field's traditional core concerns; it involves first the reinvigoration of philosophical aesthetics by figures such as Arthur Danto and Clement Greenberg, and the eventual incorporation of literature into more general theories of art by subsequent writers. Any list of figures and monographs will be insufficiently inclusive, but writers such as Noël Carroll, Peter Lamarque and Kendall Walton represent some of the most influential thinkers in the field, and one can perhaps take the 1994 publication of *Truth, Fiction, and Literature* by Lamarque and Olsen as a moment that crystallised the new approach as an alternative to traditional literary theory. It is moreover a growing field, with a number of anthologies in recent years, and one that includes a group of rising scholars.[47]

From a perspective outside the humanities, it is striking that the philosophy of literature and literary theory should be essentially two entirely different fields. Yet separate they certainly seem to be: to read the polemics between the two camps gives one the impression that deep issues regarding the nature of language, truth, meaning, knowledge and political commitment are at stake in the divide. Lamarque and Olsen give over three chapters of their book to an account of the nature of truth against the post-structuralism of Paul de Man and Jonathan Culler, and Richard Gaskin opens his *Language, Truth, and Literature* with a dauntingly complex account of what he calls the thesis of 'linguistic idealism'. Meanwhile, from the literary theory side, Terry Eagleton observes the 'curious (and quite unnecessary) relation between analytic philosophy and cultural and political conservatism', and remarks humorously (and unfairly) that there is 'one remarkable fact about philosophers of literature. Their knowledge of literary works seems to consist entirely of the Sherlock Holmes stories, along with the first sentence of Tolstoy's *Anna Karenina*.'[48] And to put the basic objection with less mockery, literary critics have faulted the philosophers of literature for failing to account for the breadth and historicity of cultural texts.[49]

Yet to see the tension between literary theory and the philosophy of literature as divided in these deep ways misses the fact that they share a common recent ancestor, perhaps even a great-grandparent. Monroe Beardsley was, after all, a philosopher of art, and the famously influential collaborations between Beardsley and the Yale New Critic William Wimsatt represent a mid-twentieth-century union between the two fields. Moreover, in several important ways literary theory and the analytic philosophy of literature have progressed through similar movements. For instance, the institutional theory of art, as suggested by Arthur Danto and developed by George Dickie, shares some of the ideas that motivate Stanley Fish's notion of interpretive communities as well as many of the critiques of canonical aesthetics that occupied literary theory in the 1980s and 1990s. What I want to suggest is that the two movements – literary theory and the philosophy of literature – should be understood as each taking one of two different but complementary reactions to the mid-century theory of literary art contained in the New Criticism.

Noël Carroll eloquently summarises Beardsley's view and its attractions:

> If one takes aesthetic experience as the central concept of one's theory of art, one can use it, as Beardsley did, to systematically answer a great many other questions about art. One cannot only define art functionally, but can go on to develop evaluative criteria for works of art in terms of the amounts of aesthetic satisfaction an artwork delivers, a critical vocabulary keyed to pinpointing the features of artwork that cause aesthetic experience, and an explanation of the value of art in light of the instrumental value of having aesthetic experiences in human life. That is, one may be attracted to the aesthetic approach because of its systematicity.[50]

In other words, if one thinks that a work of art is defined by its capacity to give rise to aesthetic experience, and that that capacity is created by certain formal features, then many other difficult questions find neat resolutions. Literary theory and the philosophy of literature broke from each other by reacting against this attractively unified and neat theory in opposing ways. Literary theory and the criticism that followed it chose to emphasise the formal features of artworks and abandoned the notion that the analysis of such forms required an appeal to aesthetic experience or satisfaction. The philosophy of literature, on the other hand, chose to emphasise the value of art and the varieties of aesthetic experience, and abandoned the notion that formalism and the formal features of artworks were the only means available for such a purpose.

This opposition is not entirely to the benefit of the philosophers. Perhaps because of its reluctance to seriously question the idea of aesthetic value, the philosophy of literature has generally looked sceptically on the political emphasis of literary theory and criticism. Alan Goldman's *Philosophy and the Novel* offers an unfortunate recent example of how this relation can weaken the scholarship; at one point in his analysis of *Pride and Prejudice*, he writes: 'The most intimate and intricate [personal relationship] is marriage, which, *despite the doubts of feminist critics*, at its best makes a perfect match between a social institution and our deepest personal needs and moral capacities.'[51] Certainly the retrograde politics here are troubling and self-undermining; insisting on the value of the institution of marriage in the midst of one's account of the philosophical nature of literature is hardly a way to convince literary critics that they have been concentrating too much on politics. But what is perhaps even worse is the gratuitous and uninformed slap at feminist scholarship: the idea that feminist thought denies the claim that traditional marriages can and do make some people happy is laughably unfair.[52] And while most of the tradition is not as bad as this, still philosophers of literature tend not to be familiar with major recent works in literary theory, and thus fail to grasp the reasons motivating the interpretive approaches that they criticise. Deconstruction in general and Stanley Fish in particular are common targets, while the influence of Michel Foucault and the varieties of historicist criticism generally go unacknowledged.

Still, and perhaps because of its distance from mainstream literary theory, the field has taken up some basic questions about the nature of literary interpretation that literary theory itself has tended to dismiss. As Rita Felski has noted, 'literary theory' is really something of a misnomer, insofar as 'the dominant figures in the theory canon are typically concerned not just with literature but also with language, history, identity, society, politics, the nature of being'.[53] To put the point generally, one might say that literary theory has tended to be more interested in various conceptions of the relationship between literature and the world than in what specifically one does in encountering the literary text. And as Felski argues, while this approach has the advantage of situating literary interpretation in a bigger picture, it has the drawback of minimising the question of 'how we read' in the interest of explaining why we should. A similar notion leads Toril Moi to claim that literary criticism 'doesn't have anything we can plausibly call competing methods'; what goes under the name of differing methods – namely, literary theory – in fact names different fields of interest.[54] What one actually does when reading and interpreting, Moi argues, is largely the same across theoretical schools: it is just attentive reading.

Moi doesn't have a problem with this fact, but we might borrow a distinction from the philosophy of literature to suggest why some methodological clarity and methodological differentiation might be worth having. Take the distinction between 'elucidation' and 'interpretation' as introduced by Noël Carroll and developed by Richard Gaskin.[55] Elucidation is a form of explanation that proceeds sentence by sentence, translating its propositional content into clearer or at any rate different terms; one might think of it as explanation from the ground up. Interpretation, on their description, proceeds from the top down, explaining how and why the major elements of the text do what they do. So an elucidation of *Hamlet* might start by glossing the conversation between Bernardo and Francisco on the walls of Elsinore, while an interpretation (on this definition) might start by saying that Hamlet was a prince of Denmark who was worried that his father had been murdered, or perhaps that Shakespeare was interested in large questions about suicide and the purpose of life and used a vacillating prince to think about them. There's nothing particularly earth-shattering about this distinction, although I will come back to it in a moment. Rather, what is striking here is that took two philosophers of literature to make it. This is after all a basic question in the method of literary interpretation: when does it make sense to explain individual lines, and when does it make sense to focus on larger elements of the text? It is revealing of how little attention literary theory has paid to this kind of garden-variety methodological question that there was space for Carroll and Gaskin to address it.

More substantively, in rejecting the neo-Kantian late modernist emphasis on literary form, and working from the premise that formalism cannot adequately capture the diversity of our responses to works of art, the philosophical approach to literature has tried to theorise the many reasons for and ways in which we value literature.[56] In the current context, that matters most insofar as such critics have tried to figure out when readers might justifiably say they have learned something discrete from a literary text, and what properties a text needs to have in order to inform and educate in this way. And, perhaps because they are philosophers, this is a form of aesthetic response to which philosophers of literature have given a great deal of attention. There are a host of sub-debates in this field – one particularly esoteric conversation involves Paul Grice's theory of the conditions that define a speech act as an assertion, and whether literary texts meet those conditions – and I will draw on this archive of thought later in this chapter and indeed throughout this book. But what is perhaps more important as a starting point is simply the attitude.[57] Consider these remarks about literary content, as opposed to the remarks from literary theorists mentioned earlier:

> Fictions, construed as propositions to be imagined, supply us with the relevant, unasserted propositional content, and in entertaining that content as the author mandates, we can be emotionally moved by fictions.[58]

> It is wrong to reject the possibility of paraphrase *tout court*: the *what* of a poem may indeed be presented by another piece of language, though (trivially) nothing else could present its *how*.[59]

> A Propositional Theory of Literary Truth could then be formulated as follows: *the literary work contains or implies general thematic statements about the world which the reader as part of an appreciation of the work has to assess as true or false.*[60]

I cite these claims not as views to agree with, but rather as evidence of how seriously the analytic philosophy of literature has taken the question of literary content and the uses of paraphrase. Even the formalists rise above pejoratives; there's no designation of their rival as someone whose practice literally cannot be described as reading. Instead, there's a sympathetic and charitable reconstruction of an approach that values literary texts for their contents. And presumably that reconstruction is necessary in part because of their interlocutors, the non-formalist philosophers who contend just that.

Lamarque and Olsen's 1994 work is illustrative in this regard. The book ultimately defends a formalist aesthetic; as they put it at one point, 'the aesthetic value defined by the creative-imaginative aspect of the concept of literature is constituted by the imposition of form on a subject', and 'appreciation, the mode of apprehension defined by the literary stance, aims at identifying the complex and coherent form of a literary work of art' (*TFL*, p. 265). In other words, they reiterate the basic New Critical and indeed Kantian idea that aesthetic engagement consists in recognising and experiencing the form of the work of art. Yet they pair this argument with a recognition that many readers want something different from literature, namely, the truth. Not caring about whether the work of art is beautiful, what matters to many readers is that the work of art conveys something true and interesting about the world. Far from dismissing this instinct, Lamarque and Olsen see the acknowledgement and incorporation of the views that guide such readers as a necessary element of their argument. They seek to 'find a proper location for intuitions about literature's "truth-telling" capacities', ultimately arguing for the importance of 'humanly interesting content' in the work of art (*TFL*, pp. 3, 265). One can question whether this attempt is persuasive; certainly other philosophers have objected to their view, and I will do so as well. But what is notable and undeniable is the very different attitude this formalism takes to the paraphrasing reader interested in content.

It is instructive to compare Lamarque and Olsen's work to contemporaneous formalist research in literary studies. Susan Wolfson's 1997 book *Formal Changes: The Shaping of Poetry in British Romanticism* is in many ways engaged in a project sympathetic to that of Lamarque and Olsen; Wolfson argues that the formal features of literary art are 'not simply conscriptable as information for other frameworks of analysis; the forms themselves demand a specific kind of critical attention'.[61] To put the point a little more directly, they are worth studying for their own sake. But the way Wolfson develops this claim is significantly different from the way Lamarque and Olsen do; her argument proceeds by contending that many of the reflections about the political effects of form – specifically those made by Jerome McGann and Marjorie Levinson – were in fact anticipated by the Romantic poets themselves.[62] Thus, in Wolfson's hands, John Keats's final poems reflect 'an investigation of poetic forms as factitious, temporary, and historically situated, thoroughly implicated with systems of experience and processes of language that they cannot transcend'.[63] The idea that an attention to literature for its own sake would primarily be an attention to form is taken for granted, indeed assumed; the reader who cares primarily about content, ideas and truth is not a rival who needs to be taken seriously. And Wolfson's interlocutors are not really critics who deny that close formal analysis of poetry is a thing worth doing. Rather, the dispute is about why and how that analysis should be conducted. The necessary argument in Wolfson's eyes is a demonstration that literary form is not an always-integrating, organicising force for unity. The underlying and implicit conditional here – that if one can show poetic form does not necessarily have the negative political dimension its critics have suggested, then its study for its own sake will be justified – is striking; when openly articulated, it's tough to see why one should agree that the consequent follows from the antecedent, and it marks how differently literary studies has conceived of the opposing approaches that a defence of formalism needs to address.[64]

The very different attitude towards literary content among philosophers of literature has reached an extensive recent articulation and defence in Richard Gaskin's 2013 *Language, Truth, and Literature*, and his text offers an excellent starting point for developing an alternative approach in literary studies. Gaskin starts with Gottlob Frege's theory of meaning, in which the content of a sentence is the proposition it conveys, and in which one can grasp the proposition by paraphrasing the sentence. Gaskin's project is to take this basic approach to meaning as an approach to a whole work. As he puts it: 'a work (or part thereof) to which the sense-reference distinction applies presents the same propositionally structured entity or entities in the realm of reference as does its paraphrase (to that extent work and paraphrase mean the same) but that work and paraphrase present that referential content in *different* ways' (*LTL*, p. 70). In the same way that 'the Sun' and 'the centre of the solar system' refer to the same object in different ways, so the literary text and its paraphrase refer to the same object but create different effects. Indeed one could almost say that the paraphrase is just the entity the work refers to, except that each paraphrase can itself be paraphrased. This view requires some elaborate wrinkles to explain how literary works that describe the real world simultaneously refer to that world and to a particular set of propositions that comprise content, but it has the attractive and intuitive implication that the content of a literary text is just what is captured by a paraphrase of the work.

But three features of this view call for exploration. First, one odd implication is the fact that a literary text's content can probably never really be known by any actual reader. The theory depends on the possibility of a 'maximally full' paraphrase of a literary work – Gaskin calls it an 'ultimate paraphrase' – to make that content clear, and such paraphrases only exist as an ideal (*LTL*, p. 90). They thus serve a 'theoretical and regulatory purpose', offering a standard against which one can recognise paraphrases that are 'partial or slanted' (*LTL*, p. 91). Second, Gaskin contends that the ultimate paraphrase of a work is at the end of the day the statement of its moral: 'paraphrase has a much grander purpose, namely to state the overall moral purpose of the work' (*LTL*, p. 86). In the process of working out this idea, he suggests that works sometimes state their own message – his example is a poem from Juvenal that includes the line 'virtue is the sole and only kind of nobility' – and concludes that it is possible for a work to '*contain* its own paraphrase' (*LTL*, p. 90). Third, and in keeping with the theory of paraphrase-as-moral, Gaskin thinks that the 'ultimate paraphrase' of a text will be 'maximally succinct': 'one cannot add anything to it without falling into repetition, irrelevance, or inaccuracy' (*LTL*, p. 90).

Each of these claims seems odd. Most importantly, it is not clear why one should agree that succinctness is a reasonable standard to use in assessing paraphrases. Such a criterion introduces what seems like a traditionally formalist aesthetic sense into an interpretive technique. Then too, it sounds strange to say that a work can contain its own paraphrase. Whatever the quote from Juvenal is, it's tough to see how it could be an ultimate paraphrase of the poem, if only because it does not capture the way the poem develops the idea. In other words, this might be the most important idea in the poem, but surely its content is more than this. And the idea that the goal of a paraphrase is only to state the purpose of the work looks strange too – what if the work doesn't have a purpose, let alone a moral one?

The idea of an ultimate paraphrase is a compelling one, but I think Gaskin's theory of it is too constrained by his emphasis on the idea that works have morals. A paraphrase is primarily a form of pointing: a way of highlighting one element of a work over another, calling attention to specific features. Conceived of in this way, an ultimate paraphrase is not an attempt to point to the real core or fundamental purpose of the text; to view literature this way is to return surreptitiously to the formalist conception of the work. Instead, an ultimate paraphrase is closer to an attempt to point at everything, from all the perspectives readers might take. To introduce an idea that Chapter 3 will develop more extensively, it is a reconstitution of the text in all of the various discourses in which it might be interesting.

An example will be useful here. Consider the famous last stanza of Matthew Arnold's 'Dover Beach':

> Ah love, let us be true
> To one another! For the world, which seems
> To lie before us like a land of dreams
> So various, so beautiful, so new,
> Hath really neither joy, nor love, nor light,
> Nor certitude, nor peace, nor help for pain;
> And we are here as on a darkling plain
> Swept with confused alarms of struggle and flight
> Where ignorant armies clash by night.[65]

One might say that the first part of the stanza contains a reasonable paraphrase of the poem itself. 'Let us be true to one another, for the world hath really neither joy, nor love, nor light, nor certitude, nor peace, nor help for pain' is not a bad approximation of Arnold's message in the poem. But to conceive of this as the ultimate paraphrase against which other paraphrases are measured misses the various ways in which Arnold's text and ideas can be reconstructed, and thus much of the content of the poem.

Consider for instance some ways in which readers have engaged with this stanza:

> Insisting on the christological character of Christian theology might at least help to preserve the theologian from indulging in the easy speeches that comfort cruel men, and from slackening the paradox that counterpoints Christian joy with the recognition that the world that lies before us, on Dover Beach, has neither 'certitude, nor peace, nor help from [sic] pain'.[66]

> The neglect of the plurality of our affiliations and of the need for choice and reasoning obscures the world in which we live. It pushes us in the direction of the terrifying prospects portrayed by Matthew Arnold in Dover Beach: 'And we are here as on a darkling plain / Swept with confused alarms of struggle and flight / Where ignorant armies clash by night.' We can do better than that.[67]

Arnold's poem, of course, is much more than a love poem, for it details his belief in the liberal subject's ability to seek out a private space of thoughtful emotion, of human intimacy, where subjects alienated in mind or body can become fully authentic and intentional in relation to themselves and to each other, in spite of the chaotic world without.[68]

It does not do much good to think of these as partial paraphrases that each approach but fail to reach some perfect epigrammatic maxim that captures the real content of the poem. Instead, each is an explication of the ideas of the stanza within a different sphere of interest: the first, in theological terms; the second, in the context of a theory of political pluralism; the third, in an account of political agency and selfhood. And we should avoid too the idea that an ultimate paraphrase is the one that appears when one reads with no sphere of interest; I will come back to this worry, but briefly the key response is that there is no obvious reason why the paraphrase this yields is more essential to the work than other paraphrases. Rather, an ultimate paraphrase is something closer to the set of all possible readings, all of the multifarious dimensions of a text's content.

This might seem, however, to stretch the notion of 'content' too far. After all, it doubles down on the idea that individual readers will never really be able to grasp a text's content. And this seems un-intuitive: it moves away from the common-sense idea that the content of a literary work is just the meaning of all its individual sentences. Gaskin is suspicious of the impulse to break a literary text down into its elements; the meaning of a work 'is not arrived at', he warns, 'by summing the senses and references of its semantically significant parts (in particular of its component sentences)' (*LTL*, p. 72). But one intuitive way of explaining this point is that what such a reading misses is precisely an understanding of form. A plausible way to describe a reader who grasps all the sentences but not the purpose behind their pattern, who can elucidate the text but not interpret it, is as precisely someone who has understood the content but not the form of a text. This seems to be what Lamarque and Olsen think: they imagine a reader of Euripides' *Hippolytus* who understands all the play's sentences but fails to grasp that the play is about deep issues of self-control, freedom and fate (*TFL*, pp. 411–12). Such a reader misses the presence of a theme, a recognition of the fact that the work's elements are organised into a coherent purpose – which is to say, that it has a form. So then why should one let the idea of content stretch to include all the varieties of paraphrase? Why not limit the idea of the content of a text to simply the individual elucidations of all the sentences that comprise its components?

A related worry is that surely it is possible to paraphrase the poem in a way that does not yield its contents – in other words, to force a set of concerns on the poem. Suppose one were to paraphrase Arnold's final stanza thus:

> It is telling that the lover in 'Dover Beach' is both nameless and voiceless. In calling for his lover to be loyal to him, in the hope that her affection can help him confront the threat of existential despair, Arnold's speaker practises the emotional vampirism so characteristic of a particular type of masculinity. Thoughtful and brooding, but always self-obsessed, Arnold's speaker is not interested in his lover's feelings, but only in how she might help him deal with his own.[69]

To call this paraphrase of 'Dover Beach' its content misses the against-the-grain nature of the argument. At best, this is an assumption that the poem rests on, or perhaps an unintentional implication. This is not to say the paraphrase is inaccurate, but it is not the poem's content, at least not in the same way the other paraphrases were. So then the question is this. In which cases – if any – does the content of a text include more than the elucidation of its component sentences? Or – and here we return to the original definitions I opened with – what does it mean for a literary text to say something?

Allegories and Examples: Towards a Content Formalism

Lamarque and Olsen put the basic problem well: 'the concatenation of predicates in a narrative structure generates and authorises inference beyond explicit content' (*TFL*, p. 134). Their own formalist solution links such inferences to the idea of theme: 'Kafka's *The Trial* is about alienation or the inhumanity of industrialised society or neurotic anxiety not because these notions are given in the content itself but only to the extent that it might be fruitful to reflect on the content through these conceptions' (*TFL*, p. 134). Terry Eagleton sympathises with this answer, arguing that it is simply inherent in the nature of literature that it calls for paraphrases which move beyond literal content. Because such texts are 'non-pragmatic', they 'invite us to generalise their significance in the way that [a circular on rubbish collection times] does not, pondering their moral implications rather than treating them simply as an empirical report' (*TFL*, p. 131). Part of regarding a work as a literary text, in other words, is to see it as inviting the connection to general topics that moves a paraphrase beyond a literal restatement of a text.

I think this approach concedes too much to the choice of interpretive method. Clearly readers can give general significance to any particular text, performing literary interpretations on almost anything. But it is also possible for texts to invite this sort of paraphrase, to include features that indicate that they intend to speak about larger issues than the particulars they depict or to which they refer. When a paraphrase captures the ways in which they engage with those larger issues, the results are just as much the text's 'contents' as a literal elucidation of the component sentences would be; a paraphrase of *Hamlet* that attends to the play's thinking about political life is just as accurate an account of its content as a line-by-line elucidation. This is to say that some texts call for thoughtful as well as immersive reading: in addition to seeking to catch readers up in absorptive engagement within a fictional world, they can encourage readers to play a double game, thinking about the broader dimensions of the story at the same time.

How do texts extend such invitations? Well, as the Finnish philosopher Jukka Mikkonen puts it in a response to Lamarque and Olsen, one answer would be to say that they do it in all sorts of ways: 'authors manifest their assertions by the form and content of their utterances, the tone and style of the narrative and the manner of representation, the design of the work, and the like'.[70] And undoubtedly this is correct if one is looking for a broad statement of the claim that is capable of capturing all possible instances. But it does not get us very far in describing the actual ways in which texts accomplish this goal as an empirical matter. Correspondingly, it leaves the nature of textual content undefined: often a literary text's content will be more than its literal elucidation, but exactly when and how can only be answered by a description of the individual text. It is possible to make this somewhat more precise, I want to argue, by suggesting that texts offer such invitations by refusing formalist appraisal; rather than calling for readings that experience form for its own sake, they indicate that they are using form as a tool to communicate.

It's worth pausing a little to specify the precise nature of the problem at stake here. A generation or perhaps even ten years ago, the hint of authorial intention behind this approach would have been the main issue that required explication and defence. But the rise of Wittgensteinian approaches in literary theory has made a less abstract theory of intention and an acknowledgement of its role in communication and interpretation more plausible.[71] Then, too, in a previous period the idea that texts refer to the world would have been the key claim: Michael Riffaterre, Roland Barthes and Paul de Man, among others, would have diagnosed an emphasis on content as a version of the 'referential fallacy'.[72] Here, following Toril Moi and Terry Eagleton, the problem is better dissolved than resolved; there is no need to explain how texts refer to the world, because there is no gap between language and the world.[73] Rather, the problem is a distinctly literary one: how can texts be about multiple things at once?

This is an issue that critics have generally understood within the terms of allegory. As Angus Fletcher writes in a famous account, in an allegory 'the poet is giving us two large-scale meanings for one'.[74] Fletcher quotes William Empson, who contends that in allegory, the reader feels that there are 'two levels of being', which 'correspond to each other in detail'.[75] And in his book *The Vitality of Allegory*, Gary Johnson follows this critical tradition in suggesting that allegory is opposed to mimesis – indeed, that one recognises that a text is an allegory precisely when it starts to violate a reader's mimetic expectations.[76] Thus, he suggests that 'allegory is figurative or symbolic, and this serves to distinguish it from mimetic fiction';[77] moreover, it is the 'tension between the figural and the mimetic' that gives a text such as Kafka's *Metamorphosis* its allegorical elements.[78] So Lamarque and Olsen are not quite right that the themes in Kafka's works are present only as a result of the decision to read them thematically, as literature; rather, the texts indicate their ideas by violating mimetic expectation. Far from requiring readers to take the literary stance, the allegory acquires its power by assuming that they do not take such a stance. Readers start with the expectation of straightforward reporting, and only realise the broader dimensions of the work, and the necessary thematic and theoretical reflection, as it proceeds.

Yet this way of defining allegory misses the way mimetic texts, in their realist form, can also invite the reader into consideration of a second level of being and a new layer of meaning precisely through realistic representation. The great novels of social realism work this way, telling the stories of particular individuals such as Gervaise Macquart and Tess of the D'Urbervilles as a way of making a broader claim about social structures. Gervaise and Tess, in exemplifying the ideas that Zola and Hardy seek to bring forward, evoke a broader level of meaning essentially identical to an allegorical meaning. So we ought to hesitate in thinking that the allegorical and the exemplary are really separate. Indeed, many of the most famous allegorical texts depend precisely on exemplary characters, as Paul Suttie points out with regard to *The Faerie Queene*:

> An exemplary character no more literally 'is' what he or she exemplifies – the individual fictional person no more literally 'is' a *kind* of person – than the sort of character we would call a personification literally 'is' that thing, impersonal in kind; both types of reading [allegorical and exemplary], equally, involve taking one thing as the sign of another.[79]

Just as Duessa is not literally the Catholic Church, Redcrosse Knight is not literally the set of brave knights, or the abstract ideal 'brave knight'. He is rather *a* brave knight, and it is part of the text's strategy to use this fact to make him a figure for brave knight-ness. In other words, exemplarity emerges as just as much a figural structure as the personification common to traditional allegory, and might reasonably be said to be a variation of allegory and not an alternative to it. Once we stop assuming the traditional tension between allegory and mimesis, moreover, it becomes clear that readers have long recognised the basic links between the two. As James Phelan has pointed out, characters can easily have mimetic and didactic functions at the same time.[80]

Given that by definition they cannot violate mimetic expectations, realist texts must thus use different strategies to achieve allegorical/exemplary effects. Commonly they do this with what Sarah Raff has called in a reading of Jane Austen 'generalizations': overt statements that seem to violate the diegetic world, addressing themselves directly to the reader.[81] The statement 'It is a truth universally acknowledged, that a single man in possession of a good fortune, must be in want of a wife' gives an allegorical dimension to the story that follows, asking readers to take the story of Elizabeth Bennett and Mr Darcy as in part a figural exemplification of an idea.

Philosophers of literature have devoted significant energy to thinking about these kinds of generalisations, since as John Searle points out they appear to be direct assertions from the author, and thus to invite overt philosophical engagement.[82] When the narrator of *Middlemarch* remarks that 'there is no general doctrine which is not capable of eating out our morality if unchecked by the deep-seated habit of direct fellow-feeling with individual fellow-men', it is easy to see Searle's point; this certainly seems to be something that George Eliot thinks and upon which she wants us to reflect. A great deal of ink has been spilled in the philosophical debate over whether such statements merit the title of assertions; perhaps they are merely 'suggestions', or ideas for readers to 'entertain'.[83] Mikkonen's approach is to regard them as 'dual layered': they 'function on two levels', as 'assertions of the fictional world, and assertions of reality'.[84] But Gaskin aptly summarises the worry about paying too much attention to these features of the literary text when he notes somewhat wryly, 'it is easy to fall into the trap of supposing that literature's principle value resides in the general applicability of these passages. Horace has been a notable victim, over the centuries, of the "good bits" approach to literature' (*LTL*, p. 81).

Lamarque and Olsen are sceptical that generalisations merit the title 'assertions', though they agree that such statements merit special attention and analysis. On their account, a literary generalisation 'invites reflection both from an internal and an external perspective'; borrowing from Thomas Nagel, they contrast an internal identification and involvement with the text against an external recognition of it as a work of art. Internally, we want Creon just to leave Antigone alone; externally, we can recognise that the play is a great work of art because he does not. But the two perspectives are not really in tension, according to Lamarque and Olsen; indeed, they 'nicely interact. For while a reader comes to acquire a deeper understanding of the character in the light of the generalization, he might also come to see an added authority in the generalization in the light of its application to the character' (*TFL*, pp. 147–8). This is the kind of reading that allegory involves, and it demonstrates how generalisations can function as invitations to allegory.

Indeed, one can see this even at the level of the sentence. Let's return briefly to the passage from *Middlemarch*:

> There is no general doctrine which is not capable of eating out our morality if unchecked by the deep-seated habit of direct fellow-feeling with individual fellow-men. But a man who believes in something else than his own greed, has necessarily a conscience or standard to which he more or less adapts himself. Bulstrode's standard had been his serviceableness to God's cause: 'I am sinful and nought – a vessel to be consecrated by use – but use me!' – had been the mould into which he had constrained his immense need of being something important and predominating. And now had come a moment in which that mould seemed in danger of being broken and utterly cast away.[85]

There are two different ways in which the opening generalisation can be explicated. One can stay at the level of this particular sentence, restating it as a philosophical proposition. But one can also note that it's a description of Mr Bulstrode – that he is the person whose general doctrine is in question, and it isn't really possible to understand the generalisation without grasping that it is also a statement about a particular person. Explicating the generalisation, in other words, leads one to recognise that this is both an attempt to describe a particular individual in mid-nineteenth-century England and a philosophical claim, and thus invites an allegorical or thoughtful reading.

Another point is worth noting. The second example of explication – recognising that the generalisation is a characterisation of Mr Bulstrode – is in some sense a recognition of the text's form. At the least, it is a recognition of the fact that the generalisation is not unconnected to the sentences around it, and that it means to pick out and describe one character instead of another. But just as obviously, this is an element of the text's form that can easily be paraphrased. Working through this passage makes clear how it is impossible to limit the content of a text to merely the explication of all its constituent sentences, and the inadequacy of the approach that defines 'content' as the sum of all the propositions in a text and gives the name 'form' to everything else. Part of explicating some sentences, like generalisations, will involve recognising their connections to other sentences. The paraphrases that follow will clearly and unquestionably convey the text's content – it seems obvious that it is part of the content of *Middlemarch* that there is a character named Mr Bulstrode who has fallen into self-deception due to a lack of sympathetic connection with others – but at no point of explicating individual sentences will that paraphrase emerge. Defining 'content' as the paraphrase of a literary text, then, necessarily involves viewing that paraphrase as something attentive to patterns in the text. We can call such patterns forms if we choose, but it's worth stressing that in their paraphrasability they lack the aesthetic properties often given to literary form. And it is necessary to distinguish those patterns from the other formal elements that comprise the 'how-it-is-said' of a text that genuinely cannot be paraphrased: no paraphrase is as funny as the joke it explains. But parsing the distinction between patterns that can be paraphrased and forms that cannot, and explaining the idea of a form as a tool for communication, requires working through a more extended set of examples. Taking up the uses of the marriage plot in the works of Anthony Trollope as a paraphrasable pattern, the next chapter gives some depth to this claim.

Notes

1. Peter Childs and Roger Fowler, *The Routledge Dictionary of Literary Terms* (London: Routledge, 2006), p. 166.
2. Other reference books of literary terms that do not offer a definition for 'content' include J. A. Cuddon, *A Dictionary of Literary Terms and Literary Theory*, 5th edn (New York: Wiley-Blackwell, 2013), which goes from 'conte dévot' to 'contests' – as in, poetry contests; Roland Greene and Stephen Cushman, *The Princeton Handbook of Poetic Terms*, 3rd edn (Princeton: Princeton University Press, 2016), which goes from 'consonance' to 'convention'; and M. H. Abrams and Geoffrey Harpham, *A Glossary of Literary Terms*, 11th edn (New York: Wadsworth, 2014), which goes from 'Contemporary Period' to 'contextual criticism'. All of these dictionaries use the term 'content' in defining dozens of other terms.
3. Chris Baldick, *Oxford Dictionary of Literary Terms* (Oxford: Oxford University Press, 2015), pp. 74–5.
4. Here it is:

    > A critical term with a confusing variety of meanings. It can refer to a *genre (e.g. 'The short story form'), or to an established pattern of poetic devices (as in the various *fixed forms of European poetry), or, more abstractly, to the structure or unifying principle in a given work. Since the rise of *Romanticism, critics have often contrasted the principle of *organic form, which is said to evolve from within the developing work, with 'mechanic form', which is imposed as a predetermined design. When speaking of a work's **formal** properties, critics usually refer to its structural design and patterning, or sometimes to its style and manner in a wider sense, as distinct from its content. (Baldick, *Oxford Dictionary of Literary Terms*, p. 134)

5. Angela Leighton, *On Form: Poetry, Aestheticism, and the Legacy of a Word* (Oxford: Oxford University Press, 2007), p. 2. See also John Lysaker, *You Must Change Your Life: Poetry, Philosophy, and the Birth of Sense* (University Park: Pennsylvania State University Press, 2002). Lysaker writes: 'The opposition between medium and message contains, therefore, a threefold distinction involving content, form, and matter' (p. 8).
6. Noël Carroll, *Philosophy of Art: A Contemporary Introduction* (New York: Routledge, 1999), pp. 139–40.
7. Daniel Albright, *Panaesthetics: On the Unity and Diversity of the Arts* (New Haven: Yale University Press, 2014).
8. Moretti, *Distant Reading*, p. 86.
9. Sandra Macpherson, 'A Little Formalism', *ELH* 82.2 (2015), p. 390.
10. Levine, *Forms*, p. 3.
11. Raymond Williams, *Keywords* (London: Fontana, 1976), p. 138.
12. Kendall Walton, 'Categories of Art', *The Philosophical Review* 79.3 (1970), p. 347.
13. Moretti, *Distant Reading*, p. 71.

14. Moretti, *Distant Reading*, p. 83.
15. The point becomes even clearer if one thinks about the relationship between the stories that comprise so-called 'fan fiction' and the features of their source texts. Surely one of the elements of the matter and not a part of the form is a character's name – the names of the characters, particularly in the tradition of literary narrative, are purposely arbitrary, meant to convey a sense of the representative nature of the character. And yet in fan fiction this situation changes. In the world of *Pride and Prejudice*, Mr Darcy is just a name – yet in the world of Jane Austen fan fiction, 'Mr Darcy' is something quite different: he is a feature, perhaps even a necessary one, whose presence shapes the other elements of the story. His name has passed, in other words, from content into form.
16. See Humphrey Carpenter, *J.R.R. Tolkien: A Biography* (London: Houghton Mifflin, 2000), for a detailing of this process.
17. See George Dove, *The Reader and the Detective Story* (Bowling Green: Ohio State University Press, 1997).
18. Sedgwick, 'Paranoid Reading and Reparative Reading', p. 130.
19. See Stanley Fish, *Is There A Text in This Class?* (Cambridge, MA: Harvard University Press, 1983).
20. Levinson, 'What is New Formalism?', p. 569. Of course, there have been ten years of formalist work since her essay, which might dispute the supposed lack of theorisation.
21. Wolfson, 'Reading for Form', p. 9.
22. Levine, *Forms*, p. 39; Nussbaum, *Love's Knowledge*, p. 152.
23. Nathan Hensley, *Forms of Empire* (Oxford: Oxford University Press, 2016); John Gibson, 'Literature and Knowledge', in Richard Eldridge (ed.), *The Oxford Handbook of Philosophy and Literature* (Oxford: Oxford University Press, 2009), p. 14.
24. Moi, *Revolution of the Ordinary*, p. 214.
25. See William Deresiewicz, 'The Right Questions to Ask About Literature', *Slate.com* (April 2011), available at <http://www.slate.com/articles/arts/books/2011/04/the_right_questions_to_ask_about_literature.html> (last accessed 18 December 2019). See Marjorie Garber, *The Use and Abuse of Literature* (New York: Pantheon, 2011).
26. Derek Attridge, *The Work of Literature* (Oxford: Oxford University Press, 2015), p. 56.
27. Attridge, *The Work of Literature*, p. 56.
28. At one point Attridge seems to concede the worry, but then immediately reiterates his point. 'While the uninventively formulaic work can achieve a degree of popularity', he concedes, 'global and enduring success is more likely to spring from an author's capacity to invent new forms and discover new subject-matter' (*The Work of Literature*, p. 206). The problems with his reliance on an unsubstantiated empirical claim about artistic popularity notwithstanding, one is tempted to say: fine, but this is no way undermines the fact that the novice reader can experience the formulaic work as fresh and inventive.

29. Attridge, *The Work of Literature*, p. 35. Frank Kermode agrees: 'If it should chance that literature as such means very little to you, having no nose you can trust, nothing you say on the subject will have a value appropriate to comment on that subject.' Frank Kermode, *Pleasure and Change: The Aesthetics of Canon* (Oxford: Oxford University Press, 2004), p. 85.
30. Gordon Williams, *Tradition and Originality in Roman Poetry* (Oxford: Clarendon Press, 1968), pp. 578–9. I am directed to this passage by Richard Gaskin, *Language, Truth and Literature* (Oxford: Oxford University Press, 2013), p. 135.
31. Ellen Rooney, 'Form and Contentment', *MLQ* 61.1 (2000), pp. 17–40.
32. It is telling that the closest Rooney can come to a scholarly opponent is a collection of 'thematic' criticism. But as she notes, even 'theme' is ultimately a formal term. Her real opponent – the defender of paraphrase – doesn't actually exist.
33. See Giorgio Agamben, 'Bartleby, or On Contingency', in *Potentialities: Collected Essays in Philosophy*, ed. Daniel Heller-Roazen (Stanford: Stanford University Press, 1999), pp. 243–71; Gilles Deleuze, 'Bartleby; or, The Formula', in *Essays Critical and Clinical*, trans. Daniel W. Smith and Michael Greco (New York: Verso, 1997), pp. 68–90; Jacques Ranciére, 'Deleuze, Bartleby, and the Literary Formula', in *The Flesh of Words: The Politics of Writing*, trans. Charlotte Mandel (Stanford: Stanford University Press, 2004), pp. 146–64; Branka Arsić, *Passive Constitutions, or 7½ Times Bartleby* (Stanford: Stanford University Press, 2007); Barbara Foley, 'From Wall Street to Astor Place: Historicising Melville's *Bartleby*', *American Literature* 72.1 (2000), pp. 87–116.
34. Nancy Ruttenberg, '"The Silhouette of a Content": "Bartleby" and American Literary Specificity', in *Melville and Aesthetics* (New York: Palgrave Macmillan, 2011), pp. 137–55.
35. Ruttenberg, 'The Silhouette of a Content', p. 142.
36. Wendy Anne Lee, 'The Scandal of Insensibility; or, The Bartleby Problem', *PMLA* 130.5 (2015), pp. 1405–19 (p. 1414).
37. A. C. Bradley, 'Poetry for Poetry's Sake', in Eliseo Vivas and Murray Krieger (eds), *The Problems of Aesthetics* (New York: Holt, Rhinehart and Wilson, 1960), p. 574, emphasis mine.
38. See Sam Rose, *Art and Form: From Roger Fry to Global Modernism* (University Park: Penn State University Press, 2019), for an enlightening discussion of the way this account of the literary work complemented the similar theory of visual art developed by Roger Fry and Clive Bell.
39. Peter Kivy, *Philosophies of Art: An Essay in Differences* (New York: Cambridge University Press, 1997), p. 109.
40. Kivy, *Philosophies of Art*, p. 115.
41. Brooks, *The Well-Wrought Urn*, pp. 180, 188; Bradley, 'Poetry for Poetry's Sake', p. 574.

42. Nicholas Gaskill explains this point well in a recent essay, 'The Close and the Concrete: Aesthetic Formalism in Context', *New Literary History* 47.4 (2016), pp. 505–24. And my argument here is consistent with his general point that formalism has survived much longer than the theory of the text that made it make sense has.
43. Brooks, *The Well-Wrought Urn*, p. 188.
44. Toril Moi has recently made a very similar point. In a new book *Character*, co-authored with Rita Felski and Amanda Anderson, she writes: 'I have shown that the taboo on treating characters as if they were real is intertwined with the promotion of a specific understanding of modernist aesthetics [and] that the taboo rests on no sound philosophical grounds.' Toril Moi, Rita Felski and Amanda Anderson, *Character: Three Inquiries in Literary Studies* (Chicago: University of Chicago Press, 2019), p. 61. Indeed: the idea that form and content cannot be separated is just such another taboo, and similarly rests merely on a preference for certain artistic experiences.
45. Peter Lamarque and Stein Haugom Olsen, *Truth, Fiction, and Literature: A Philosophical Perspective* (Oxford: Clarendon Press, 1994). Subsequent citations, abbreviated *TFL*, are given in parentheses in the text.
46. See David Lewis, 'Truth in Fiction', *American Philosophical Quarterly* 15.1 (1978), pp. 37–46 for the canonical discussion.
47. Jonathan Gilmore offers an informative guide to this scholarship; see his 'Philosophy of Literature', *Oxford Bibliographies Online* (New York: Oxford University Press, 2013). Major anthologies include Peter Lamarque and Stein Haugom Olsen (eds), *Aesthetics and the Philosophy of Art: The Analytic Tradition* (Oxford: Blackwell, 2004); David Davies and Carl Matheson (eds), *Contemporary Readings in the Philosophy of Literature: An Analytic Approach* (Toronto: Broadview, 2008); Eileen John and Dominic McIver Lopes (eds), *Philosophy of Literature: Contemporary and Classic Readings* (Oxford: Blackwell, 2004); and Noël Carroll and John Gibson (eds), *Philosophy of Literature: A Contemporary Introduction* (New York: Routledge, 2017).
48. Terry Eagleton, *The Event of Literature* (New Haven: Yale University Press, 2012), ch. xi, p. 108. Eagleton's charitable parenthetical is meant, I think, to acknowledge the deeply radical politics of Bertrand Russell.
49. An influential example here might be Nicholas Dames's critique of Martha Nussbaum in *The Physiology of the Novel: Reading, Neural Science, and the Form of Victorian Fiction* (New York: Oxford University Press, 2007). Citing Nussbaum's defence of literature as a valuable tool for cultivating thoughtful readers, Dames points out that the novel was faulted in the nineteenth century for doing exactly the opposite, cultivating 'inattentive, uncritical uptake' in its readers. His recommendation is for a historicist formalism, an account of how 'various artistic forms [. . .] can enter into social history by inflecting and revising' the 'social norms of cognition' (p. 19).

50. Noël Carroll, *Beyond Aesthetics: Philosophical Essays* (New York: Cambridge University Press, 2001), p. 39.
51. Alan Goldman, *Philosophy and the Novel* (Oxford: Oxford University Press, 2013), p. 132.
52. The question of a 'match between a social institution and our deepest personal needs' is an issue to which feminist thought has devoted a good deal of attention. For an introduction to such analysis, see Eve Feder Kittay and Linda Alcoff (eds), *The Blackwell Guide to Feminist Philosophy* (London: Blackwell, 2007).
53. Rita Felski, 'From Literary Theory to Critical Method', *Profession* (2008), p. 109.
54. Moi, *Revolution of the Ordinary*, p. 179.
55. See Noël Carroll, *On Criticism* (London: Routledge, 2009); Gaskin, *Language, Truth and Literature*, p. 86.
56. See, for instance, Kivy, *Philosophies of Art*.
57. See Jukka Mikkonen, *The Cognitive Value of Philosophical Fiction* (London: Bloomsbury, 2013), particularly pp. 58–60, for an example of and an introduction to this scholarship. This text is a revision and expansion of a number of Mikkonen's earlier essays, including two – 'Implicit Assertions in Literary Fiction' and 'Assertions in Literary Fiction' – that played a significant role in the article version of the introduction to this book: Patrick Fessenbecker, 'In Defence of Paraphrase', *New Literary History* 44.1 (2013), pp. 117–39.
58. Carroll, *Beyond Aesthetics*, p. 235.
59. Gaskin, *Language, Truth and Literature*, p. 89. Subsequent citations, abbreviated *LTL*, are given in parentheses in the text.
60. Lamarque and Olsen, *Truth, Fiction, and Literature*, p. 325.
61. Wolfson, *Formal Changes*, p. 30.
62. See Jerome McGann, *The Romantic Ideology: A Critical Investigation* (Chicago: University of Chicago Press, 1983), and Marjorie Levinson, *Wordsworth's Great Period Poems* (Cambridge: Cambridge University Press, 1986).
63. Wolfson, *Formal Changes*, p. 191.
64. Wolfson's sense of the logical gap in her argument appears in the last paragraph of the book, where she writes, 'I want to conclude this book, however, by urging attention to form not only defensively, in terms of its potential agency [. . .] but also affirmatively' (*Formal Changes*, p. 232). The sentence functions most to show how absent an affirmative argument in the preceding pages has been, and to mark the extent to which the aesthetics of the formalist attitude are assumed rather than explicated or defended.
65. Matthew Arnold, 'Dover Beach', in Thomas Collins and Vivienne Rundle (eds), *The Broadview Anthology of Victorian Poetry* (Peterborough, ON: Broadview, 2005), p. 375.
66. Nicholas Langrishe Alleyn Lash, *Theology on Dover Beach* (Eugene, OR: Wipe and Stock, 1979), p. 21.

67. Amartya Sen, *Identity and Violence: The Illusion of Destiny* (New York: Penguin, 2007), p. xiv.
68. Elaine Hadley, 'On a Darkling Plain: Victorian Liberalism and the Fantasy of Agency', *Victorian Studies* 48.1 (2005), pp. 92–102 (p. 93).
69. This is my own interpretation, inspired by Daniel M. Lavery's account of emotional vampires in *The Merry Spinster: Tales of Everyday Horror* (New York: Holt, 2018).
70. Mikkonen, *The Cognitive Value of Philosophical Fiction*, p. 59.
71. See *Revolution of the Ordinary*, chs 5, 6 and especially 9, where Moi explains her theory of reading as 'acknowledgment'. Moi responds to and qualifies a famous argument from Steven Knapp and Walter Benn Michaels for the essential importance of authorial intention; see W. J. T. Mitchell (ed.), *Against Theory: Literary Studies and the New Pragmatism* (Chicago: University of Chicago Press, 1985).
72. This is the title of an article by Riffaterre – 'The Referential Fallacy', *Columbia Review* 57.2 (1978), pp. 21–35. A more influential expression of the key view occurs in his 'Intertextual Representation: on Mimesis as Interpretive Discourse', *Critical Inquiry* 11.1 (1984), pp. 141–62.
73. As Eagleton puts it, 'In Wittgenstein's eyes, however, language neither corresponds to nor constitutes reality. Instead, it provides us with criteria for determining what kinds of things there are and how we are to speak of them' (*The Event of Literature*, p. 156).
74. Angus Fletcher, *Allegory: The Theory of a Symbolic Mode* (Ithaca: Cornell University Press, 1964), p. 70. I am indebted to Will Coker's unpublished essay on Bela Tarr's allegories for an introduction to Fletcher and this body of scholarship.
75. William Empson, *The Structure of Complex Words* (London: Vintage, 1951), pp. 346–7. Quoted in Fletcher, *Allegory*, p. 70.
76. Gary Johnson, *The Vitality of Allegory: Figural Narrative in Modern and Contemporary Fiction* (Columbus: Ohio State University Press, 2012). I have expanded on the issues discussed here in my review of Johnson's book, 'How Do You Know an Allegory When You See One?', *Diegesis* 3.2 (2014), available at <https://www.diegesis.uni-wuppertal.de/index.php/diegesis/article/view/172/239> (last accessed 16 January 2020).
77. Johnson, *The Vitality of Allegory*, p. 13.
78. Johnson, *The Vitality of Allegory*, p. 66.
79. Paul Suttie, 'Exemplary Behaviour in *The Faerie Queene*', *The Journal of English and German Philology* 99.3 (2000), pp. 313–33.
80. James Phelan, 'Character, Progression, and the Mimetic-Didactic Distinction', *Modern Philology* 84.3 (1987), pp. 282–99.
81. Sarah Raff, *Jane Austen's Erotic Advice* (New York: Oxford University Press, 2014).
82. See John Searle, 'The Logical Status of Fictional Discourse', in Lamarque and Olsen (eds), *Aesthetics and the Philosophy of Art*, pp. 320–7. In a

heavily disputed portion of his argument, Searle writes: 'Sometimes the author of a fictional story will insert utterances which are not fictional and not part of the story' (p. 327).
83. See Mikkonen, *The Cognitive Value of Philosophical Fiction*, pp. 74–7, for a clear summary of this line of scholarship.
84. Mikkonen, *The Cognitive Value of Philosophical Fiction*, p. 54.
85. George Eliot, *Middlemarch* (New York: Penguin, 1985), p. 668.

Chapter 2

Anthony Trollope on Akrasia, Self-Deception and Ethical Confusion

As a number of critics have noted, Anthony Trollope tended to reuse a particular version of the marriage plot.[1] What Victoria Glendinning calls his 'Ur-story' is a version of the romantic triangle: protagonists, usually though not always male, commit to marrying one character, but then find themselves drawn to a second.[2] Trollope varies the specific plot dynamics; sometimes the protagonist will succeed in returning to the first character, sometimes he will abandon his previous commitment, and often complications produce other outcomes. This aesthetic fact leads to a recurring consideration of a particular issue in philosophical psychology; moral philosophers have long been interested in situations where moral agents know what they ought to do but do not do it.[3]

At the most general level, the theoretical problem involved in such states, which philosophers describe as instances of 'weakness of the will' or 'akrasia', is a question in the logic of moral psychology: how can agents will something and not will it at the same time?[4] On what one might call the simple philosophical model, ordinary action proceeds by an agent judging that a given action is worth performing; this decision constitutes an intention and produces an action. Hence it is not immediately clear how akratic action – which occurs somehow *against* an agent's judgement – is possible. Since agents frequently do seem to act against their better judgements, the simple model of intentional action must be inadequate in some way, yet this model is so intuitive that philosophers have often thought that akrasia proper in fact rarely occurs, and that most cases of weakness of will involve a sort of confusion about what one's judgements actually are. For example, the first account of the problem, Plato's discussion in the *Protagoras*, claims axiomatically that 'to make for what one believes to be evil' is not in 'human nature'.[5] When agents appear to do so, they are really confused about what course of action is best; as Amelie Rorty explains, Plato's 'account of *akrasia* explains away counterexamples by re-describing them as cases of deception of some sort'.[6] In depicting at length characters who cannot bring their romantic actions into accord with their own best judgements about how to act, Trollope reflects extensively on this issue, ultimately questioning the status of reflective deliberation for the functioning of rationality; Frank Greystock, in *The Eustace Diamonds*, offers a typical example.

There is no doubt in Frank's mind that he loves Lucy Morris more than his cousin Lizzie Eustace; early in the novel, he proposes to Lucy, and refuses as well to give up the engagement even though it is against his material interests.[7] Despite this commitment, however, he continually finds himself violating his own judgement – yet he maintains the recognition of his wrongness all along. After he flirts with and kisses Lizzie Eustace, the narrator notes that 'What [Frank] was doing was not only imprudent – but wrong also. He knew that it was so' (*ED*, p. 256); similarly, he fails to defend Lucy in conversation, while knowing that 'such silence was in truth treachery to Lucy' (*ED*, p. 311); more dramatically, after Lucy makes their engagement public, Frank is at first irritated, but then admits, 'the truth is, we are, all of us, treating Lucy very badly' (*ED*, p. 361). Alongside Frank's own reflections on his nature, Trollope's narrator considers his irrationality at some length. For instance:

> [T]here are human beings who, though of necessity single in body, are dual in character; – in whose breasts not only is evil always fighting against good, – but to whom evil is sometimes horribly, hideously evil, but is sometimes also not hideous at all [. . .] Such men, – or women, – may hardly, perhaps, debase themselves with the more vulgar vices [. . .] but ambition, luxury, self-indulgence, pride, and covetousness will get a hold of them, and in various moods will be to them virtues in lieu of vices. Such a man was Frank Greystock. (*ED*, p. 199)

Passages such as this move from a depiction of akrasia to an analysis of it. Trollope conceives of weakness of will as the product of a sort of Manichean psychological oscillation: akratic moral agents contain opposing impulses towards good and evil, which alternate in causing the agent's actions. This causation happens not through compulsion, in such a way that the agent recognises the evil as such but is powerless to overcome it, but rather through a change in beliefs, one akin to that Plato had in mind. Frank's judgements about the good temporarily change: evil changes to 'not hideous at all', 'ambition, luxury, pride' become 'virtues in lieu of vices'.

This is to say that Frank is susceptible to a particular sort of self-deception: while he is not self-consciously immoral, his ethical judgement is not immune to influences. Significantly, the narrator and the novel are deeply interested in the process by which the vices 'get a hold' of men like Frank Greystock; in particular, the narrator explains, sexual desire can temporarily lead him astray: 'In his very heart Greystock despised [Lizzie]', yet 'he loved her after a fashion, and was prone to sit near her, and was fool enough to be flattered by her caresses' (*ED*, pp. 627–8). Trollope thus suggests, through Frank's narrative, a particular way of thinking about how actions against best judgements are possible: desire can temporarily reform such judgements. Notably, Frank can recognise the wrongness of his relationship with Lizzie when he is away from her; this shows his judgement correcting itself.

The point here is to not to offer a reading of *The Eustace Diamonds*, but to demonstrate the interpretive usefulness of a concept from moral philosophy. Because of his distinctive versions of the marriage plot, Trollope returns frequently to weak-willed agents such as Frank. Recognising this fact has two key benefits. First, the attention to moral psychology can clarify an interpretive debate about the tension in Trollope's fiction between ethics and psychology; in fact, Trollope is interested in precisely the areas where the two discourses intertwine. Second and more substantively, the recognition of the role of akrasia in the main romantic plots allows a new dimension of Trollope's art to emerge; his novels contain dozens of depictions of irrational action and self-deception, and these depictions and his narratorial explanations of them complement each other in philosophically revealing ways. In particular, Trollope's works combine to offer a series of arguments against models of rationality that depend on the role of reflective judgement and conscious decision making. The critical tradition has long recognised that Trollope's novels see ideal ethical deliberation as an instinctive process, suggesting that any substantive ethical principle is incapable of acknowledging the particularities of a given situation.[8] What an attention to irrationality suggests is that Trollope does not hold this view merely because of the inability of such judgement to achieve sufficient nuance; the defence of instinct stems also from a deep worry about the psychology of rational judgement.

Trollope and Morality

The contemporary critical debate about Trollope's ethics remains indebted to Ruth apRoberts's 1971 book *The Moral Trollope*. The centrepiece of her argument is the contention that Trollope accepted a 'situation ethics': a sense of moral evaluation that emphasised sensitivity to situational particulars.[9] As she puts it, 'Trollope's interest in complex cases is thoroughly and frankly and insistently ethical. His tender casuistry demands the most careful, detailed consideration of the circumstances, even those of a crime.'[10] Put another way, Trollope's novels depict the inadequacy of the application of general ethical principles to specific situations; by portraying moral problems with the full richness of accumulated detail, Trollope reveals the insensitivity of simple rules to the complexity of human ethical life. Trollope famously refused to define his key moral concept, the 'gentleman', suggesting that those who use the term know what it means without being able to articulate it propositionally.[11] Significantly, this throws the idea of moral truth into some question: as apRoberts puts it, 'Trollope's art, his religion, and his philosophy are all demonstrably consistent; and his distinguishing consistency [. . .] can best be thought of as a relativism'.[12]

Yet, as James Kincaid has pointed out, for all his ethical sensitivity, there is nevertheless a discernible moral code in Trollope's works. Kincaid explains:

> It is true that [Trollope's] novels consistently attack all forms of purism and absolutism, but not generally to establish simple relativism in their place. The standards are all there; they are made more difficult to apply and far more difficult to define; most of all, there is less communal agreement on what they are. But they are dependent on codes which are not to be defined by situations.[13]

Kincaid grants apRoberts's claim about casuistry, agreeing that Trollope emphasises the adjustments that moral agents must make to apply general ethical rules. However, it does not follow from this emphasis that *everything* is relative to the situation; the principle being applied necessarily depends on 'extra-situational' criteria. The question of how to act 'honestly' in a given situation is only meaningful if the word 'honesty' has a meaning independent of the description of the situation. For Kincaid, then, Trollope's moral philosophy is concerned with how best to live out a moral code. Rather than relying on the careful deductive application of a general rule such as the categorical imperative, Kincaid's Trollope advocates a moral model – the 'gentleman' – who instinctively senses how to behave and specifically how to be honest.

Amanda Anderson has criticised this interpretive strain by pointing out that many of Trollope's most memorable characters become so by virtue of precisely the conflict between their own psychological features and the moral code by which they are attempting to live. As she puts it,

> They manifest not exactly integrity but rather a kind of stubbornness or obsession that often shades into perversity. The tense imbrication of morality and psychology, the irreversible mediation of morality by psychology, thus becomes a fundamental narrative interest, and problem, for Trollope. Any account of ethics in Trollope that does not appreciate this fact – as in readings of Trollope as a situation ethicist (Ruth apRoberts) or even as a writer who foregrounds the delicacy required to live within the terms of a code (James Kincaid) – fails to acknowledge the prominent issue of recalcitrant psychologies.[14]

Anderson's point is that both apRoberts and Kincaid fail to acknowledge that Trollope's depiction of the difficulties of ethical life is in some significant sense the result of his interest in characters whose psychological make-up inevitably frustrates their moral agency; Anderson goes on to discuss such 'recalcitrant psychologies' in the context of modernity. Thus, the problem Trollope is invested in is not so much about how difficult it is to apply moral rules to specific situations – which is in some sense a problem outside the moral agent – but rather about how difficult it is to live according to a moral rule given the stubborn, intractable and possibly perverse thing that oneself is, which is in some sense a problem inside the moral agent.

Anderson suggests that the focus on psychology supplants a focus on morality: 'Trollope is always putting into question the limits of morality by focusing on recalcitrant psychological impulses and on the transformations that psychological habit effects on affirmed principle.'[15] As the interpretive use of akrasia suggests, however, it is possible to see Trollope's investment in such psychological issues as reflecting the importance of a particular kind of moral problem, rather than a belief about the limited scope of the moral realm. In this sense, it is possible to follow apRoberts and Kincaid in seeing Trollope as invested in the nuances of ethical life, but to follow Anderson in thinking of the problems that ensue as the result of internal, psychological difficulties.

In considering these moral-psychological problems, Trollope's work complements and is complemented by an important minor strain in Victorian moral philosophy. For the most part, the dominant Utilitarian thinkers failed to recognise akrasia as a problem. Relying on the simple model of philosophical agency, they saw it as a necessary truth that agents would reliably pursue whatever end they judged would maximise their own pleasure; thus, moral development hinged not on learning to bring one's actions into accord with one's judgement, but rather developing oneself in such a way that one's pleasures stemmed from moral actions.[16] The notion that an agent might judge that an action maximised happiness for her and then not do it – that is, that she might act akratically – is impossible in the psychology of Jeremy Bentham and John Stuart Mill. But as Jerome Schneewind has noted, the intuitionist moral philosophers took as emblematic of morality in general those problems 'in which the agent knows what to do but finds it difficult to bring himself to do it'.[17] And the pre-Freudian psychologists who theorised the 'morally insane', as well as novelists such as Trollope, took as central the issue of self-control, offering sophisticated accounts of moral rationality and the ways it can fail.[18]

After the Victorian era, Anglo-American moral philosophers – still largely working within the utilitarian tradition – continued to defend the simple model of agency.[19] In the last quarter of the twentieth century, however, such philosophers increasingly recognised the importance of irrationality for a full account of moral agency. In particular, a seminal 1970 paper by Donald Davidson reignited the philosophical conversation by spelling out the intuitions behind the simple model of agency and acknowledging the problem that akrasia presents to it.[20] The response to Davidson has been rich and varied, and when combined with elements of the minor strains of Victorian moral philosophy, it allows an underlying coherence in Trollope's myriad depictions of irrationality to emerge. The akratic protagonist whom Trollope depicts most often, including Frank Greystock but also the Duke of Omnium and Phineas Finn, manifests a kind of self-deception importantly different from that implied by Davidson's view. Rather than holding that such irrationality is a *state*, where an agent both believes and doesn't believe something at the same time, Trollope shows how it is a *process*, whereby the ordinary means by which agents decide on actions and beliefs are misled by desires. When he depicts situations where agents are not self-deceived, and act freely against a better judgement of which they are aware, Trollope moreover demonstrates scepticism about the assumption, central to Davidson's view, that judgements carry motivational power. Trollope's depiction of 'conscious akrasia' in George Vavasor and Glencora Palliser suggests that the reasonableness of a judgement may have little actual impact on an agent's actions. Perhaps most profoundly, Trollope questions models of rationality that define reasonable behaviour as that which accords with one's judgement. Through 'ethically confused' characters such as Alice Vavasor, Trollope shows how agents can act irrationally precisely by acting in accord with their best judgement; correspondingly, he indicates that such agents would have been better off acting akratically, trusting recalcitrant impulses. Trollope's fiction accordingly contributes to the debates around akrasia in three ways: he shows how self-deception can easily mislead judgement, how such judgement can fail to motivate even when it is not self-deceived, and finally how even unbiased deliberation can still be mistaken. Taken together, Trollope's depictions of the psychology of irrationality thus concord with his emphasis on casuistry to criticise the assumption that reflective judgement is the primary capacity for moral life, and to support the sophisticated but instinctive moral agency of the gentleman.

Akrasia and Self-Deception

Davidson argued for the possibility of akrasia by distinguishing between three kinds of judgements: 'prima facie' judgements, which judge that a given action is preferable over another in the light of some specific respect; 'all things considered' judgements, which judge that a given action is preferable in all respects; and 'all-out' judgements, which decide to perform a given action.[21] Akrasia is possible, Davidson claims, because of the gap between 'all things considered' judgements and 'all-out' judgements; an agent can conclude that, all things considered, it would be best to turn off the television and go to sleep – but then fail to form the all-out judgement that consists in the actual intention to turn off the television. In such situations, on Davidson's model, the agent falls back on some prima facie judgement. Thus self-control depends on connecting 'all-out' judgements to 'all things considered' judgements and accordingly avoiding the akratic break.[22]

Explaining akrasia by appeal to a gap between judgements allows Davidson to preserve the basic theory of agency that the simple philosophical model affords: judgements still produce intentions, which cause actions. If these are not exactly separable as mental phenomena, they are nevertheless distinguishable as components of the process of action. The psychological notion at work here is one that Davidson calls a 'mild form of "internalism"'; the term refers to the view that an agent's judgements about what is worth pursuing have motivational and thus causal force.[23] In other words, the view holds that the causes of an action are internal to the deliberative process that produces the belief that the action is worth doing: colloquially, what happens in my conscious mind leads to what my body does. This internalist commitment explains why Davidson emphasises prima facie judgements: even in cases of akratic action, there is a judgement that produces the movement of the agent's body; the judgement just does not happen to be the agent's 'all things considered' judgement. This solution comes, however, at a philosophical cost: in claiming that actions can sometimes stem from a partial judgement not representative of the full deliberative process, Davidson imagines the self as divisible, so that there are moments when 'part' of a moral agent acts rather than the whole agent. This 'partitioning of the mind' is implausible, Davidson's critics have argued, for it posits the existence of 'semi-autonomous structures' within the mind that can serve as 'mental causes for other mental states' without being 'reasons'; this is to say that they can somehow cause action without being constitutive of full judgement.[24]

It is possible to see more clearly the problem here by extending Davidson's analysis to self-deception, where he defended a similar strategy. One way to make sense of the peculiar state where an agent appears to both know and not know a given thing – say, that their spouse is faithful – is to claim that this is in fact precisely what is going on: there is a 'part' of the agent that knows the spouse is faithful, while the rest of the agent believes that the spouse is not.[25] This is to see self-deception as structurally analogous to interpersonal deception: the deceiver and the deceived are separate agents. But surely, the critique goes, this is implausible; as with the approach to akrasia, this way of addressing the problem posits a number of dubious mental phenomena – sites of knowledge that exist within a person without being constitutive of that person.

Alfred Mele among others has suggested an alternative approach, arguing that self-deception and akrasia do not describe states of conflict within an agent's mind, but rather indicate failures in the ways agents arrive at action and form beliefs. Self-deception, from this perspective, is not a split between two contradictory beliefs, but one belief arrived at in an irrational – because motivationally influenced – way. In similar fashion, akrasia is not a state where a tension between a judgement and an action splits an agent, but rather a state where the operation of practical reason has been misled. Mele offers as an explanatory thought experiment in this regard 'Gordon', a high-level CIA agent accused of treason.[26] For Gordon's parents, the costs of believing falsely that Gordon is innocent are not much different from a belief based on good evidence, whereas believing falsely that he is guilty will carry a very high cost. This is to say that it does not hurt them if their belief in his innocence is wrong, since his crimes would not affect them; however, if they believe he is guilty and he is not, they will have ruined their relationship with their son for a bad reason.

For the CIA, though, the costs of believing falsely that Gordon is innocent are much higher. They will have given a spy access to state secrets if they improperly believe him innocent, whereas they will simply be lacking a presumably replaceable employee if they improperly believe him guilty. Thus, their motivation will require Gordon to prove his innocence at a much higher standard of evidence than Gordon's parents require. Self-deception appears, for Mele, in precisely these sorts of features of our belief-acquisition process: even if Gordon is innocent of treason, the CIA may deceive themselves into thinking that he is guilty simply by setting the level of evidence required to prove his innocence impossibly high. Conversely, even if Gordon is guilty, his parents may deceive themselves into thinking he is innocent by setting the level of required evidence extremely low. But in both cases, Mele avoids 'partitioning' the self: he does not say that there is a 'part' of the CIA that knows Gordon is innocent but wants to believe that he is guilty, and thus persuades the rest; likewise, Gordon's parents are not somehow partially aware of Gordon's guilt and then subsequently persuaded at a conscious level by those parts of their psyches that love their son.

It is this alternative view to Davidson's that Trollope's representation of self-deception supports, and this particular kind of irrationality – that is, self-deception, as opposed to what this chapter terms 'conscious akrasia' or 'ethical confusion' – is the most common form of weakness of will in his fiction. The prevalence of such self-deception appears most strikingly in the fact that even Plantagenet Palliser – Trollope's 'idea of a perfect gentleman' – succumbs to it.[27] *The Duke's Children*, typically, opens with a marriage crisis, with Palliser's daughter in love with a man he does not approve of. His beloved and now-deceased wife, however, encouraged the relationship behind his back, and thus Palliser (now the Duke of Omnium) irrationally redirects his anger against his wife's best friend, Mrs Finn, who has advised the young couple. As the narrator explains, he is 'driven by the desire of his heart to acquit the wife he had lost of the terrible imprudence, worse than imprudence, of which she was now accused'.[28] Wanting his wife to have been innocent of manipulating him, the Duke's desire to 'acquit' her affects the way he assesses the situation and drives him into self-deception.

Palliser's sort of irrationality does not result from his holding contradictory beliefs (*à la* the Davidsonian account); rather, it stems from motivationally influenced belief formation. Put another way, what Palliser wishes to be true affects how he sees the evidence. Trollope's narrator represents the process with some subtlety:

> He struggled gallantly to acquit the memory of his wife. He could best do that by leaning with the full weight of his mind on the presumed iniquity of Mrs. Finn. Had he not known from the first that the woman was an adventuress? And had he not declared to himself over and over again that between such a one and himself there should be no intercourse, no common feeling? He had allowed himself to be talked into an intimacy, to be talked almost into an affection. And this was the result! (*TDC*, pp. 49–50)

As the analysis the narrator offers in the first two sentences fades into a passage of free indirect discourse representing Palliser's increasingly self-deceived stream of thoughts, the way that motivation affects the understanding of evidence becomes clear. Rather than remembering his wife's willingness to manipulate love affairs – a fact present to him a moment before – his thoughts redirect into the irrelevant beginnings of his relationship with Mrs Finn, to whom the old Duke, Plantagenet's father, had proposed at the end of his life. The fact that the then Madame Goesler declined the proposal is dismissed; for Omnium at this moment, the piece of evidence that rises to consciousness is the accusation of her as an 'adventuress'.

In thus attending to irrelevant pieces of evidence, the Duke exemplifies self-deception through what Mele calls 'error costs', which involve the pain an agent will suffer if a belief turns out to be false.[29] If the Duke believes wrongly that his wife is innocent, the mistake is largely harmless – but if he wrongly believes that she is guilty, he will have unfairly condemned the woman he loved. As such, he unreflectively sets the standard of evidence for proof of his wife's guilt extremely high, and the standard for proving Mrs Finn's guilt much lower:

> He had come to entertain an idea that Mrs. Finn had been the great promoter of the sin, and he thought that Tregear [his daughter's lover] had told him that that lady had been concerned with the matter from the beginning. In all this there was a craving in his heart to lessen the amount of culpable responsibility which might seem to attach itself to the wife he had lost. (*TDC*, p. 55)

The narrator makes clear that the hope of 'lessening' the fault that his wife committed affects the Duke's belief formation. Since it would cost him a great deal of suffering to believe that his wife was manipulating him behind his back, the mere assertions from Tregear and Mrs Finn of his wife's involvement in the affair do not constitute sufficient evidence to prove her guilt. Conversely, the Duke's desires lead to him setting the bar of evidence needed to convict Mrs Finn of 'iniquity' and 'treachery' quite low. She briefly interceded with Tregear as a mentor, and while her primary advice was for him to confess everything to the Duke, the mere fact of the intercession, along with her past flirtation with the old Duke, becomes sufficient evidence to demonstrate that she is the 'great promoter of the sin'.

Even after it becomes clear that Mrs Finn's behaviour has been praiseworthy, the Duke somewhat wilfully continues to condemn her. As Trollope depicts it, this is again a result of error cost: it would cost the Duke a great deal to believe that he had treated her unfairly. Thus, after receiving a letter from Mrs Finn accusing him of injustice, he reflects on his behaviour:

> He tried to set himself to the task in perfect honesty [. . .] he had to own that her intimacy with his uncle and his wife had not been so much of her seeking as of theirs. It grieved him now that it should have been so, but so it was. And after all this, – after the affectionate surrender of herself to his wife's caprices which the woman had made, – he had turned upon her and driven her away with ignominy. That was all true. As he thought of it he became hot, and was conscious of a quivering feeling round his heart [. . .] If he could make it good to himself that in a matter of such magnitude as the charge of his daughter she had been untrue to him [. . .] Then would his wrath be altogether justified! Then would it have been impossible that he should have done aught else than cast her out! (*TDC*, pp. 100–1)

The Duke is overtly trying to avoid deceiving himself; he consciously aspires to 'perfect honesty' in evaluating his conduct. And he starts well, first recognising that Mrs Finn was not really an 'adventuress' and admitting the deep friendship between her and his wife. And yet a 'feeling round his heart rises' when he begins to realise how inappropriate his own conduct has been; 'driving' Mrs Finn away 'with ignominy' in his wrath will only be justified if he can 'make it good to himself' that she was in fact 'untrue'. Thus he misleads himself into believing that she was unfaithful; tellingly, the narrator remarks, 'as he thought of this, he felt sure she had betrayed him!' His sureness here relies not on any piece of evidence, but on how heavily his own need for self-approval depends on Mrs Finn's betrayal.

In keeping with the gentlemanly ideal that he exemplifies, the Duke eventually overcomes his self-deception, apologises to Mrs Finn, and admits his wife's failures. The perception involved in such self-mastery – where an agent frees himself from the biases of desires – is central to Trollope's conception of 'honesty'. Thus in his writing on Cicero, Trollope remarks:

> To be believed because of your truth, and yet to lie; to be trusted for your honesty, and yet to cheat; to have credit for patriotism, and yet to sell your country! The temptations to do this are rarely put before a man plainly, in all their naked ugliness. They certainly were not so presented to Cicero by Caesar and his associates [. . .] But at last [Cicero] saw his way clear to honesty.[30]

Cicero refuses to let his actions be guided by 'temptations', masters his motivations and acts on his own best judgement; in this way he avoids weakness of will. But the more specific problem that Cicero confronts is self-deception. The 'bait' does not appear in its 'naked ugliness' and is 'not repellent', Trollope explains, but instead appears in a form 'fitted to deceive and powerful almost to persuade'; the influence relies on a disguised appeal to desire, in the same way that the Duke's desire to believe that his wife was innocent led him to believe that Mrs Finn was manipulating his children. Thus, it is not so significant that Cicero is open with others; rather, he is admirable in Trollope's gloss because he is honest with himself, able to see desires as they are.

The strains of Victorian moral philosophy that recognised akrasia cohere closely with Trollope's depictions of self-deception. Somewhat ironically, one finds a particularly clear expression of this view in the generally utilitarian thought of Henry Sidgwick.[31] Arguing primarily that the philosophical tradition has refused to recognise what he terms 'unreasonable action', Sidgwick suggests that weakness of the will most commonly arises from fallacious chains of practical reasoning that the agent momentarily fails to recognise as fallacious:

> [W]hen a general resolution is remembered, while yet the particular conclusion which ought to be drawn is not drawn, the cause of the phenomenon is a temporary perversion of judgement by some seductive feeling [. . .] [given] a hard and distasteful task which he regards it as his duty to do, [a man] then rapidly but sincerely persuades himself that in the present state of his brain some lighter work is just at present more suited to his powers.[32]

Further, when a 'seductive feeling' prevents an agent from drawing a particular conclusion that he or she rationally should, the feeling 'operates not by producing positively fallacious reasoning, but by directing attention to certain aspects of the subject, and from certain others'.[33] Thus, an akratic agent often senses 'that he might come to a different view of his position if he resolutely faced certain aspects of it tending to reduce his personal claims; but he consciously refrains from directing attention to them'.[34] As in Trollope's account, there is no sense that the man somehow knows and does not know a given belief. Rather, a 'seductive' feeling has 'perverted' his judgement, self-deceptively convincing him that 'some lighter work' is more suitable than the difficult task he initially decided to do. Moreover, the man's irrationality arises in a way similar to the Duke of Omnium's: his motivations determine the 'aspects of the subject' to which he directs 'attention', and – as with the Duke's desire to believe well of himself – his 'personal claims' lead him astray.

If *The Duke's Children* thus essentially corroborates the account of self-deception as motivated reasoning in Mele and Sidgwick, *Phineas Finn* considers but ultimately rejects Davidson's account of self-deception as a contradiction between internal states. Phineas Finn tries to convince himself that he is in some sense two agents; crucially, however, Trollope presents Phineas's belief not as a lucid account of his actual internal division, but as itself a product of motivated self-deception. In the first eponymous novel, Phineas finds himself after election to Parliament in a series of romantic entanglements – first with Lady Laura Standish, then with Violet Effingham, and finally with Madame Max Goesler. All the while, however – much like Frank Greystock – he is in an implicit way engaged to a woman back home: Mary Flood-Jones, whom Phineas grew up with in Ireland. Phineas deals with the tension by imagining that he is two different people:

> He felt that he had two identities, – that he was, as it were, two separate persons, – and that he could, without any real faithlessness, be very much in love with Violet Effingham in his position of man of fashion and member of Parliament in England, and also warmly attached to dear little Mary Flood-Jones as an Irishman of Killaloe. He was aware, however, that there was a prejudice against such fullness of heart, and, therefore, resolved sternly that it was his duty to be constant to Miss Effingham.[35]

And similarly, after giving up his pursuit of Violet Effingham, the reader hears:

His Irish life, he would tell himself, was a thing quite apart and separate from his life in England. He said not a word about Mary Flood-Jones to any of those with whom he lived in London. Why should he, feeling as he did that it would so soon be necessary that he should disappear from among them? (*PF*, p. 500)

As these passages reveal, Phineas makes sense of himself by partitioning his agency; he has 'two separate identities', is 'two separate persons', with an 'Irish life' quite different from his 'life in England'. But Trollope's narration clarifies the extent to which Phineas is mistaken in these beliefs about these conflicted states; his mental division represents only what Phineas 'would tell himself', what he 'feels', and – importantly – what allows him to think that he is not guilty of 'faithlessness'. Phineas thus evades what Richard Moran has called the responsibility of the authority that arises from a first-person relation to one's actions; by pretending that the person in Ireland is different from and not in control of the person in England, Phineas avoids having to deal with his own duplicity.[36] And his inchoate recognition of this fact appears in his awareness of the 'prejudice against such fullness of heart'.

What Frank Greystock, the Duke of Omnium and Phineas together reveal is the extent to which self-deceived irrationality is a structuring element of Trollope's fiction. Indeed, Phineas's subsequent narrative makes this particularly clear: Mary Flood-Jones dies after the end of *Phineas Finn* but before the beginning of *Phineas Redux*.[37] The woman to whom Phineas has committed himself, whose marriage with Phineas represents the triumph of his self-control, immediately disappears from the rest of the story. Insofar as Mary's death reopens the possibility of weakness of will in Phineas's romantic life, her death is necessary for Trollope's narrative logic. A Phineas with fully integrated motivations would not allow Trollope to depict the distortions and deceptions that corrupt his practical reasoning. Early in *Phineas Redux*, the narrator criticises Phineas, remarking, 'In his character there was much of weakness, much of vacillation, perhaps some deficiency of strength.' It is precisely because of the philosophical complexities of these failings, of course, that the character is of such interest to Trollope.[38]

Conscious Akrasia

Alongside these portrayals of self-deception, however, Trollope occasionally depicts conscious akrasia, where an agent recognises that a given action is a mistake but then performs it anyway. Although the bulk of the novel is concerned with self-deception, the climax of *Phineas Finn* points towards a more conscious kind of irrationality. Phineas visits Madame Max Goesler, believing that she will propose marriage to him and intending to decline it in order to marry Mary. No longer self-deceived, complete self-mastery still eludes him; he must deliberately remind himself of his commitment to Mary in order to prevent irrational flirtation:

> [T]here was a care about his person which he would have hardly taken had he been quite assured that he simply intended to say good-bye to the lady whom he was about to visit. But if there were any such conscious feeling, he administered to himself an antidote before he left the house. On returning to the sitting-room he went to a little desk from which he took out the letter from Mary which the reader has seen, and carefully perused every word of it. 'She is the best of them all', he said to himself, as he refolded the letter. (*PF*, p. 533)

The passage emphasises first of all the recalcitrance of desire. Despite his overt intentions, Phineas unreflectively dresses attractively for the meeting – in Henry Sidgwick's terms, the desires draw his attention to certain kinds of clothing in a way that warps his ordinary deliberation. Second, and crucially, Phineas here demonstrates what Mele calls self-control as an 'ability', after demonstrating over the course of the novel that he lacks it as a 'trait'.[39] Mele means by this distinction to capture the difference between self-control through reflective techniques and self-control as a property of character: for an example, one might think of the difference between agents who get themselves out of bed through a complex series of alarm clocks and agents who get out of bed simply as a result of waking up. The latter 'exceptionally resolute' agents have 'no need to make an effort of self-control even when faced with strong competing desires'.[40] It is because Phineas lacks this kind of resolve that he must consciously work to control himself. Because he knows his judgement may fail to motivate when the chips are down, in an encounter fraught with temptation he bolsters the motivational strength of his judgement by re-reading a letter from Mary.

This weakness arises from a surprisingly common evaluative instability. Trollope's narrator criticises Phineas's attempt to bolster himself by judging that Mary is the 'best' of the women he might marry, explaining: 'I am not sure that it is well that a man should have any large number from whom to select a best; as, in such circumstances, he is so very apt to change his judgement from hour to hour' (*PF*, p. 533). In the offhand remark that a man is 'so very apt to change his judgement', this passage expresses a deep scepticism about the stability of character. The fundamentally malleable nature of evaluative judgements emerges moreover in the narrator's registering of how quickly they change. Thus Phineas's weakness is not merely a result of his lack of resolve, but results more substantively from the weak nature of human judgement: his judgements fail to motivate him, the passage implies, because they are so changeable.

These passages suggest Trollope's rejection of what Davidson called 'internalism', the position that judgements are intrinsically motivational. On the opposing 'externalist' view, akrasia results from the difference between an 'agent's assessments or rankings of the objects of his wants and the motivational force of those wants'.[41] Self-control is difficult and akrasia common because the connection between judgements and actual motivations is so tenuous; merely judging that an action is worthwhile may have little effect on what an agent actually does. To put the objection in Davidson's terms, akrasia happens not because an agent falls back on a prima facie judgement, but because the motivational power of some other option outweighs the motivational power of an all-things-considered judgement. The point is not that the desire overwhelms and compels such agents; rather, the claim is that when they decide to act, their reasons play less of a role in the decision than the motivations created by their desires.

This rejection of internalism appears in a number of different ways in Trollope's works, but *Can You Forgive Her?* offers a particularly vivid example. George Vavasor approaches self-conscious villainy in calling himself a 'rascal'. When after their engagement Alice Vavasor refuses to embrace him, he recognises that she does not love him, but concludes that he will take her money anyway. The narrator explains:

> When Alice contrived as she had done to escape the embrace he was so well justified in asking, he knew the whole truth. He was sore at heart, and very angry withal. He could have readily spurned her from him [and] would have done so had not his need for her money restrained him. He knew that this was so, and he told himself that he was a rascal.[42]

Here, George differs from the self-deceived characters in openly recognising the wrongness of his actions, yet he does them anyway; his judgement that they are wrong simply fails to motivate him.

Trollope is at pains to explain how George can simultaneously recognise himself as a rascal and yet treat Alice in such a fashion. The narrator remarks:

> Vavasor had educated himself to badness with his eyes open. He had known what was wrong, and had done it, having taught himself to think that bad things were best . . . [yet he] would sometimes feel tempted to cut his throat and put an end to himself, because he knew that he had taught himself amiss. Again, he would sadly ask himself whether it was yet too late; always, however, answering himself that it was too late. (CY, p. 481)

And, a moment later:

> He believed in his own ability, he believed thoroughly in his own courage; but he did not believe in his own conduct. He feared that he had done, – feared still more strongly that he would be driven to do, – that which would shut men's ears against his words, and would banish him from high places. No man believes in himself who knows himself to be a rascal, however great may be his talent, or however high his pluck. (CY, p. 482)

In George Vavasor, a true separation between evaluations and intentions emerges; the internalist notion that evaluations have motivational power has become entirely untrue for him. The fact that he knows himself to be a rascal is not sufficient to lead him to change – it is 'too late' to do so. One might think that he is self-deceived, in the same way Phineas is; one key line in the passage, which indicates that George 'had taught himself to believe that bad things were best', could suggest that he has fooled himself into thinikng that immoral actions were in fact praiseworthy.

The emphasis, however, is crucially on George's awareness of what he has been doing: he 'educated himself to badness with open eyes', and has done wrong things despite the fact that he 'had known what was wrong'. Then, too the context is revealing: the narrator is comparing George to Mr Bott, a fellow new Member of Parliament, who, though he 'meant to do well', was 'born small'. The narrator explains further that Mr Bott 'did not know that he was doing amiss in seeking to rise by tuft-hunting and toadying. He was both mean and vain [. . .] [but] was troubled by no idea that he did wrong' (CY, pp. 480–1). The point here is that Mr Bott suffers from a garden variety form of self-deception; he is acting immorally, but has no awareness of the fact. Given that the passage draws a contrast between the two, one must understand George as caught in a much darker state of agency – a state where, due to his self-education in immorality, he is helpless to act from what Trollope calls the 'better part of his nature'.

If George knows that what he does is wrong, and Mr Bott does not know that what he does is wrong, Lady Glencora Palliser knows that what she *would* do is wrong. Although situational constraints do not allow Glencora to act on her desires, her impulse to act against her own judgement parallels George Vavasor's. She is drawn to Burgo Fitzgerald and away from her husband in a way she recognises as wrong but which she is powerless to stop:

> I know what I am, and what I am like to become. I loathe myself, and I loathe the thing that I am thinking of. I could have clung to the outside of a man's body, to his very trappings, and loved him ten times better than myself! – ay, even though he had ill-treated me, – if I had been allowed to choose a husband for myself. (CY, p. 306)

As with George, Glencora is a conscious akratic: she would have run with away with Burgo, but exterior forces – her husband and her family – prevented her from acting at all.

But here the distinction between Lady Glencora and George emerges, as we see her deploying self-control as an ability. She alters her circumstances to prevent an elopement by avoiding Burgo socially and enlisting Alice in the service of preventing any sort of meeting between her and her ex-lover. As the narrator describes Glencora, 'She was as one who, in madness, was resolute to throw herself from a precipice, but to whom some remnant of sanity remained which forced her to seek those who would save her from herself' (CY, p. 453). This is closely related to Phineas's decision to fortify his resolution through the 'antidote' of a re-reading of Mary's letter; Glencora's decision to draw on forces outside herself represents an awareness of the gap between her reasons and her actual motivations. Believing that if she is left to her own devices she will elope, because her love for Burgo will outweigh the motivation arising from a recognition of the act's wrongness, she does not – as George does – let the chips fall where they may, but instead adds additional motivational strength to her reasons. In this way, Glencora and George offer a philosophically significant juxtaposition: if George represents Trollope's awareness of the motivational gap, Glencora represents his suggestion about how moral agents ought to address such a condition.

In suggesting that agents are capable of overcoming their own desires in this way, Trollope points to the complexity of akrasia – though akratic agents are driven by their desires, they are not compelled by them. As Glencora demonstrates, akratic agents are in some sense free to overcome the desires that move them. Trollope expands upon the tension involved here in *Framley Parsonage*, in the character of Mr Sowerby. The narrator describes Mr Sowerby thus:

> That Mr. Sowerby had been a rogue, I cannot deny. It is roguish to lie, and he had been a great liar. It is roguish to make promises which the promiser knows he cannot perform, and such had been Mr. Sowerby's daily practice. It is roguish to live on other men's money, and Mr. Sowerby had long been doing so [. . .] But, for all that, in spite of his acknowledged roguery, Lord Lufton was too hard upon him in his judgement. There was yet within him the means of repentance, could a *locus penitentiae* have been supplied to him.[43]

Mr Sowerby has long been a self-aware rogue who nevertheless recognises himself as such; however, in the same way that George finds it 'too late' to change, Mr Sowerby lacks a habit-breaking opportunity that would lead him back to a praiseworthy life.

Crucially, the narrator in *Framley Parsonage* reflects on this sort of thinking, contending that 'A man always can do right, even though he has done wrong before. But that previous wrong adds so much difficulty to the path – a difficulty which increases in tremendous ratio, till a man at last is choked in his struggling, and is drowned beneath the waters.'[44] On the one hand, the narrator appears to dismiss the hopelessness that George and Sowerby feel as foolish by simply declaring that 'a man can always do right'; on the other hand, the comment also lays out why they might feel such hopelessness, since their actions 'add difficulty' to the path, until they choke and drown 'beneath the waters'. The point here is that the capacity to be resolute – that is, self-control as a trait – is a habit, and can disappear if it is consistently overridden. It is always possible to exert self-control as an ability, which involves consciously bringing oneself into accord with a better judgement; this is the assumption that lies behind the narrator's assertion that a 'man can always do right'. But if a moral agent continually lets desires overwhelm their judgement, such exertions will become increasingly necessary, as he 'drowns' in a succession of irresolute, weak-willed actions.

Rational Akrasia

All of the instances of irrationality presented thus far do not quite yet question the role of deliberative judgement within an account of rational behaviour. If self-deceived characters demonstrate Trollope's recognition of the ways judgement can be misled and conscious akratics demonstrate his recognition of the ways judgement can fail to motivate, both sorts of moral problem still reinforce the importance of judgement. In other words, both deliberative problems imply that moral action requires freeing one's judgement from bias and bringing one's behaviour into accord with it. But the depth of Trollope's reflection on the issue appears in the fact that he also considers what is in some sense the opposite problem. Challenging the assumption that correct judgement is essential to rational behaviour, Trollope depicts extended states of 'ethical confusion', where a character's sincere, honest and careful deliberative judgement is nevertheless deeply mistaken. In such moments, he represents feelings and desires not as biases that produce irrationality, but instead as sub-reflective guides that point to a moral agent's real reasons. Correspondingly, in such situations a character's rationality does not lie in finding ways to overcome those feelings and act in accord with their best judgement, but in trusting her feelings and acting against that judgement itself.

The suggestion that weakness of the will might be rational represents a powerful challenge to the Davidsonian view. Nomy Arpaly, in her essay 'On Acting Rationally Against One's Best Judgement', points out that one's 'all things considered' or best judgement is, after all, just another belief, and can be mistaken in the ways that any other belief can.[45] Arpaly argues that there is no guarantee that reflection, even under ideal circumstances, can never make mistakes. Even if one limits the conception of rationality to what Arpaly calls the 'coherence of the agent's mental states', the possibility of reflective error remains; the point is that even when the only question is which action best serves an agent's interests, the agent can still err through confusion about what her interests actually are.[46] When caught up in such confusion, Arpaly argues, akrasia is not necessarily irrational. More specifically, given two irrational actions, where one is against an agent's real interests and desires but in accord with her judgement, and the other is against an agent's best judgement but in accord with her real interests and desires, the fact that the latter is akratic is inconsequential, given its deeper reasonableness. In a state of ethical confusion, furthermore, an agent's recalcitrant emotions and instincts can be guides to her genuine interests or real reasons. Thus akrasia matters less than one might think; agents who act on the basis of recalcitrant emotions might be procedurally irrational, but they are better off than they would be if they insisted on following their judgement.

To motivate this claim, Arpaly offers the following thought experiment:

> Emily's best judgement has always told her that she should pursue a Ph.D. in chemistry. But as she proceeds through a graduate program, she starts feeling restless, sad, and ill motivated to stick to her studies. These feelings are triggered by a variety of factors which, let us suppose, are good reasons for her, given her beliefs and desires, not to be in the program. The kind of research that she is expected to do, for example, does not allow her to fully exercise her talents, she does not possess some of the talents that the program requires, and the people who seem most happy in the program are very different from her in their general preferences and character. All these factors she notices and registers, but they are also something that she ignores when she deliberates about the rightness of her choice of vocation [. . .] One day, on an impulse, propelled exclusively by her feelings, she quits the program, calling herself lazy and irrational but also experiencing a (to her) inexplicable sense of relief. Years later, happily working elsewhere, she suddenly sees the reasons for her bad feelings of old, cites them as the reasons for her quitting, and regards as irrationality not her quitting, but rather the fact that she held onto her conviction that the program was right for her as long as she did.[47]

What Emily has experienced, then, is a moment when her best judgement about how to behave has become so systematically mistaken that akratic action against that judgement is more rational than action in accord with it. In other words, she is so blind to herself, so lacking in awareness about her genuine interests and capacities, that despite her careful deliberations in deciding to do a PhD in chemistry, she acts incoherently. In this state, her unhappiness and frustration represent instinctive guides to her real interests – for instance, they stem from the fact that her work does not permit her to fully exercise her talents – rather than impulses that she must overcome to act rationally.

In *Can You Forgive Her?*, Alice Vavasor's extensive reflections on whom to marry exemplify the kind of irrationality that Arpaly describes. As Trollope's representation indicates, ethically confused deliberations can be quite sophisticated; indeed, the implication is that their extent and depth are part of the problem. Alice's deliberation has led her to vacillate – she has been engaged to George Vavasor, is engaged to John Grey at the novel's beginning, returns to George, and then ends the novel by marrying John. The narrator criticises Alice's deliberations thus:

> That Alice Vavasor had thought too much about it, I feel quite sure [. . .] She had gone on thinking of the matter till her mind had become filled with some undefined idea of the importance to her of her own life [. . .] If [a woman] shall have recognised the necessity of truth and honesty for the purposes of her life, I do not know that she need ask herself many questions as to what she will do with it. Alice Vavasor was ever asking herself that question, and had by degrees filled herself with a vague idea that there was a something to be done; a something over and beyond, or perhaps altogether beside that marrying and having two children; – if she only knew what it was. She had filled herself, or had been filled by her cousins, with an undefined ambition that made her restless without giving her any real food for her mind. (CY, pp. 140–1)

The point here is that Alice's extensive reflections on what to do with her life misled her; she has created a 'vague idea' that a life spent in married domesticity is inadequate. This undefined ambition is irrational; not only does it not offer 'food for her mind', which would presumably take the shape of definite projects to pursue, but it may result from the manipulations of her cousins George and Kate Vavasor. Trollope's alternative is revealing as well, since he does not suggest that Alice ought to have deliberated differently, but instead that she should not have deliberated at all. Once they have recognised the importance of 'truth and honesty', agents need not think very much about what to do with their lives more generally.

Now, as Kate Flint has noted, Trollope's portrayal of Alice undoubtedly reflects Victorian sexual politics.[48] Certainly, Trollope reveals a version of separate-spheres ideology in the suggestion that Alice's confusion arises from her belief that she should do something with her life besides 'marrying and having two children'.[49] The antifeminist impulses inherent in the view become more obvious in the narrator's explanation that Alice has become confused after listening to a 'flock of learned ladies'.[50] As such, it is difficult not to see ideological content in Trollope's suggestion that Alice should not reflectively deliberate, but instead just feel and act. Nevertheless, the destabilisation of rational judgement is interesting. For instance, the narrator returns to the relationship between rationality and coherence in a series of counterfactuals:

> When she told herself that she would have no scope for action in that life in Cambridgeshire which Mr. Grey was preparing for her, she did not herself know what she meant by action. Had any one accused her of being afraid to separate herself from London society, she would have declared that she went very little into society and disliked that little. Had it been whispered to her that she loved the neighbourhood of the shops, she would have scorned the whisperer. Had it been suggested that the continued rattle of the big city was necessary to her happiness, she would have declared that she and her father had picked out for their residence the quietest street in London because she could not bear noise; – and yet she told herself that she feared to be taken into the desolate calmness of Cambridgeshire. (CY, p. 141)

The passage points out a tension between Alice's real reasons and the conclusions to which she has come. Alice does not like London society, London shops or London noise, and each of these facts about her desires represents a reason to marry John Grey. But her desires are opaque to her in this matter; without being self-deceived, she has concluded that the 'desolate calmness' of John's estate in Cambridgeshire represents a reason not to marry him. This sort of disjunct between desires and agents' conclusions about them is what rational incoherence involves, and it is significant that the problem is that Alice had thought too much about them. In thinking about herself, she has distanced herself from the sort of immediate reaction that feelings involve.[51] As the narrator indicates, if one asks her directly whether she likes London, she says no – but she loses the clear connection to her desires when she moves to the larger question of whom she wants to marry.

Correspondingly, John persuades Alice to marry him through a critique of her reasoning:

> I think you have been foolish, misguided, – led away by a vain ambition, and that in the difficulty to which these thing brought you, you endeavoured to constrain yourself to do an act, which, when it came near to you, – when the doing of it had to be more closely considered, you found to be contrary to your nature. (CY, p. 769)

Alice's response is revealing: 'Now, as he spoke thus, she turned her eyes upon him, and looked at him, wondering that he should have had power to read her heart so accurately' (CY, p. 769). This diagnosis is consistent with what John thinks throughout the novel; elsewhere he thinks of Alice as 'one wounded, and wanting a cure' and as brought to 'a sad pass' by 'her ill judgement' (CY, pp. 138, 395). He thus portrays Alice's conscious beliefs as a medical condition; a 'vain ambition' has so misdirected her assessment of what she should do that it is comparable to a kind of insanity. Moreover, John points briefly but suggestively to a theory of rationality in discerning a part of Alice that resists this condition: he appeals to her 'nature', suggesting that it was ultimately in some sense smarter than she was. When, to paraphrase his point, push came to shove and it was time to marry George Vavasor, Alice's unreflective nature found the action 'contrary', and rose against her judgement. Alice confirms this psychological diagnosis in her reaction, and the plot does as well; tellingly, even after saying she would marry George, Alice involuntarily resists his embrace (CY, p. 380).

The appeal to Alice's 'nature' as an entity that opposes her judgement has two important implications. First, it helps explain the tension between Alice's actions and her advice to Lady Glencora. As Juliet McMaster has observed, Alice 'can be astonishingly sententious in her judgements on Glencora's behaviour, and in the very matters in which she is herself most at fault'; she is insistent that Glencora maintain her marriage vow, for instance, when she has broken her own promises a number of times.[52] This sort of hypocrisy is, of course, common; as McMaster puts it, 'Most of us have at some time irritably responded to cavillers: "Don't do what I do, do what I say!"'[53] Ordinarily, such statements function to point out duplicity, noting that a moral agent is not living up to her ideals. But what Trollope suggests, through John Grey's diagnosis, is that they can also be indicative of ethical confusion. If in commonplace hypocrisy the problem is that agents need to bring what they do in line with what they say, in ethical confusion the problem is that agents need to bring what they say in line with what they do.

Ted Hinchman calls this 'upstream reasoning'.[54] In moments of 'rational akrasia', where an agent acts rationally in acting against her best judgement, he argues that such agents should manifest what he calls 'reasonable self-mistrust'.[55] Maintaining a healthy scepticism about the limited capacity of one's rational abilities, such agents take their inability to perform the action that they have judged they should do to be indicative of a reason that they have overlooked. As opposed to reasoning 'downstream', where an agent forms a judgement and then acts, such agents thus reason 'upstream': having found that they cannot act, they reform their judgement.

Second, the fact that Alice experiences the reason-responsiveness of her 'nature' through her feelings suggests that agents' non-deliberative feelings can be better guides to their actual reasons than their deliberations are. In this light, it is significant that Alice's ethical confusion arose in part from a dismissal of her emotions: 'it was not her love for [George] that prompted her to run so terrible a risk. Had it been so, I think that it would be easier to forgive her. She was beginning to think that love [. . .] did not matter' (CY, p. 342). The positive reason for marrying George, the narrator explains, is surprisingly haphazard:

> She had not so much asked herself why she should do this thing, as why she should not do it [. . .] 'If I can do him good why should I not marry him?' In that feeling had been the chief argument which had induced [Alice] to return such an answer as she had sent to [George]. (CY, pp. 373, 374)

This dismissal of the importance of love is necessary, because Alice never denies that she loves John: 'With all her doubts Alice never doubted her love for John Grey' (CY, p. 140). In concluding that it does 'not matter' whether she loves George, Alice dismisses the reasons to which her love for John attends. Rather than trusting that her affection attends to genuinely valuable properties that she cannot consciously articulate – and not least, the fact that loving someone is by itself a good reason for marrying him – she distrusts her own emotions.

In the suggestion that emotional reactions can be rational, and that Alice acts irrationally in dismissing them, Trollope speaks to an important trend in moral philosophy. As Karen Jones has described it, such feelings can significantly be 'reason-trackers'. She explains: 'When an agent's emotional responses are shaped, fine-tuned, and sometimes even radically transformed through the process of character formation', they can become 'reliable at latching on to the reasons that obtain' for her.[56] The point here is that explanations of rationality need to account for those moments when agents act rationally without recognising that they are doing so; when well-developed emotions respond to a fact and subsequently move agents to act in the same way they would have had they recognised the fact and deliberated about it, the insistence that such deliberation is necessary for rational action seems implausible.[57] The Duke of St Bungay seems to be summarising this view when he remarks, 'I would a deal sooner trust to instinct than to calculation' (CY, p. 619).

The Rationality of the Gentleman

In concluding that Trollope criticises the view that moral deliberation should involve a process of reflective judgement and that he advocates an instinctive version of moral agency, the arguments here align with the critical consensus about Trollope's moral philosophy.[58] James Kincaid points out that 'the most common standard for moral behaviour in Trollope is the code centred on the word "gentleman"'.[59] While, as we saw, there is critical disagreement about just how substantive this code is, critics agree that it is not identifiable with a particular principle for action; one cannot be a gentleman by following a rule. A degree of situational sensitivity, which one can model but not articulate, is required. In so doing, Trollope differs substantively from the neo-Kantian tradition, and aligns himself with the Aristotelian or virtue ethics theory. The all-important 'style' of a gentleman, which includes his instinctive sense of which situational nuances are relevant and how to behave accordingly, represents a Victorian version of the deliberative sense that Aristotle called 'practical wisdom', and a clear alternative to the Kantian picture of deliberation through the categorical imperative.[60]

What the arguments here have contributed to this interpretation is a sense of Trollope's coherence. Rather than demonstrating his rejection of principle-based judgement by showing how it cannot properly evaluate the complexities of specific situations, this chapter has sought to show how Trollope questions the psychology of judgement itself. Through his diverse representations of irrationality, Trollope contends that the deliberative judgement of practical reasoning is easily misled into self-deception, that it can fail to motivate even when it is not biased by desire, and finally that even unbiased judgement can still be profoundly mistaken. Thus, Trollope offers a moral psychology that complements his view of moral deliberation: the gentleman represents an ideal for moral agency not only because he will be appropriately sensitive to situational particularities, but also because – in minimising the ethical role of judgement – he will avoid irrationality. In making this suggestion, Trollope alters the moral psychology in the Kantian strain of Victorian morality in a significant way.

By way of conclusion, however, a slight qualification of my argument indicates a path for future analysis. On the basis of the arguments here, one might reasonably conclude that for Trollope, reflective moral deliberation – susceptible as it is to self-deception, motivational gaps and sheer error – is always a mistake, and that moral agents ought to aspire as much as possible to purely instinctive lives. But this would not be quite right; there are, importantly, scenes of sincere and admirable deliberation in Trollope, where agents make difficult decisions and act on them. Perhaps the most famous scene in this regard is Plantagenet Palliser's decision in *Can You Forgive Her?* to reject an opportunity to become the Chancellor of the Exchequer in order to try to save his marriage. Having learned that his wife is in love with Burgo Fitzgerald and not with him, he concludes that he must do everything in his power to try to make Glencora happy, even though this means he will miss the political opportunity he has wanted all his life. Trollope represents this decision without irony: the narrator and the novel both admire the Duke for his sacrifice. Thus, it seems that deliberation can occasionally be rational in Trollope.

In her recent work, Arpaly has emphasised the fact that deliberation is itself an action; in the same way that situational facts make ordinary actions reasonable – a falling piano makes it reasonable for me to move – so there might be situational facts that make careful reflective consideration of reasons a rational action to perform.[61] That is to say that virtuous people will indeed occasionally deliberate reflectively; it is just that they will only do so when the situation calls for it. Having thus recognised in this chapter the many ways in which judgement can fail in Trollope's fiction, a complementary analysis, along the lines laid out above, might seek to find the moments in which it succeeds.

* * *

Let me return to a point considered briefly at the beginning of this chapter. Each of the novels considered is structured around a marriage plot, which is often considered a clear example of a narrative form. But that has not been how I have regarded it. This refusal of formalism appears in a variety of ways in the chapter, perhaps most obviously in refusing the common critical move of appealing to philosophical ideas as explanatory tools for a text's formal structure. And in the few moments that did turn to formal considerations, the emphasis has been on the way they enable certain treatments of particular problems. One way to put this is to say that wherever possible I have turned the form of the marriage plot into content, from a repeatable and architectural pattern into a dense and specific paraphrase. This chapter has tried to demonstrate that this is neither reductive nor impossible: texts yield much of what makes them interesting to paraphrases, and the idea that a paraphrase is a 'heresy' requires viewing the features that cannot be paraphrased as both the only interesting elements of the literary text and the characteristics that distinguish it as literature. Neither assumption is tenable, particular with regard to an author such as Trollope.

Some of the hard issues in aesthetics that these claims introduce will reappear in Chapter 5, but for now there's a more obvious problem. To read for the content is of necessity anachronistic: it involves connecting the ideas in the text one reads to issues that particular readers care about. This chapter has more or less openly treated Trollope as if he could speak directly to Nomy Arpaly and Karen Jones. But of course, he can't. And a generation of scholarship in literary criticism and indeed the humanities more generally has regarded this sort of anachronism as a deep error, an impulse that must be refused in order to grasp the text in its place and time. Since many of the most recent and influential methods in literary study have justified themselves as versions of historicism, it is necessary to take those arguments head on. Such is the goal of the next chapter.

Notes

1. As Sharon Marcus puts the point, 'a typical Trollope novel charts the dilemmas of a heroine who must choose between two or more suitors and arrive at a decision final in both senses: timed to coincide with the novel's end and pronounced with the permanence of a marriage vow'. Marcus, *Between Women*, p. 233. John Dustin goes so far as to divide Trollope's *oeuvre* into three categories on the basis of their plots: 'category B' centres on the young man 'who makes an error in moral judgement' and spends the novel dealing with it, and thus includes many of the novels where the romantic triangle appears. John Dustin, 'Thematic Alternation in Trollope', *PMLA* 77.3 (1962), pp. 280–8 (p. 281).
2. Victoria Glendinning, *Trollope* (London: Hutchinson, 1992), p. 135.
3. Miller, *The Burdens of Perfection*, p. 77. This chapter is in some ways an extended reflection on a brief comment from Miller, who notes in passing that Trollope's *Prime Minister* is 'a novel much concerned with the weakness of will'.
4. For an excellent introduction to this issue, see Sarah Stroud's entry on 'Weakness of Will' in *The Stanford Encyclopedia of Philosophy*, ed. Edward N. Zalta, available at <http://plato.stanford.edu> (last accessed 18 December 2019).
5. 'Protagoras', in *The Collected Dialogues of Plato*, ed. Edith Hamilton et al., trans. Lane Cooper et al. (Princeton: Princeton University Press, 1963), 358d.

6. Amelie Rorty, 'Plato and Aristotle on Belief, Habit, and "Akrasia"', *American Philosophical Quarterly* 7.1 (1970), pp. 50–61 (p. 54).
7. Anthony Trollope, *The Eustace Diamonds* (New York: Penguin, 1969), pp. 311–12. Subsequent citations, abbreviated *ED*, are given in parentheses in the text.
8. This chapter will touch more substantively on this suggestion in a moment, but for a good discussion of the various versions of this argument, see 'Three Moral Trollopes', the final chapter of Jane Nardin, *Trollope and Victorian Moral Philosophy* (Athens: Ohio University Press, 1996).
9. Ruth apRoberts, *The Moral Trollope* (Athens: Ohio University Press, 1971), p. 52.
10. apRoberts, *The Moral Trollope*, p. 42.
11. In the autobiography, Trollope considers a man who uses the term in specifying the qualifications for a position, suggesting that 'he would be defied to define the term, – and would fail should he attempt to do so. But he would know what he meant.' *Autobiography of Anthony Trollope*, ed. Michael Sadleir et al. (New York: Oxford University Press, 2009), p. 40.
12. apRoberts, *The Moral Trollope*, p. 125.
13. James Kincaid, *The Novels of Anthony Trollope* (Oxford: Clarendon Press, 1977), p. 12.
14. Amanda Anderson, 'Trollope's Modernity', *ELH* 74 (2007), pp. 509–34 (p. 511); see also the updated version of this argument in Amanda Anderson, *Bleak Liberalism* (Chicago: University of Chicago Press, 2016).
15. Anderson, 'Trollope's Modernity', p. 515.
16. See, for instance, Jeremy Bentham's claim that 'Nature has placed mankind under the governance of two sovereign masters, pain and pleasure. It is for them alone [. . .] to determine what we shall do.' The notion that an action might maximise an agent's pleasure, yet somehow not be performed, goes unexamined. Jeremy Bentham, 'Principles of Morals and Legislation', in *Utilitarianism and Other Essays*, ed. Alan Ryan (New York: Penguin, 1987), p. 65. The notion that societies should develop individuals so that their pleasures stem from moral action is central to John Stuart Mill's thought, and in particular constitutes his notion of an 'internal sanction' for morality; see John Stuart Mill, 'Utilitarianism', in *Utilitarianism and Other Essays*, ed. Ryan.
17. Jerome Schneewind, 'Moral Problems and Moral Philosophy in the Victorian Period', *Victorian Studies* 9 (September 1965), pp. 29–46 (p. 33).
18. A number of examples of this tradition are brought together in the anthology of Victorian psychology compiled by Jenny Bourne Taylor and Sally Shuttleworth, *Embodied Selves: An Anthology of Psychological Texts* (New York: Oxford University Press, 1998), pp. 1830–90. See,

for instance, J. C. Prichard's explanation that moral insanity involves 'a disordered condition of the mind', which 'displays itself in a want of self-government, in continual excitement [. . .] in thoughtless and extravagant conduct' (p. 254).
19. The agenda of twentieth-century moral philosophy was set by G. E. Moore's *Principia Ethica*, which emphasised questions about the precise meaning of ethical terms over questions of the logic of agency. See Scott Soames's account of Moore in *Philosophical Analysis in the Twentieth Century* (Princeton: Princeton University Press, 2005).
20. See Stroud, 'Weakness of Will'.
21. Donald Davidson, 'How is Weakness of the Will Possible?', in *Essays on Actions and Events* (Oxford: Oxford University Press, 1980), pp. 21–42.
22. Davidson, 'How is Weakness of the Will Possible?', p. 41.
23. This term is regrettably loaded in ways that obfuscate the debate to the non-specialist. As used in contemporary moral philosophy, 'internalism' and 'externalism' denote two ends of a continuum of views of the motivational force of an agent's judgements – the internalist holding that a judgement is powerfully motivating, while the externalist sees such judgements as only weakly so. Both ends of the continuum are equally unattractive. For an important study that sets out a number of the terms of the debate, see Stephen Darwall, *Impartial Reason* (Ithaca: Cornell University Press, 1983).
24. See Alfred Mele, *Irrationality: An Essay on Akrasia, Self-Deception, and Self-Control* (New York: Oxford University Press, 1992), pp. 75–6.
25. As Mele notes, David Pears has committed the Davidsonian account to just this view by positing a 'sub-system' within the mind of the self-deceiver, one 'built around the wish for the irrational belief [. . .] although it is a separate centre of agency within the whole person, it is, from its own point of view, entirely rational' (*Irrationality*, p. 87).
26. Alfred Mele, *Self-Deception Unmasked* (Princeton: Princeton University Press, 2001), pp. 64–5.
27. Trollope, *Autobiography of Anthony Trollope*, p. 361.
28. Anthony Trollope, *The Duke's Children* (New York: Oxford University Press, 1999), p. 38. Subsequent citations, abbreviated *TDC*, are given in parentheses in the text.
29. Mele, *Self-Deception Unmasked*, p. 42.
30. Anthony Trollope, *The Life of Cicero* (New York: Kessinger, 2004), p. 194.
31. Henry Sidgwick, 'Unreasonable Action', in *Practical Ethics: A Collection of Addresses and Essays* (London: Swan Sonnenschein, 1898), pp. 235–60. In particular, Sidgwick writes of the philosophical tradition, 'I find that such writers are apt to give an account of voluntary action which – without expressly denying the existence of what I call subjective irrationality – appears to leave no room for it' (p. 246).

32. Sidgwick, 'Unreasonable Action', p. 255.
33. Sidgwick, 'Unreasonable Action', p. 258.
34. Sidgwick, 'Unreasonable Action', p. 259.
35. Anthony Trollope, *Phineas Finn: The Irish Member* (New York: Oxford University Press, 1999), p. 263. Subsequent citations, abbreviated *PF*, are given in parentheses in the text.
36. Richard Moran, *Authority and Estrangement: An Essay on Self-Knowledge* (Princeton: Princeton University Press, 2001). Moran observes that one of Jean-Paul Sartre's 'themes is the thought that the person cannot simply *accept* such a theoretical conclusion [about their likely weakness of will], however empirically well-grounded, without that opening him to the charge of indulging in *acquiescence* in his weakness under cover of being hardheaded and without any illusions about himself' (p. 81). Phineas does something very similar: by implying that his weak will is an inevitable result of his dual lives, he acquiesces to the weakness.
37. Anthony Trollope, *Phineas Redux* (New York: Oxford University Press, 2002), p. 10.
38. Trollope, *Phineas Redux*, p. 79.
39. Mele, *Irrationality*, p. 58.
40. Mele, *Irrationality*, p. 59.
41. Mele, *Irrationality*, p. 11.
42. Anthony Trollope, *Can You Forgive Her?* (New York: Penguin, 1972), p. 406. Subsequent citations, abbreviated *CY*, are given in parentheses in the text.
43. Anthony Trollope, *Framley Parsonage* (New York: Oxford University Press, 2002), p. 531.
44. Trollope, *Framley Parsonage*, p. 150.
45. Nomy Arpaly, 'On Acting Rationally Against One's Best Judgement', *Ethics* 110.3 (2000), pp. 488–513 (p. 512).
46. Arpaly, 'On Acting Rationally', p. 496.
47. Arpaly, 'On Acting Rationally', p. 504.
48. Kate Flint, 'Trollope and Sexual Politics', in Anthony Trollope, *Can You Forgive Her?* (Oxford: Oxford University Press, 1982).
49. The idea that Victorian social and especially economic life was separated into masculine and feminine 'spheres' is the main argument of the groundbreaking work by Leonore Davidoff and Catherine Hall, *Family Fortunes: Men and Women of the English Middle Class, 1780–1850* (Chicago: University of Chicago Press, 1987). It has drawn a wide variety of responses and evoked some changes in the argument from Davidoff and Hall; for a helpful discussion, see Nancy Henry, *Women, Literature and Finance in Victorian Britain: Cultures of Investment* (New York: Palgrave, 2018).
50. Flint, 'Trollope and Sexual Politics', p. 140.
51. Daniel Wright argues that it is the very obviousness of the reasons for marrying John Grey – in his phrasing, their tautological clarity and

certainty – that makes Alice suspicious of them. Daniel Wright, *Bad Logic: Reasoning about Desire in the Victorian Novel* (Baltimore: Johns Hopkins University Press, 2018), pp. 82–3.
52. Juliet McMaster, '"The Meaning of Words and the Nature of Things": Trollope's *Can You Forgive Her?*', *Studies in English Literature* 14.4 (1974), pp. 603–18 (p. 612).
53. McMaster, '"The Meaning of Words and the Nature of Things"', p. 613.
54. Ted Hinchman, 'Rational Requirements and "Rational" Akrasia', *Philosophical Studies* 166.3 (2013), pp. 529–52.
55. Hinchman, 'Rational Requirements', p. 530.
56. Karen Jones, 'Emotion, Weakness of Will, and the Normative Conception of Agency', *Royal Institute of Philosophy Supplement* 52 (2003), pp. 181–200 (p. 196).
57. The rich philosophical conversation responding to Arpaly's claims has centred around this issue. See, for instance, Niko Kolodny, 'Why be Rational?', *Mind* 114 (July 2005), pp. 509–63, and Nomy Arpaly and Tim Schroeder, 'Deliberation and Acting for Reasons', *Philosophical Review* 121.2 (2012), pp. 209–39. I shall return to these questions in a moment.
58. Certainly, apRoberts emphasises such a sensitivity in her notion of Trollope's 'casuistry', but Shirley Robin Letwin captures a very similar idea: 'The manners of a gentleman are not a set of choreographed movements and they cannot be found in a code or a manual.' Shirley Robin Letwin, *The Gentleman in Trollope: Individuality and Moral Conduct* (Pleasantville, NY: Akadine, 1982), p. 115.
59. Kincaid, *The Novels of Anthony Trollope*, p. 12.
60. See Rosalind Hursthouse, *On Virtue Ethics* (Oxford: Oxford University Press, 1999), pp. 56–62.
61. See Arpaly and Schroeder, 'Deliberation and Acting for Reasons'. They suggest that deliberation is made reasonable by facts to which an agent is sensitive without deliberating; in such moments, deliberation assists an agent's instinctive reason-responsiveness, rather than overwhelming it.

Chapter 3

Justifying Anachronism

By way of beginning, it is worth considering whether content-based interpretations should concern themselves with historical context at all. If one is interested in the ideas in a text, why does it matter where they come from, or even whether they are really there? With apologies to J. Hoberman and Noël Carroll, we might call this a history of ideas version of the *Plan 9 from Outer Space* problem. Carroll writes:

> *Plan 9 from Outer Space* is a cheap, slapdash attempt to make a feature film for very little, and in cutting corners to save money it violates – in outlandish ways – many of the decorums of Hollywood filmmaking that later avant-gardists also seek to affront. So insofar as the work of contemporary avant-gardists is aesthetically valued for its transgressiveness, why not appreciate *Plan 9 from Outer Space* under an analogous interpretation? Call it 'unintentional modernism', but it is modernism none the less and appreciable as such.[1]

How should one regard it when a text is accidentally genius, so to speak? Presentist critics are, as they say frequently, uninterested in history for its own sake. So if there is a surprising connection between a text from the past and something we care about, why does it matter how authors came to write the books they did? If some readers find the content of a text interesting and insightful insofar as it speaks to some problem they are thinking about, then it seems at least prima facie questionable to insist on the work's historical context, even if (let us suppose) the connection between the issue the reader is thinking about and the work of art is insubstantial and arbitrary, disappearing once the fuller context is taken into account.

This is a deep problem that does not admit of an easy solution, and variations on the problem have occurred in a variety of fields. Correspondingly my argument here proceeds accretively, connecting up different versions of the *Plan 9* problem to elaborate a clearer way of thinking about the competing intuitions at work in it. Ultimately, I contend that the lack of a generally accepted solution is not an accident, and that the root of the problem lies in opposed but necessary elements of the reading experience – the impulse to understand what someone is saying on the one hand and the impulse to consider it as possible truth on the other.

Contemporary Presentisms

The prima facie intuition that validates the 'unintentional modernism' of *Plan 9* is one of the motivations behind the rise of 'presentism' in literary studies. Following Margreta De Grazia's injunction to 'Always Anachronise!' and Marjorie Garber's diagnosis of the threat of 'historical correctness', a group of primarily Shakespeare scholars has organised an overtly anti-historicist method.[2] Presentist critics such as Hugh Grady, Terence Hawkes, Evelyn Gajowski and Linda Charnes insist on connecting the literary text in question to current issues, and emphasising the way 'the art-work continues to produce meanings in historical eras different from that in which it was created'.[3] Such critics have developed a number of different terms for such connections: Charnes refers to 'wormholes', those moments in a text where 'an idea' appears 'in advance of its historical "context"', while Hawkes speaks of 'eruptions', whose appearance requires the application of later terminology.[4] These terms accord reasonably well with recognisably presentist approaches in other subfields of literary criticism; for instance, Wai Chee Dimock's notion of 'resonance', which involves a 'kind of historicism' that is 'diachronic' and that 'allows texts to be seen as objects' that travel 'across space and especially across time', relies on much the same metaphor as Charnes for approximately the same reasons.[5] The arguments for such approaches rely heavily on our inevitable situation in a given time and the impossibility of a critical stance outside of it. Hawkes and Grady summarise the point: 'The truth is that none of us can step beyond time. The present can't be drained out of our experience. As a result, the critic's own "situatedness" does not – cannot – *contaminate* the past.'[6] It is a mistake to grade interpretations on the basis of their success at removing present concerns; such removal is impossible, and we should not think of it as a goal.

Such critics use this argument to counter certain assumptions about the possibility of valid interpretation. Hawkes and Grady go on to say: 'Facts, after all, do not speak for themselves. Nor do texts. This doesn't mean that facts or texts don't exist. It does mean that all of them are capable of genuinely contradictory meanings, none of which has any independent, "given", undeniable, or self-evident status'.[7] Indeed, the notion of fidelity to the text stops seeming like a reasonable foundation for literary criticism, and starts to seem like a politically and ethically naive ontology. As Gajowski puts the point, presentist approaches 'are overt acts of shouldering responsibility for constructing meanings in Shakespeare's texts'.[8] She explains: 'It is [. . .] a matter of ethical responsibility, of owning up to meanings that we construct in Shakespeare's texts [. . .] Shakespeare scholars would likely agree, I think, that none of us can know with any degree of certitude what was in Shakespeare's mind.'[9] The logic of this argument is somewhat startling. From a pre-reflective standpoint, after all, the notion that there could be 'ethical responsibility' in interpretation sounds odd: the point of interpretation is to understand something, and success or failure in that understanding is the only rubric by which one could hold an interpreter 'responsible'. The key phrase that explains Gajowski's point is 'owning up to meanings that we construct'. For her, all Shakespeare critics engage in the same fundamental practice of imposing their own 'constructed' meanings on his works, rather than discovering facts about them. What such critics ought to do is admit or 'own up' to the fact that this imposition is what they are really doing, since 'none of us can know' Shakespeare's mind.[10]

This abandonment of validity points to a controversial aspect of presentist approaches. For instance, one of the critics Gajowski cites approvingly is Jonathan Dollimore, whose 'cultural materialism' represents an important antecedent to contemporary presentism.[11] One key element of Dollimore's groundbreaking text *Radical Tragedy* is not only his own anti-essentialist views about the self, but the impulse to find such views in early modern thinkers. Dollimore sees, for example, Francis Bacon as recognising the culturally constructed nature of the self, in part because of a line from his essay 'Of Custom and Education' that reads, 'Nature, nor the engagement of words, are not so forcible as custom.'[12] But as Tom McAlindon and Robin Headlam Wells have argued, this contention misses a great deal of the relevant context: 'In the companion piece Bacon characteristically put the other side of the argument, asserting the inviolability of that essential self which exists at a deeper level and is not affected by the vagaries of social behaviour: "nature is often hidden, sometimes overcome, seldom extinguished".'[13] The point here is not that Dollimore misreads the line, exactly, but rather that he fails to place the line in proper context with the rest of a writer's work – a fact caused, presumably, by his philosophical interests. Thus, the anachronistic framing is caused by and causative of a dismissal of key elements of the text. Instead of reflecting an honest 'shouldering' of the constructed nature of literary interpretation, then, presentists can be guilty of theoretical bias, insofar as their own philosophical views elide parts of the text supposedly under interpretation.

I take this worry to be similar to John Holbo's. In a scathing attack on this formulation of 'presentism', Holbo has accused critics such as Hawkes and Grady of committing themselves to error for its own sake. As he flatly states, '"presentism" means relatively more historicist injustice than historicism, or it means nothing'.[14] What is striking about this group of thinkers is the idea that presentism as such would need a defence; all responsible historians are prepared to concede the basic point that one always sees the past from one's present location, which is always limited and partial, and that they are in part driven by present concerns. But those facts in themselves do not license the dismissal of what historical facts it is possible to know – as Holbo puts it, 'from the fact that one always sees from some perspective [. . .] it hardly follows that we should set out to do the wrong thing'.[15]

Moreover, he continues, the presentists are not really so much concerned with the 'present' as they are with 'theory'. This iteration of 'presentism' is directed against David Kastan's *Shakespeare After Theory*, and for Holbo the interest in theory is the key to their real argument: 'Grady and Hawkes are hinting at an identification between "theory" and "what is present." Then the hint is dropped that, therefore, we ought to study Shakespeare with a special eye for relating him to "theory," since what we want is present relevance.'[16] Holbo doesn't think that they are actually doing theory – though 'they are not doing anything else', either – but it seems to me that the presentists are defending something like the right to do theory under the name of interpretation.[17] If I am correct, that points to an expanded version of the worry about Dollimore, and about interpretations that emphasise content more generally – namely, that they stop being interpretations, and start becoming theoretical or philosophical arguments, using the literary text as a sort of jumping-off point or mediator but not as an object worth understanding.

It was concerns such as this that motivated Kastan's critique in the first place, and led to his emphasis on the historical Shakespeare: 'only by attending to the actual conditions of playwriting in England', he writes, can critics save the historical Shakespeare from 'the mystifying moves of poststructural theory'.[18] There is a specificity to Shakespeare that can disappear when the text is treated in a vacuum, and when – to use Grady's interpretation as an example – Shakespeare, Nietzsche and Althusser are simply treated as contemporaries, able to talk to each other seamlessly across time. So, this debate in Shakespeare scholarship is interesting for the way it introduces a large worry. To dismiss the role of history threatens to dismiss the text too; having been started down an interesting theoretical road by some aspect of a text, the presentist critic is happy to continue without feeling any constraint on further theorising from the rest of the text. In the urge to find sophisticated theorising, such unrestrained anachronism ignores what the text actually has to offer.

History and Form

But of course, the more common kinds of anachronistic criticism are sensitive to this worry, balancing a presentist concern for contemporary problems with a sense of the historical forces that led to a text's composition. Perhaps the most influential presentist approach is the symptomatic criticism developed by Marxist and psychoanalytic critics, especially via Fredric Jameson's influential combination of the two approaches. For Jameson, the idea of a necessary tension between anachronism and historicism misses the way the two can and should be reconciled. As he famously explained in *The Political Unconscious*, literary form represents the imaginative solution of a real political problem, and understanding the text involves understanding it in the context of that problem. In that sense, the text's form is a 'symptom', the product of an underlying condition the text cannot acknowledge. As such, any criticism that understands the symptomatic relationship must necessarily be anachronistic, drawing on an understanding of the underlying problem not available to the author herself. In short, the problem is repressed by its author, and interpretation involves 'restoring to the surface of the text the repressed and buried reality' of class struggle.[19]

Jameson's invocation of form here exemplifies an essential element of contemporary literary criticism: the close interweaving of historicism and formalism. The two are often presented as opposed methods; Stephen Cohen calls 'form and history' the 'two mighty opposites' of literary criticism.[20] But one need only think of the work of the most influential critics of the last generation to realise how inadequate that characterisation is. To writers such as Jameson, Catherine Gallagher and Michael McKeon, historicism and formalism are not merely not opposed: they require each other for either to be properly done.²¹ As Joe North puts it in a laconic footnote, the idea that the field oscillates between form and history 'is a popular view, but it does not seem right'.²² Indeed, to the reader interested in content and struck by the pervasiveness of form, what is notable in the union between the two is the way contemporary formalisms derive much of their strength from their presentation as historically justified. As such, developing an alternative to formalism requires redescribing the intuitions that motivate concern for the historical origins of literary texts, showing that it is possible to account for the views that motivate such reading in non-formalist ways.

A historical approach to content would help address a tension often apparent in historicist formalism – the tendency to suggest that some authors are inchoately aware of the underlying process driving formal change. In 'Authentic Ressentiment', his chapter on George Gissing in *The Political Unconscious*, Jameson attributes to Gissing a sense of problems he cannot quite understand: 'What is interesting about Gissing is that he is locked into this program at the same time that he sees through it and arraigns it violently'.²³ This awareness, which cannot appear overtly in Gissing's thought, appears in the form of his novel *The Nether World* in the idea of philanthropy for the poor as an orienting vocation. Jameson sees an attempt to 'resolve the dilemmas of totality' in the philanthropic mission, because it takes 'as its object not a single individual but a whole class', which correspondingly moves 'the ethical' act to the point 'beyond which it must necessarily become political'.²⁴ This technique is similar to a strategy common in deconstructive criticism, which often praised texts on the basis of a semi-awareness of the inevitable failure of referential language. To pick another famous example, D. A. Miller's reading of *Middlemarch* starts from a sense of the novel's combination of 'deconstructive insights' with 'a confident reenactment of traditional form'.²⁵ In Dorothea's belief that marriage with Casaubon would create a world where 'Everyday-things with us would mean the greatest things', Miller sees her desiring 'a world in which daily experience would have a cognitive transparency'.²⁶ Yet the text demonstrates its recognition of the impossibility of such transparency, since the climactic moments of sympathy that end the novel are each moments of silence.

This strategy, which depends on the positing of an underlying process that requires anachronistic description, but which subsequently attributes awareness of the process to the text on the basis of its form, has been deployed in a number of arguments since. As two of the most influential writers in the last generation of literary criticism, Jameson and Miller helped inspire a generation to attribute significant philosophical insight to texts on the basis of formal innovation, and to see that insight as the half-aware, partial grasp of a theoretical problem that the author lacked the perspective or terminology to grasp.[27] And it reflects one of the most important impulses motivating the desire to read for the content: the desire to recognise in literary authors insight and awareness. But it runs the risk of something like aggrandised textuality. Authors are generally posited as 'continuous with unreflective forms of power', but on the other hand 'strange exceptions occur, wherein certain historical subjects are exempted from networks of power'.[28] Such critics want, roughly speaking, to have it both ways; the figures they consider are at once subject to constitutive and determinative historical forces, while being simultaneously aware of and sufficiently detached from such forces to manipulate them. Thus the account of form is contradictory, on the one hand the register of history, and on the other an at least partial awareness that the better-informed critic, writing with the help of theoretical advances, can subsequently grasp.

Precisely because of the vexed nature of the agency in question, Jameson has to describe the events that demonstrate anachronistic insight in the passive voice: 'In [Gissing's] later work the inevitability of frustration has been secretly bracketed'.[29] It is a similar position, moreover, that leads him to diagnose Gissing's as an 'Unhappy Consciousness'. Accordingly, the details in the novel do not reflect Gissing's own contingent decisions, but instead the necessary consequences of the problem he was engaging; realist novelists are 'forced' and 'necessarily threatened', while the conclusion of Gissing's novel *Demos* is 'inescapable'.[30] As Rita Felski has written of this approach, for the Jamesonian critic 'nothing is random or accidental; every textual detail harbours a hidden purpose and pulsates with fateful meaning'.[31] And this appeal to necessity jars harshly with the sort of semi-awareness attributed to writers such as Gissing, who are determined only until they aren't.

Finally and perhaps most significantly, historicist formalism often requires precisely dismissing what insights texts do have to offer when they don't fit the model of an inchoate awareness realised in the form. The clearest version of this objection comes appropriately enough from a psychoanalytic critic. Shoshana Felman's emphasis on the distinction between implication and application in theoretical literary criticism captures an important objection to anachronism via the symptomatic model. Let us turn to that objection now.

Implication/Application

In her famous 1977 essay 'Turning the Screw of Interpretation', Shoshana Felman argued that Henry James's *The Turn of the Screw* anticipated and confounded the Freudian interpretations famously applied to it. Edmund Wilson's 1934 essay 'The Ambiguity of Henry James' inspired a legacy of criticism and a fierce debate by arguing through a 'Freudian reading' that the ghosts in James's story did not in fact exist, and were instead the psychic product of the governess's repression of her sexual drives.[32] For Felman, what is most revealing about this tradition of criticism is how it attempts to eliminate the ambiguity of the story. As she puts it,

> the Freudian reading is no doubt 'true', but no truer than the opposed positions which contradict it. And it is 'false', indeed, to the extent that it *excludes* them. These opposed positions which assert the text's contradiction in the very act of denying it, are thus 'true' to the extent that they are 'false'.[33]

It is the combination of the two opposing interpretations that best captures the real dynamic of the story, which invites scepticism about the truth of the governess's experience without ever confirming the sceptical view decisively.

Felman goes on to suggest that the story thus indicts the attitude towards literature characteristic of psychoanalytic criticism:

> This, then, is what psychoanalytical interpretation might be doing, and indeed is doing whenever it gives in to the temptation of *diagnosing* literature, of indicating and of situating *madness* in a literary text. For in shutting madness up in literature, in attempting not just to explain the literary symptom but to explain away the very symptom of literature itself, psychoanalysis, like the governess, only diagnoses literature so as to justify itself, to insure its own control of meaning, to deny or to negate the lurking possibility of its own madness.[34]

The governess believes she is sane by diagnosing madness in the children she is supervising. Unintentionally and ironically, Wilson duplicates this gesture, preserving the sane and sensible nature of psychoanalysis by diagnosing madness in the governess. But by calling the governess's sanity into question, the story also questions the suspicious attitude she demonstrates. And this is the same suspicious attitude of psychoanalysis: to see criticism as a diagnostic gesture of locating the symptoms of a psychic disorder in a story and establishing a firm diagnosis is to deny the possibility of one's own failures.

In particular, it is to dismiss the literary as such, which consists in the kind of ambiguity that resists the kind of definitive interpretation the governess seeks to give. 'The position *par excellence* of *meaning* in the *literary utterance*', Felman explains, is a 'rhetorical position, implying a relation of mutual subversion and of radical, dynamic contradiction between utterance and statement'.[35] The psychoanalytic critic tries to situate himself outside literature, looking in at it and offering a clear explanation of its structure. But this is impossible, as there isn't an outside to literature, to language: 'Wilson's error is to try to *situate* madness and thereby situate *himself outside it* – as though it were possible, *in* language, to *separate* oneself from language'.[36] What criticism must do instead is recognise its limitations and resign itself to the impossibility of definitive explanations.

But what is striking here is the way the Jamesian aesthetic and its refusal to convey a clear meaning becomes definitive of the literary as such. This gesture, which Felman initially treats as a suggestion but which by the end of the essay has become a general truth, is highly significant; in particular, it cuts off all the aesthetic effects that literary texts create through the use of clarity and referential language as not actually 'literary'. As Rita Felski points out, 'any form of reading for meaning' for Felman 'wreaks deadly violence on the literary text'.[37] Yet when engaging literary effects that depend on clarity, to look past such content and insist on the text's 'radical, dynamic contradictions' is precisely to duplicate the suspicious gesture that Felman means to criticise. In cases where a text has a clear meaning it seeks to convey, to insist on the failure of that conveyance is once again to posit the critic as engaging in diagnosis, seeing the fundamental truths underneath the text's symptoms.

There's a parallel objection to Jameson's version of political criticism. Jonathan Arac, in a response to Jameson's reading of Joseph Conrad, pointed out how much overt political thinking in the text Jameson had to dismiss in the process of attributing political significance to the narrative's form. As he puts it, Jameson 'must hide the political in order to find it elsewhere'.[38] Conrad is, after all, certainly interested in questions in political theory, and it is only by dismissing the relevance of the overt ideas that his novels consider that Jameson can attribute so much importance to the text's political 'unconscious'. Correspondingly, the diagnostic certainty of the critic, very much what Felman means to call into question, is an essential part of the symptomatic gesture.

That is to say that this worry is really an updated version of Felman's own objection to Wilson. Indeed, a terminology she develops can help capture it. In 'To Open the Question', her introduction to the issue of *Yale French Studies* that contains her discussion of James, Felman reiterates that the 'relationship between literature and psychoanalysis' usually ends up being one of 'subordination, a relation in which literature is submitted to the authority, to the prestige of psychoanalysis. While literature is considered as a body of *language* – to be *interpreted* – psychoanalysis is considered as a body of *knowledge*, whose competence is called upon to interpret.'[39] She calls this problem one of 'application': the naive psychoanalytic critic simply applies his theoretical frame to the text, and thus inevitably overlooks its complexity. As an alternative, Felman suggests that psychoanalytic critics practise 'implication', which she describes thus:

> The notion of application would be replaced by the radically different notion of implication: bringing analytical questions to bear upon literary questions, involving psychoanalysis in the scene of literary analysis, the interpreter's role would here be not to *apply* to the text an acquired science [. . .] but to act as a go-between, to generate implications between literature and psychoanalysis [. . .] each one finding itself enlightened, informed, but also affected, displaced by the other.[40]

Rather than positing one discourse as 'an acquired science', the goal here is rather to posit the discourses as equally valid approaches to a related set of problems. Each has its own standard for generating claims and establishing their validity, but since they pursue importantly related goals, the claims of one discourse might 'affect' or 'displace' those of the other. Thus, rather than granting the status of 'knowledge' only to psychoanalysis, Felman suggests that literary texts merit equal recognition. Rather than treating literature simply as a site where one might find the evidence of psychoanalytical truths, Felman suggests a criticism that sees literature as a kind of thinking, one that might usefully revise certain tenets of psychoanalytic thought.

Subsequent responses to Felman have not taken up this important distinction, but it's a useful way to think about anachronism.[41] Its inside/outside logic suggests that the worry about anachronism is a worry about theoretical material derived from a source external to the work. Felman's additional metaphors reinforce this way of conceiving interpretation: implicative criticism acts as a 'go-between', moving from within the literary work to the broader discourse of psychoanalysis. Correspondingly, the problem that leads to unjustified application is a refusal to recognise the artwork as capable of independent thought. Though Felman does not put it quite this way, what implicative reading seems to require is a recognition of and willingness to engage with the thinking a literary text offers, rather than dismissing it in order to fit it to the application of a psychoanalytic frame.

Yet one of the main worries that motivated the symptomatic approach remains. Even if the symptomatic attitude and its dismissal of the overt ideas in a text shares in the diagnostic surety that Felman criticises, it is nevertheless responsive to the text's location in history. What is needed, then, is a way of accounting for this fact, a way to take seriously the historicity of the content in a literary text, but which does not consist in a diagnostic attitude. Another debate, this time about anachronism in historiography, offers additional conceptual resources.

Contextualism in the History of Ideas

The publication in 1969 of Quentin Skinner's famous essay 'Meaning and Understanding in the History of Ideas' represented the cresting of a new wave in the historiography of political theory.[42] As J. G. A Pocock described the shift in 1971, 'during the last ten years scholars interested in the study of systems of political thought have had the experience of living through radical times, which may amount to a transformation in their discipline'.[43] The transformation Pocock had in mind involved the overt rejection of the methodology for the history of ideas first articulated by Arthur Lovejoy, who emphasised the analysis of the broad 'unit-ideas' that lay un-articulated underneath the intellectual debates of a given period, and subsequently the way they developed.[44] In the history of political thought, this approach in practice meant the isolation of a canon of texts of political theory, running from Plato to Marx, which critics would then compare and discuss.[45] Against this canonisation, Skinner, Pocock and their allies insisted on the fundamental historicity of an idea; as Skinner argued, 'the notion that any fixed "idea" has persisted is spurious' (MU, p. 35). Instead, historians must understand an idea in terms of its original illocutionary force (MU, p. 39), in Skinner's phrase, and restore it to the particular political language of its period, in Pocock's terms.[46] Skinner's 'Meaning and Understanding' summarises both the critique of the Lovejoy model that such 'contextualists' articulated and the methodology they offered in its place, and the debate surrounding Skinner's essay offers a rich theoretical archive for the defence of theoretical anachronism.

Skinner is, first, suspicious of interpretations based on an attempt to grasp a text's stance on some issue that the interpreter sees as timeless, which he calls the 'mythology of doctrines' (MU, p. 7). In his diagnosis, 'the essential belief that each of the classic writers may be expected to consider and explicate some determinate set of "fundamental concepts" of "perennial interest" [. . .] seems to be the basic source of the confusions engendered by this approach' (MU, p. 5). As he goes on to explain, the notion – for instance – that a historian might see Plato, Locke and Hegel as all addressing the nature of an entity called the 'state' is methodologically pernicious; it leads to a series of misleading anachronisms, as theorists are faulted for not properly addressing issues of later concern or praised for 'anticipating' them (MU, pp. 11–13). Both approaches, Skinner argues, raise an essential question: 'whether any of these writers ever intended, or even could have intended to do, what they are thus castigated [or praised] for' (MU, p. 16). Moreover, this interpretive impulse can lead to more damaging anachronisms, as the failure to properly situate a given text within its context can lead the philosophical critic to mistakenly assume the presence of a later view and thus overlook real complexity; thus he explains, 'the historian may conceptualise an argument in such a way that its alien elements are dissolved into an apparent but misleading familiarity' (MU, p. 27). As his example of the tempting but mistaken impulse to see John Locke's notion of the right to revolt as connected to his remarks on 'government by consent' demonstrates, our later ways of addressing an issue can blind us to a writer's actual view (MU, p. 28).

Additionally, such an approach tends to produce a 'mythology of coherence' in the figures it considers; when guided by an attention to 'perennial problems', as Skinner contends, 'it will become dangerously easy for the historian to conceive it as his task to supply or find in each of these [classic] texts the coherence which they may appear to lack' (MU, p. 16). Whatever issue an interpreter might be interested in will guide his interpretation in such a way as to turn whatever scattered remarks a historical figure makes about it into a key for addressing the *oeuvre*, so that a reconstructed and newly coherent thinker will appear to be discussing the problem in a way the actual texts never individually did. Skinner is characteristically scathing: 'The history thus written becomes a history not of ideas at all, but of abstractions: a history of thoughts which no one ever actually succeeded in thinking, at a level of coherence which no one ever actually attained' (MU, p. 18). Such an impulse has additional problems as an interpretive heuristic, since it inevitably dismisses what a writer actually says about his purpose, and, in its insistence on coherence, it leaves the possibility that writers simply contradict themselves unexplored (MU, pp. 19–20).

Against this approach, Skinner recommended a renewed interpretive focus on a writer's intentions. Drawing on J. L. Austin's theory of speech acts, he argued that linguistic behaviour involved understanding more than just what a speaker's words meant; one had to grasp what the speaker meant to do with them. Such an approach is essential to grasping, for instance, irony; in Skinner's example, the words in Daniel Defoe's tract on dissenting might literally recommend the beheading of nonconformists, but what he was doing with that meaning was recommending religious toleration (MU, p. 32). He explains the point further in an overt rejection of Wimsatt and Beardsley's analysis of the 'intentional fallacy', arguing that the comprehension of an utterance 'will be equivalent to an understanding of that agent's primary intentions in issuing that particular utterance'.[47] In order to grasp such intentions, a careful focus on a writer's context is essential – not because it is 'the determinant of what is said', but because it is 'an ultimate framework for helping to decide what conventionally recognizable meanings in a society of *that* kind, it might in principle have been possible for someone to have intended to communicate' (MU, p. 49).

Both a positive and a negative methodological principle follow from this emphasis. Positively, Skinner insists on capturing the 'mental world' of the writer: 'No agent can eventually be said to have meant or done something which he could never be brought to accept as a correct description of what he had meant or done' (MU, p. 29). Such descriptions can thus never be anachronistic: 'It follows that any plausible account of what the agent meant must necessarily fall under [. . .] the range of descriptions which the agent himself could at least in principle have applied' (MU, p. 29). This criterion, famous enough that Richard Rorty calls it 'Skinner's maxim', makes writers' own sense of their goals central. Negatively, Skinner insists on the repudiation of presentist impulses. In the essay's most famous passage, he writes:

> This reformulation and insistence on the claim that there are no perennial problems in philosophy [. . .] is not even a denial of the possibility that there may be apparently perennial *questions*, if these are sufficiently abstractly framed. All I wish to insist is that whenever it is claimed that the point of the historical study of such questions is that we may learn directly from the answers, it will be found that what *counts* as an answer will usually look, in a different culture or period, so different in itself that it can hardly be in the least useful even to go on thinking of the relevant question as being 'the same' in the required sense after all. *More crudely: we must learn to do our thinking for ourselves.* (MU, p. 52, emphasis mine)

There is an interesting concession here in the notion that 'perennial questions' are possible when 'sufficiently abstractly framed'; I shall return to this in a moment. Nevertheless, the opposition to presentism is clear; central to Skinner's historical methodology is the refusal to think that we might learn from historical texts how to solve our own philosophical problems. Because earlier generations, if they share our political problems at all, will have conceived of them in such different ways and as admitting of such different possible solutions, we contemporary theorists need to simply 'think for ourselves'.

One can direct Skinner's objections with almost no translation against presentist literary criticism. Certainly, the interpretation I offered in Chapter 2 is vulnerable to them; there is no question that I have considered Anthony Trollope's moral philosophy as worthy of attention in part because it anticipates more recent thinking in moral psychology. Moreover, in collecting his remarks about weakness of will from across his fiction, there can be no doubt that I have posited a mythological coherence. Even if I am right about some central themes in Trollope's thinking about ethics, my interpretation undeniably lends that thinking a systematic nature and scholarly provenance that the reading of any individual text would not support. Fortunately, Skinner's work produced an immediate, wide-ranging and provocative response, now sustained through a generation of historiographers, and it is possible to mine that response for a defence of anachronism.

First, a number of critics have pointed out Skinner's concession that some 'questions' might be perennial, even if their answers are not, and moreover argued that Skinner seems to overlook the obvious point that historical figures often overtly engage each other. As Mark Bevir contends, 'Political theorists often discuss classic works, and when they do so they thereby create chains in which their concerns link up with those of the authors of these works.'[48] So in some ways anachronism will appear not merely permissible but obviously so; we can meaningfully ask contemporary Marxists what they think about the nature of capital, and whether Marx might agree. More generally, whether a question in political theory is 'perennial' seems upon reflection to be an empirical question, one much different from whether there are 'eternal' questions. Robert Lamb puts the point thus: 'Scepticism about perennial issues is scepticism about the longevity of philosophical problems', and the notion that some problems 'simply cannot last a long time seems not only not self-evident [. . .] but also severely counterintuitive'.[49] More importantly, even in situations where thinkers from the past are not straightforwardly addressing our current issues, it is not obvious that the point of historical scholarship should be to understand them in their own terms. David Hull makes this point by drawing on a wonderful passage from Lewis Carroll:

> 'What do you consider the largest map that would be really useful?'
> 'About six inches to the mile.'
> 'Only six inches!' exclaimed Mein Herr. 'We very soon got to six yards to the mile. Then we tried a hundred yards to the mile. And then came the grandest idea of all! We actually made a map of the country, on the scale of a mile to the mile!'
> 'Have you used it much?' I enquired.
> 'It has never been spread out, yet', said Mein Herr: 'the farmers objected: they said it would cover the whole country, and shut out the sunlight! So we now use the country itself, as its own map, and I assure you it does nearly as well.'[50]

The point here, of course, is that it is not an objection to maps to say that they are abstractions and simplifications of the territory they represent. They are supposed to be all of those things, because that is how we use them. Similarly, it might not be a problem that an interpretation of a writer from the past translates that writer's concerns into abstract issues relevant for a present reader: in offering a contemporary guide, it serves its purpose. Denying this goal culminates in the abandonment of interpretation, under the theory that all texts are interpretations of themselves.

The editors of another response to Skinner make a similar point: 'To say that [presentist] histories are anachronistic is true but pointless: they are *supposed* to be anachronistic.'[51] They compare such historians to anthropologists, and suggest that anthropological work that merely describes the rituals of a given tribe in the tribe's own terms has not done its job – 'what we want to be told is whether that tribe has anything interesting to tell *us*'.[52] If someone were to refuse this task because 'such filtering and paraphrase' would 'distort and betray' the tribe's culture, then there is a sense in which he 'would no longer be an anthropologist, but a sort of cultist'.[53] The same holds true for an intellectual historian – to give up explaining a historical figure's insights in terms that contemporary readers can understand and appreciate as important is to cease to work 'for us'.

Richard Rorty, one of the editors, added to this argument a distinction between 'historical' and 'rational' reconstructions of a writer's view. Historical reconstructions will follow 'Skinner's maxim', and will constrain themselves to offering only descriptions that the writer in question could in principle endorse. Rational reconstructions, on the other hand, will offer as charitable an account of the writer as possible given our current best beliefs about the truth of the matter:

> By filtering out certain sentences as irrelevant to his concerns, and to the concerns the author himself would have had if he had known more about the way the world is, while giving a sympathetic rendering of the remainder, the historian of philosophy helps the dead philosopher put his act together for a new audience.[54]

This sort of interpretation is the 'mapping' of intellectual history. In the same way that cartographers might dismiss features of the landscape that users are not interested in and emphasise elements that they are interested in, so rational reconstructors will 'filter', dismissing certain elements of the text as not essential, emphasising others as compelling, and organising the whole into a package for a new group of readers. In so doing, such interpreters will overtly look for moments where a writer anticipates a later development; they will let their own more informed position show them how to restate the writer's views as plausibly as possible.

Importantly, Rorty resists the impulse to say that either 'rational reconstruction' or 'historical reconstruction' captures what a given text really 'means':

> It is natural to describe Columbus as having discovered America rather than Cathay, and not knowing that he had done so. It is almost equally natural to describe Aristotle as unwittingly describing the effects of gravity rather than of natural downward motion. It is slightly more strained, but just a further step along the same line, to describe Plato as having unconsciously believed that all words were names [. . .] It is fairly clear that in [the historical] sense of 'mean' Plato meant nothing like this. When we anachronistically say he 'really' held such doctrines we mean that, in an imagined argument with present-day philosophers about whether he should have had certain other views, he would have been driven back on a premise which he never formulated, dealing with a topic he never considered – a premise which may have to be suggested to him by a friendly rational reconstructor.[55]

While Rorty claims that critics ought to be careful about admitting which project they are engaged in – that is, whether the reconstruction is historical or rational – there is no reason to give either side a monopoly on the word 'meaning'. As he puts it later, 'grasping the meaning of an assertion is a matter of placing that assertion in a context', and 'whether we privilege the context which consists of what the assertor was thinking about around the time he or she made the assertion depends upon what we want'.[56] The rational reconstructor will be happy to concede that she is using terms the historical figure could not have, because the interpretive goal is different.

Rorty's examples are worthy of some attention, because they suggest how the appeal to the truth works as an interpretive matter – we say that Columbus discovered America without knowing it because we believe that the landmass Columbus approached was in fact America (and not India). Similarly, many of the objects Plato thought of as metaphysical entities we now see as linguistic and conceptual, and the translation Rorty has in mind involves turning Plato's claims about 'forms' into claims about language. In this way, the critic sees Plato as approaching a certain problem, one that she now better understands. This self-conscious rational reconstruction represents, I contend, a version of presentism that survives Skinner's worries. Of course, rational reconstruction will necessarily contain a good deal of purely historical reconstruction – as Rorty notes, 'one cannot figure out whether Spinoza got anything right before figuring out what he was talking about'.[57] And in this way rational reconstruction holds itself to an expanded version of Skinner's claim that an interpretation is only viable if a figure could be brought to accept it. Rorty explains: 'We are interested not only in what the Aristotle who walked the streets of Athens "could be brought to accept as a correct description,"' but 'in what an ideally reasonable and educable Aristotle' could accept.[58] The rational reconstructor works primarily by imagining not the particular historical writer, but that writer ideally informed. The goal here is still to capture what the writer intended to say, but we imagine that writer as more fully aware than she could ever have been.

We can thus redefine the worry about anachronism as a worry about the kinds of constraints historical reconstructions exert on rational reconstructions. Strict criteria in this realm are probably impossible; as Kenneth Minogue argued in his response to Skinner, it is not clear that interpretations in the history of ideas are susceptible to clear methodological rules.[59] To borrow from Mark Bevir, there is no such a thing as an interpretive 'method', in the form of a clear procedure guaranteed to yield true results, but one can perhaps nevertheless speak of heuristics – general hermeneutic principles that tend to produce persuasive analyses.[60] Chapter 2 followed three such heuristics, which we can now articulate. The first is a close attention to the repetition of ideas across a text and across a writer's work. Each of the chapters here ranges widely across an *oeuvre*; the goal is to ensure that the ideas central to a presentist analysis are not, so to speak, cherry-picked, justifying the anachronistic frame only through a selective attention to the evidence. There is a cost, insofar as the interpretations are thus invariably guilty of the mythology of coherence, but this is just to admit that the reconstructions are rational ones.

The second heuristic is a close attention to the overt ideas expressed in a text, in the form of passages where a narrator or a character openly discuss a philosophical claim. Chapter 1 suggested that such passages mattered importantly in the question of whether a literary text was inviting a certain kind of paraphrase; properly understood, this point also matters for the question of the justification of presentism, for such passages offer the best evidence for establishing the historical reconstruction of how an author thought about a given issue. And they matter for a further reason. One might object to the arguments so far by denying that rational reconstructions are a genre worthy of much attention. Yes, perhaps Lewis Carroll was right, and any interpretation must be somewhat abstracted and presentist, but the goal ought to be to minimise this factor as far as possible – the map ought to be as close to the land as it can be. Our impulse to reconstruct rationally reflects our own bias, and as such ought to be marginalised as much as is compatible with the need to address the *explanandum* in terms comprehensible to a contemporary reader.[61] I will argue in a moment that this is not the case. Writers and their texts call for rational reconstructions, and we do them an interpretive disservice if we think we can ignore this call. Central to this argument are a text's overt theoretical statements.

The third heuristic connects back to Rorty's point about the 'mapping' of intellectual history and the uses of interpretation, and requires a bit more explanation. A striking feature of work in the history of philosophy is how often it presents the idea of a reasonable middle ground between rational and historical reconstruction as straightforward, as if it is clear why it's a good idea or how it might proceed. Thus Robert Pippin: 'one would like to think that a submissive textualism and restrictive historicism on the one hand' or 'what one hears sometimes called "textfrei" interpretations on the other' are 'not the only alternatives'.[62] Or Aloysius Martinich:

> there is no good reason for the Analyst to be ignorant of or indifferent to the historical context of his text or for the Historian to be ignorant of or indifferent to the best analytic methods. Consequently, there is a third, and, I think, superior, way of studying the history of philosophy. It is the way that uses the methods of both the Analyst and the Historian.[63]

And (a very different thinker) Mortimer Adler: '*scholarship and history need not be* substituted *for philosophy*. Therein lies the reconciliation of the two false extremes [. . .] we correct the excess of historicism by placing scholarship in the service of an intelligent reading of books.'[64] Remarks such as this gesture at solutions to the problem but are really better thought of as names for it. It is clear that many writers working in the history of philosophy want to incorporate philosophical argument with historical interpretation. What is less clear is whether there is a broad agreement on what this sort of incorporation involves.

Pressed on in this way, Rorty's phrase 'the historian of philosophy helps the dead philosopher put his act together for a new audience', Pippin's phrase 'one would like to think', and Adler's notion of 'the intelligent reading of books' appear as more interesting than they might at first have seemed. The uncomfortable truth that these writers don't quite admit is that reading philosophy can be enjoyable, and that rationally reconstructing a philosophical text is often just what it means to enjoy it. To put it in a word, then, the most basic justification for rational reconstruction might ultimately be aesthetic, a way of pointing at the elements of a text that make it worthy of attention. That sounds troubling: the philosophical pursuit of truth is supposed to be more serious than the experience of art. But the discomfort stems only from a naive conception of what art and philosophy are; reconstructing Trollope's account of akrasia is not really different from an artistic interpretation. The experience of truth is an artistic experience. Thus the final heuristic is about the goal of this kind of interpretation – one assesses the value of a rational reconstruction insofar as it makes authors interesting when they otherwise might not have been. But of course this introduces the difficult question of truth.

The Impulse Towards Allegory

One of the most recurring objections to Skinner's contextualism disputed his assertion that he could dismiss as interpretively irrelevant the question of which ideas were true or false. As Charles Taylor puts the point, for Skinner texts in political theory 'are attempts to manipulate the terms of debate in which the political identity of a society is established and continued. But they can be identified as such as independent of any judgement of their truth or validity.'[65] However, Taylor goes on to argue, the historian's use of his own 'explanatory language' cannot help but imply the belief that such language is 'more accurate, more precise – more truthful', and thus the 'bracketing of the issue of truth is never successfully achieved'.⁶⁶ Additionally, a number of Skinner's critics pointed out that regardless of what he thought about the foolishness of timeless problems in political philosophy, authors from earlier periods certainly thought the issues they were addressing were timeless, and thus interpreters misunderstand them in insisting on understanding them only in the terms of their discourse. John Patrick Diggins contends: 'Authors use texts to convert ideas into truths that are not intended to have a context.'⁶⁷ In other words, Skinner's attempt to make authorial intent the central feature of analysis ironically leads to the restoration of philosophical truth as an interpretive criterion: 'We may discover past thinkers who felt their thoughts would have little value if there were determined by historical circumstances. Thus in some instances the intellectual historian could hardly be a contextualist if he or she seriously wanted to understand the thought of a political thinker exactly as the thinker understood it.'⁶⁸

There was always a limited sense in which Skinner was prepared to acknowledge this point. In particular, he suggests that his goal is to make the subjects of his interpretation appear as 'rational as possible', and some fundamentally timeless assumptions are necessary for any such interpretive endeavour – for instance, that the writer of the text in question meant his utterances to contain true propositions. Thus he remarks:

> Some of [the texts under study] may be pervasively marked by hidden codes such as irony. But we have no option but to assume that, in general, they can be treated as straightforward expressions of belief. Unless we can assume such a convention of truthfulness, we cannot hope to make any headway with the project of explaining what they believed.⁶⁹

And more, the critic must assume that the writers have certain attitudes towards belief formation; for example, the interpreter must posit a desire to be consistent, since 'to espouse a given belief as well as its contradictory is to hold at least one belief that must be false'.⁷⁰ Similarly, positing rationality requires that one see the objects of interpretation as 'concerned with the kinds of coherence, and where appropriate the kinds of evidence, that give them grounds for concluding that their affirmations of belief can in fact be justified'.⁷¹ The point here is that these three interpretive assumptions – that writers take to be true the things they say, that they will be consistent when possible, and will be concerned with the grounds for their beliefs, whether evidentiary or logical – are not avoidable, and to this extent a concern for truth is an essential part of interpretation.

One must take these presentist impulses a step further, I want to argue, and the step is suggested by the objection to Skinner that writers often intend to address issues of timeless import. In 'Transhistorical Intentions and the Persistence of Allegory', E. D. Hirsch argues that literary texts often contain 'allegorical intentions': they intend to make themselves 'applicable to (allegorizable to) unforeseen situations'.[72] Drawing on, among other examples, the Fourteenth Amendment to the US Constitution, Hirsch points out that writers frequently 'intend their writings to have meanings that go unforeseeably beyond their original literal contents'.[73] The interpreter must go beyond the literal content upon detecting the allegorical intention; to do otherwise is to dismiss the spirit of the text for the letter. But he must never let this 'going beyond' stretch too far away from the letter of the text, for this is another way of dismissing the spirit – after all, his sense of the spirit is based entirely upon the writer's literal, historical intention.[74] What Hirsch is talking about here is very close to the necessary imbrication of historical and rational reconstruction. Respecting the spirit of texts requires that one try to make as much sense of them as possible, including going beyond their strict historical meaning when doing so is required by their allegorical intentions.

One might well wonder how to decide if a text intends readers to take it allegorically, and it seems to me that overt statements of ideas necessarily intend precisely this. Trollope's comment that 'there are human beings who, though of necessity single in body, are dual in character' (*ED*, p. 199) offers a useful example. One needs, of course, to reconstruct this historically, connecting it to Victorian debates about moral psychology and making sense of what Trollope might have meant by the idea of a 'dual' character. Upon finishing this reconstruction, however, grasping the logic of the statement requires more than this; after all, the statement does not say that it is limited to Victorian England. Rather, Trollope's narrator means to make a statement of general philosophical truth, and the critic does a disservice to the novel by failing to engage with it on that level. In this sense, parsing Trollope's moral psychology and putting it in conversation with more recent thinkers is a way of responding to the 'spirit' of the text, of reconstructing it 'rationally', and of recognising the philosophical ideas that it 'implies'.

Hans-Georg Gadamer's hermeneutics make this point central. He writes:

> Precisely because it entirely detaches the sense of what is said from the person saying it, the written word makes the understanding reader the arbiter of its claim to truth. The reader experiences what is addressed

to him and what he understands in all its validity. What he understands is always more than an unfamiliar opinion: it is always possible truth.[75]

To encounter a written statement of an idea is always to engage it as potentially true for oneself, now; as Gadamer puts it, it is always 'possible truth', not just an 'unfamiliar opinion' that must be placed in some other context to become comprehensible. And per Gadamer, one might redescribe the relationship between historical and rational reconstruction as a version of the hermeneutic circle. As Rorty puts it, the two tasks 'will continually be correcting and updating the other'.[76] Thus, one reconstructs historically an author's intention to address a certain issue; then, upon discovering that she intended to make a statement of general philosophical truth, one rationally and anachronistically extends that account. However, grasping the way that she would extend that view requires further historical reconstruction, and the process thus continues.

That is to say that the stance of needing to know what to believe, now, is the stance that requires anachronism; in deciding what to think, all new ideas one encounters are possible truths and at the same level as each other. One might think of this as the stance of agency. Srinivas Aravamudan puts it thus in his essay 'The Return of Anachronism':

> The subject of anachronism [. . .] goes beyond historicism by refashioning an explanation of himself or herself in the wake of the multiple futures that exist in the now, rather than by yielding to the tyranny of a totalised now that purportedly leads to a singular future. The return of anachronism is nothing more than the return of the subject [. . .] no longer the unitary humanist subject but a fragmented, fragmentary subject, the object, abject, or even reject of historicism.[77]

In their capacity to make sense of and explain themselves, agents demonstrate both the possibility and necessity of anachronistic explanations. Rather than deferring to the necessary temporality of a historical determinism, agents can emphasise different aspects of themselves and their pasts to help realise one or another of the multiple possibilities present in a given moment.

Walt Whitman and the History of Ideas

Let me try to illustrate how the distinction between rational and historical reconstructions might be useful via a brief example, taken from the critical history of Walt Whitman's 'Song of Myself', and in particular the interpretations of one famous description of the poet: 'He judges not as the judge judges, but as the sun falling around a helpless thing.'[78] For Wai Chee Dimock, Whitman thinks of political participation as necessarily involving the process of eliminating most of my identity, insofar as it is contingent and unnecessary and thus not suitable for consideration when thinking about the nation as a whole. I must aspire to be a 'thin self' when participating in the democratic process, and think only about the thin selves of others. This involves judging 'not as the judge judges, but as the sun falling around a helpless thing', where 'unfastidious, unconditional generosity' eliminates everything about the considered subject that is accidental, non-essential or 'lucky'.[79]

For Martha Nussbaum, political participation involves the ability to sympathise with and erotically imagine the other people I encounter, an ability that I can only acquire by recognising my own eroticism. Far from involving a 'thinning' of the self, the essential step for Nussbaum's Whitman in effective political citizenship is the ability to assume the correct affective relationship to other people. The poet is a model for this relationship because 'he judges not as the judge judges, but as the sun falling around a helpless thing', which involves 'seeing its every nook and crevice, seeing its helplessness sharply but with the illumination of love'.[80]

For George Kateb, the key is to recognise that every person is in fact a composite of potentialities; this facilitates democratic participation because it creates an 'openness to others', each of whom is granted a reality equal to one's own.[81] In a view that is somewhere in between Dimock and Nussbaum, this entails that 'one learns to see others in order to become properly attached to them, but first one must be somewhat detached from oneself'. Correspondingly, for Kateb, Whitman incites us 'to see rather than to overlook, to accept rather than to disdain, to judge "not as the judge judges, but as the sun falling around a helpless thing"'.

And there are many more. For Paul Lauritzen, the key is emotion: 'Bioethics has too frequently encouraged physicians to judge as the judge judges and too seldom as the sun falling round a helpless thing [...] it is crucial for bioethics to provide a place for the emotional dimension of the clinical encounter.'[82] For Peter Bellis, the key is Whitman's rejection of representation as a model for poetic language; the poet 'is "to judge not as the judge judges but as the sun falling down around a helpless thing." Poetry is not a second-order activity, a response to a preexisting fact or event. Verbal expression is like the fall of sunlight.'[83] And in 'The Solar Judgement of Walt Whitman', Jane Bennett has argued that Whitman is advocating a kind of judging that is outside of and indeed in opposition to moral judgement: 'Good judgement may require one to inhabit the role of falling sun, for this accepting, nonranking illumination can reveal things as possessing a certain performativity.'[84]

These discrepant interpretations might appear to be a disagreement about how to interpret Whitman, but in fact they are really disagreements at the level of theory; these are alternate rational reconstructions. In that sense, what is going on here is not so much a disagreement about the details of Whitman's poem as a disagreement about which theoretical debate can benefit the most from a reconstructed Whitman. And as Rorty points out, rational reconstructions are 'unlikely to converge, and there is no reason to think they should', since the same text can offer diverse and perhaps even contradictory insights when taken up in radically different theoretical conversations.[85]

The dispute between Jane Bennett and Martha Nussbaum about how to interpret the line is particularly revealing. For Bennett, the line is about a form of judging that is free of the assumed primary of human agency, free of the axiom that the self is an active entity with reflective self-control operating among 'passive objects'.[86] As a result, she thinks that Nussbaum's reading is mistaken; conceding her point that it advocates a form of judgement that refuses abstract principles in favour of situational specificity, Bennett's Whitman goes further, contending that to judge like the sun is to refuse the distinction between oneself and other objects, recognising the fundamental materiality of the self. But Bennett's representation of this dispute is striking: 'The primacy Nussbaum gives to moral agency', Bennett writes, 'leads her to focus on just those lines and phrases in "By Blue Ontario's Shore" that I tend to elide or treat as secondary, and to them with the stress on the poet's distinctively human powers of decision.'[87]

Bennett goes on to offer three 'things' that Nussbaum supposedly overlooks, but none of them is really evidence from the poem itself – one, for instance, is a 'certain iconoclasm' that Whitman shared with Emerson and Thoreau, which would require the suspension of the 'ordinary moral criteria' that Nussbaum defends.[88] Instead, the key point is her admission that the question is one of emphasis – whether one emphasises, as Nussbaum does, the passages that stress the human agency of the judgement of the poet, or whether one elides those passages and emphasises, as Bennett does, the passages that collapse the distinctions between persons and objects (passages that Nussbaum elides). This difference in emphasis is precisely the filtering Rorty had in mind when talking about rational reconstruction. And in that sense, Bennett and Nussbaum are not really disagreeing with each other so much as they are talking past each other from different disciplinary standpoints. Nussbaum has asked what Whitman's poetry might say if we put it in conversation with theories of deliberation in contemporary moral philosophy, while Bennett has asked what it might say if we put it in conversation with Bruno Latour and Actor-Network Theory. That Whitman's poetry has interesting but different things to say in those different conversations is not surprising, and the conflict between these two reconstructions is not troubling, so long as one keeps in mind that the poem by itself cannot arbitrate between the two.

* * *

In March 2015 a group of younger scholars of Victorian literature released a 'Manifesto' for Victorian Studies in the twenty-first century.[89] The most controversial item in the Manifesto, as assessed from subsequent debate on the webpage of the 'V21 Collective', was its first item, which claimed that 'Victorian Studies has fallen prey to *positivist historicism.*' Without accepting either the term 'positivism' or the implications of the metaphor 'fallen prey', it does seem fair to characterise the last generation of literary criticism as dominated by the sense that critical interpretation must be historicist in nature, in what Joe North calls the 'Historicist/Contextualist' paradigm.[90] As Lauren Goodlad and Andrew Sartori summarised this position in the introduction to a special issue of *Victorian Studies* devoted to the 'Ends of History', 'We think historicism cannot but be part of our critical practice. For it is that aspect of the critical enterprise that strives to illuminate the concrete conditions from which our aspirations spring.'[91] Because our political goals are after all the products of historical forces, and because the literary text is after all the product of specific 'relations' that enable 'its coherence as an object', literary criticism – even politically driven criticism – must allow at least a partial role for historical analysis in its methodology.[92]

I have argued that this attentiveness to the forces that produced the object is not the only way to be historically responsible. Quentin Skinner's emphasis on historical reconstruction, on considering what writers' words would have meant in their conceptual world, is another way of acknowledging the same constraint that historicity requires. Yet the anachronistic impulse cannot be ignored; because we must decide who we think we are and what to believe now, anachronism is a necessary feature of our experience of reading. In that sense, this chapter is in sympathy with another part of the V21 Manifesto, which claims that 'The variations of and alternatives to presentism as such have not yet been adequately described or theorised.' Rorty and Skinner point the way towards one such variation, a kind of anachronism that balances presentism and historicism, but in a way much different from the historicist formalism of writers such as Jameson, and in a way that can promisingly respond to the importance of both aspects of the interpretive endeavour. Chapter 2 demonstrated to a certain extent what a historicist way of reading for the content would look like; having made clear the importance of the issue and its centrality to my argument, Chapter 4 will spend more time clarifying the intellectual history surrounding its interpretive claims, this time taking George Eliot as the key example.

Notes

1. Carroll, *Beyond Aesthetics*, p. 175.
2. 'Always Anachronise!' was the title of a talk that Margreta de Grazia gave at the MLA in 2005; I have been unable to find a published version of these remarks, but the phrase has been an important touchstone for presentist critics; see, for example, Linda Charnes, 'Anticipating Nostalgia: Finding Temporal Logic in a Textual Anomaly', *Textual Cultures* 4.1 (2009), pp. 72–83 (p. 76). The reference is, of course, to Fredric Jameson's injunction to 'always historicise', of which more in a moment. 'Historical Correctness' is the title of the final section of Marjorie Garber's book *A Manifesto for Literary Studies* (Seattle, WA: University of Washington Press, 2003); Garber is worried about the assumption that 'history grounds and tells the truth about literature' (p. 49).
3. Hugh Grady and Terence Hawkes, *Presentist Shakespeares* (New York: Routledge, 2007), p. 4. See Hugh Grady, *Shakespeare's Universal Wolf: Postmodernist Studies in Early Modern Reification* (New York: Oxford University Press, 1996); Terence Hawkes, *Shakespeare in the Present* (New York: Routledge, 2002); Evelyn Gajowski, 'Beyond Historicism: Presentism, Subjectivity, Politics', *Literature Compass* 7/8 (2010), pp. 674–91; and Charnes, 'Anticipating Nostalgia'.
4. Charnes, 'Anticipating Nostalgia', p. 76; Hawkes, *Shakespeare in the Present*, p. 20.

5. Wai Chee Dimock, 'A Theory of Resonance', *PMLA* 112.5 (1997), pp. 1060–71 (p. 1061). Dimock redefines context 'as a diachronic relation', in which current theory that on a simple historicism would seem to 'interfere' with genuine interpretation, in fact 'remakes a text while unmaking it', giving birth to 'newly possible meaning' (p. 1062).
6. Grady and Hawkes, *Presentist Shakespeares*, p. 3. See also Michael Bristol, 'Macbeth the Philosopher: Rethinking Context', *New Literary History* 42.4 (2011), pp. 641–62.
7. Grady and Hawkes, *Presentist Shakespeares*, p. 3.
8. Gajowski, 'Beyond Historicism', p. 680.
9. Gajowski, 'Beyond Historicism', p. 686.
10. A movement called the 'New Unhistoricism' in queer theory shares this sense of a political perniciousness in standard assumptions about interpretation and history. See Madhavi Menon, *Unhistorical Shakespeare: Queer Theory in Shakespearean Literature and Film* (New York: Palgrave Macmillan, 2008), p. 1.
11. Gajowski, 'Beyond Historicism', p. 683.
12. Jonathan Dollimore, *Radical Tragedy: Religion, Ideology, and Power in the Drama of Shakespeare and His Contemporaries* (Durham, NC: Duke University Press, 2003), p. 11.
13. Robin Headlam Wells, 'Historicism and Presentism in Early Modern Studies', *The Cambridge Quarterly* 29.1 (2000), pp. 37–60 (p. 49).
14. John Holbo, 'Shakespeare Now: The Function of Presentism at the Critical Time', *Literature Compass* 5/6 (2008), pp. 1097–110 (p. 1098).
15. Holbo, 'Shakespeare Now', p. 1098.
16. Holbo, 'Shakespeare Now', p. 1102; David Kastan, *Shakespeare After Theory* (London: Routledge, 1999).
17. Holbo, 'Shakespeare Now', p. 1102.
18. Kastan, *Shakespeare After Theory*, p. 31.
19. Jameson, *The Political Unconscious*, p. 20.
20. Stephen Cohen, *Shakespeare and Historical Formalism* (Aldershot: Ashgate, 2007), p. 1.
21. See, for instance, Catherine Gallagher, *The Industrial Reformation of English Fiction, 1832–1867* (Chicago: University of Chicago Press, 1988), or Michael McKeon, *The Origins of the English Novel: 1600–1740* (Baltimore: Johns Hopkins University Press, 2002).
22. Joseph North, *Literary Criticism: A Concise Political History* (Cambridge, MA: Harvard University Press, 2017), p. 141.
23. Jameson, *The Political Unconscious*, p. 192.
24. Jameson, *The Political Unconscious*, p. 194.
25. D. A. Miller, *Narrative and Its Discontents: Problems of Closure in the Traditional Novel* (Princeton: Princeton University Press, 1981), pp. 107–8.
26. Miller, *Narrative and Its Discontents*, pp. 137–8.

27. One might note this influence in the presence of the phrase 'the novel anticipates' in critical discourse, where what the novel anticipates is some post-structuralist theoretical insight. It is crucial that the novel does the anticipating and not the author: the narrative's form and its independence from the author permits, apparently, insight not available to the writer. See, for instance, David Collings, 'The Romance of the Impossible: William Godwin in the Empty Place of Reason', *ELH* 70.3 (2003), pp. 847–74, and Gage McWeeny, *The Comfort of Strangers* (Oxford: Oxford University Press, 2016). I will return to this interesting critical gesture in Chapter 5.
28. I allude here to Amanda Anderson's influential critique of 'aggrandised agency'. Amanda Anderson, 'The Temptations of Aggrandised Agency: Feminist Histories and the Horizon of Modernity', in *The Way We Argue Now: A Study in the Cultures of Theory* (Princeton: Princeton University Press, 2006), pp. 46–66 (p. 47).
29. Jameson, *The Political Unconscious*, p. 205.
30. Jameson, *The Political Unconscious*, pp. 193, 202.
31. Felski, *The Limits of Critique*, p. 96.
32. Edmund Wilson, 'The Ambiguity of Henry James', in *The Triple Thinkers* (New York: Harcourt, 1938), pp. 88–132.
33. Shoshana Felman, 'Turning the Screw of Interpretation', *Yale French Studies* 55/56 (1977), pp. 94–207 (p. 117). All emphasised passages from this essay are in the original.
34. Felman, 'Turning the Screw of Interpretation', p. 196.
35. Felman, 'Turning the Screw of Interpretation', p. 200.
36. Felman, 'Turning the Screw of Interpretation', p. 201.
37. Felski, *The Limits of Critique*, p. 106.
38. Jonathan Arac, *Critical Genealogies: Historical Situations for Postmodern Literary Studies* (New York: Columbia University Press, 1987), p. 279.
39. Shoshana Felman, 'To Open the Question', *Yale French Studies* 55/56 (1977), pp. 5–10 (p. 5).
40. Felman, 'To Open the Question', pp. 8–9.
41. Typical of this response is Peter Brooks, 'The Idea of a Psychoanalytic Literary Criticism', *Critical Inquiry* 13.2 (1987), pp. 334–48. Brooks opens by claiming that 'psychoanalytic literary criticism has always been something of an embarrassment', and cites Felman as pointing out 'more effectively than any other critic' the problem with pairing psychoanalysis 'and' literature (p. 335). He does not, however, take up and expand her distinction.
42. Quentin Skinner, 'Meaning and Understanding in the History of Ideas', *History and Theory* 8.1 (1969), pp. 3–53. Subsequent citations, abbreviated MU, are given in parentheses in the text. The following discussion will cite a number of thinkers who claim foundational importance for Skinner's essay, but for a retrospective discussion sympathetic to Skinner's

concerns, see J. G. A. Pocock, 'The State of the Art', in *Virtue, Commerce, and History* (New York: Cambridge University Press, 1985), pp. 4–5.
43. J. G. A. Pocock, 'Languages and their Implications: The Transformation of the Study of Political Thought', in *Politics, Language, Time* (Chicago: University of Chicago Press, 1971), pp. 3–41 (p. 3).
44. Arthur Lovejoy, *The Great Chain of Being* (Cambridge, MA: Harvard University Press, 1936), p. 20.
45. Pocock, 'Languages and their Implications', pp. 4–5.
46. Pocock, 'Languages and their Implications', pp. 18–19. In emphasising the discursive nature of knowledge and the impossibility of comparing intellectual formations between periods, Skinner and Pocock shared both explicitly and implicitly in the broad critiques of the philosophy of science offered by Michel Foucault and Thomas Kuhn.
47. Quentin Skinner, 'Motives, Intentions, and the Interpretations of Texts', in James Tully (ed.), *Meaning and Context: Quentin Skinner and his Critics* (Princeton: Princeton University Press, 1988), p. 74.
48. Mark Bevir, 'Are there Perennial Problems in Political Theory?', *Political Studies* 42 (1994), pp. 662–75 (p. 668).
49. Robert Lamb, 'Quentin Skinner's Revised Historical Contextualism: A Critique', *History of the Human Sciences*, 22.3 (2009), pp. 51–73 (p. 68). Skinner gave ground on this point in later remarks; referring to this passage, he writes: 'My way of putting the point appeared to deny the obvious fact that western traditions of philosophy have contained long continuities.' Quentin Skinner, 'A Reply to My Critics', in Tully (ed.), *Meaning and Context*, pp. 231–88 (p. 283).
50. David L. Hull, 'In Defence of Presentism', *History and Theory* 18.1 (1979), pp. 1–15.
51. Richard Rorty, J. B. Schneewind and Quentin Skinner, 'Introduction', in Richard Rorty, J. B. Schneewind and Quentin Skinner (eds), *Philosophy in History: Essays on the Historiography of Philosophy* (Cambridge: Cambridge University Press, 1984). This introduction is an interesting text. Given that Skinner reiterated his original views in a new version of his foundational essay in 1988, it seems unlikely to me that he in fact agreed with this introduction; this is perhaps gestured at in a somewhat pregnant line from the preface, 'the editors do not think with one mind or speak with one voice' (p. ix). For reasons of alphabetical preference, I shall refer to the author of this essay as 'Rorty', but one should keep in mind that the authorial situation is rather more complicated than that.
52. Rorty, Schneewind and Skinner, 'Introduction', p. 6.
53. Rorty, Schneewind and Skinner, 'Introduction', p. 7.
54. Rorty, Schneewind and Skinner, 'Introduction', p. 6.
55. Richard Rorty, 'The Historiography of Philosophy: Four Genres', in Rorty, Schneewind and Skinner (eds), *Philosophy in History*, pp. 49–75 (p. 53).
56. Rorty, 'The Historiography of Philosophy', p. 51.

57. Rorty, Schneewind and Skinner, 'Introduction', p. 10.
58. Rorty, 'The Historiography of Philosophy', p. 51.
59. Minogue writes: 'It all depends on the contingent matter of putting acute and penetrating questions into the heads of intellectual historians. Hence there is room to doubt whether they ought to sympathise with Skinner in feeling "an increasing need to look for renewed philosophical help".' Kenneth Minogue, 'Method in Intellectual History', in Tully (ed.), *Meaning and Context*, pp. 176–93 (p. 183).
60. Mark Bevir, *The Logic of the History of Ideas* (New York: Cambridge University Press, 2002). Bevir writes: 'All methods differ from heuristic techniques in that they are either sufficient or necessary to ensure a correct conclusion about something, whereas heuristic techniques merely provide a potentially fruitful way of reaching a correct conclusion about something' (p. 10).
61. This is, of course, John Holbo's point vis-à-vis the presentists.
62. Robert Pippin, *Hegel's Practical Philosophy: Rational Agency as Ethical Life* (New York: Cambridge University Press, 2008), p. 33.
63. Aloysius Martinich, 'Philosophical History of Philosophy', *Journal of the History of Philosophy* 41.3 (2003), pp. 405–7.
64. Mortimer Adler, *Reforming Education: The Opening of the American Mind*, ed. Geraldine Van Doren (New York: Collier and Macmillan, 1990), p. 32. This is a reprint of his 'Two Essays on Docility'.
65. Charles Taylor, 'The Hermeneutics of Conflict', in Tully (ed.), *Meaning and Context*, pp. 218–28 (p. 219). Taylor develops a similar argument against Michel Foucault in his essay 'Foucault on Freedom and Truth', *Political Theory* 12.2 (1984), pp. 152–83.
66. Taylor, 'Hermeneutics of Conflict', p. 220.
67. John Patrick Diggins, 'The Oyster and the Pearl: The Problem of Contextualism in Intellectual History', *History and Theory* 23.2 (1984), pp. 151–69 (p. 155). Robert Lamb makes a similar point: 'if a thinker seems to have been pitching his or her arguments at an abstract, philosophical level, there would be no reason to privilege a contextualist understanding of that argument' ('Quentin Skinner's Revised Historical Contextualism', p. 58).
68. Diggins, 'The Oyster and the Pearl', p. 161.
69. Skinner, 'A Reply', p. 246.
70. Skinner, 'A Reply', p. 239.
71. Skinner, 'A Reply', p. 240.
72. E. D. Hirsch, 'Transhistorical Intentions and the Persistence of Allegory', *New Literary History* 25.3 (1994), pp. 549–67 (p. 552).
73. Hirsch, 'Transhistorical Intentions', p. 555.
74. Hirsch, 'Transhistorical Intentions', pp. 557–8.
75. Hans-Georg Gadamer, *Truth and Method* (New York: Continuum, 1975), p. 396.
76. Rorty, Schneewind and Skinner, 'Introduction', p. 10.

77. Srinivas Aravamudan, 'The Return of Anachronism', *MLQ* 62.4 (2001), pp. 331–53 (pp. 351–2). This is consistent as well with Michael Bristol's version of anachronism: he thinks that to deny the anachronistic elements of our initial reading of a text is to 'depersonalise' the first-person stance of the reader ('Macbeth the Philosopher').
78. The line is from the 'Preface' to the original 1855 edition of *Leaves of Grass*. See *Leaves of Grass* (New York: Dover, 2012), p. 6.
79. Wai Chee Dimock, 'Whitman, Syntax, and Political Theory', in Betsy Erkkila and Jay Grossman (eds), *Breaking Bounds: Whitman and American Cultural Studies* (New York: Oxford University Press, 1996), pp. 62–79. Dimock elaborates on her view in *Residues of Justice: Literature, Law, Philosophy* (Berkeley: University of California Press, 1996), esp. pp. 113–24.
80. Martha Nussbaum, *Upheavals of Thought: The Intelligence of Emotions* (New York: Cambridge University Press, 2001), p. 671.
81. George Kateb, *The Inner Ocean: Individualism and Democratic Culture* (Ithaca: Cornell University Press, 1994), p. 167.
82. Paul Lauritzen, 'A Poetic Bioethics', in G. P. McKenny and J. R. Sande (eds), *Theoretical Analyses of the Clinical Encounter* (New York: Kluwer, 1994), pp. 151–69.
83. Peter Bellis, 'Against Representation: The 1855 Edition of Leaves of Grass', *The Centennial Review* 43.1 (1999), pp. 71–94.
84. Jane Bennett, 'The Solar Judgement of Walt Whitman', in John Seery (ed.), *A Political Companion to Walt Whitman* (Lexington: University of Kentucky Press, 2011), pp. 131–48.
85. Rorty, 'The Historiography of Philosophy', p. 51.
86. Bennett, 'The Solar Judgement of Walt Whitman', p. 131.
87. Bennett, 'The Solar Judgement of Walt Whitman', p. 137.
88. The other two arguments are: 1) Nussbaum misses how Whitman uses 'the sound and sense of poetry' to create a capacity to perceive 'nonhuman agencies' alongside persons, and 2) Whitman uses the experience of agency outside the self to help develop sensitivity to the 'nonhuman agencies inside the self'. Such a dispute is no longer really about the poem but about the nature of judgement and selfhood: the 'sound and sense of poetry' are not, I submit, the sort of evidence that might unequivocally lend weight to one side or the other of this disagreement.
89. V21 Collective, 'Manifesto of the V21 Collective', available at <http://v21collective.org/manifesto-of-the-v21-collective-ten-theses/> (last accessed 29 June 2015).
90. North, *Literary Criticism: A Concise Political History*, p. 1.
91. Lauren Goodlad and Andrew Sartori, 'The Ends of History: Introduction', *Victorian Studies* 55.4 (2013), pp. 591–614 (p. 610). As the combination of the debate in Victorian studies with the debate surrounding new presentist approaches in Shakespeare criticism might suggest, the role of history in literary criticism is perhaps the dominant current question in

considerations of methodology. This is exemplified, briefly, by a recent special issue of *New Literary History* addressed to 'context', and perhaps especially by Rita Felski's contribution, 'Context Stinks!', *New Literary History* 42.4 (2011), pp. 573–91. Studies of American literature have also been pressing on this question: the 100th issue of *American Literary History* was also devoted to the role of history in literary criticism, and saw a range of attitudes towards the issue. As Matthew Taylor argues in the issue's conclusion, one might break the responses into roughly two groups: the first group holds that literary criticism can and should be 'exorcising the sin of historical omission'; trusting the 'New Historicist assumption that literature is symptomatic of the sociocultural field in which it is produced', literary criticism can thus be a way of recovering the impact of suppressed events, tracing the suppression in the very way that texts hide it. The second group is more sceptical of the possibility and the value of doing history in this way, with attitudes ranging from Jennifer Fleissner's argument that one must strike a middle ground between 'total identification' with the past or the belief in a 'total difference from it', to Wai Chee Dimock's contention that the past is not a 'stable thing in itself' and correspondingly that 'History is updatable', to Walter Benn Michaels's suggestion in 'Forgetting Auschwitz' that the past must be forgotten so as not to be paralysed by it, accepting the implicit premise that turns 'history into identity'. Matthew Taylor, 'The Ends of History', *American Literary History* 25.4 (2013), pp. 944–57 (p. 947). My approach here falls, fairly clearly, into the second group, and to imagine ways of moving past New Historicist approaches.
92. Goodlad and Sartori, 'Ends of History', p. 596.

Chapter 4

The Scourge of the Unwilling: George Eliot on the Sources of Normativity

In a notebook of 1876, George Eliot engages at one point in a bit of philosophical musing. The 24th page of the notebook reads thus:

> The impulse of virtue
> The criterion of virtue
> The sanction of virtue
> Of what stuff is virtue made?
> How do we discriminate the genuine from the false?
> By what means is the making to be stimulated?
> How far is virtue knowledge, feeling, habit?
> Is it to be tested by its relation to human welfare, or is it to be ascertained a priori?
> Where is the scourge of the unwilling?[1]

We see Eliot here speculating on some of the hardest questions in moral philosophy. While musing about the role of emotion in moral judgement and the tension between utilitarian and Kantian ethics, Eliot goes further and asks about the real motivational force supporting moral norms – what she calls the 'sanction of virtue'. Of course, the rubber hits the road on this question when one asks about moral sceptics: how is it possible to persuade those who deny the existence of moral reasons? Where might one find 'the scourge of the unwilling'?

In asking this question, Eliot was participating in the analysis of a problem that deeply worried her contemporaries. As John Stuart Mill put it, 'The question is often asked, and properly so, in regard to any supposed moral standard [. . .] what is the source of its obligation? Whence does it derive its binding force?'[2] Mill is looking for what analytic philosophers call an explanation of 'normativity', for an account as to how it can be true that agents are obliged to do something. Christine Korsgaard calls this 'the normative question'; as she writes: 'the day will come, for most of us, when what morality commands, obliges, or recommends is hard [. . .] And then the question – why? – will press, and rightly so. Why should I be moral?'[3]

Mill's own answer to the question was famously inadequate. He writes in *Utilitarianism*:

> No reason can be given why the general happiness is desirable, except that each person, so far as he believes it to be attainable, desires his own happiness. This, however, being a fact, we have not only all the proof which the case admits of, but which it is possible to require [. . .] each person's happiness is a good to that person, and the general happiness, therefore, a good to the aggregate of all persons.[4]

The 'therefore' in that last sentence covers up some significant assumptions. One might easily concede that 'each person's happiness is a good to that person' without thinking that this shows anything at all about either what the aggregate of persons should do or any duty an individual has towards that aggregate. So Mill hasn't really addressed the sceptic, a point that Henry Sidgwick brought out in his 1874 treatise *The Methods of Ethics*:

> [A]n aggregate of actual desires, each directed towards a different part of the general happiness, does not constitute an actual desire for the general happiness, existing in any individual, and Mill would certainly not contend that a desire which does not exist in any individual can possibly exist in an aggregate of individuals.[5]

But at the end of the day Sidgwick didn't have a better answer; what he termed the 'Dualism of Practical Reason' is precisely the conflict between two forms of rational justification – justifications that appeal to the general good, and justifications that appeal to one's own good. So far from seeing how to fix the conflict, Sidgwick ended dramatically by claiming that 'the Cosmos of duty is thereby reduced to a Chaos', and then spent the rest of life looking for evidence of the paranormal, which might be able to demonstrate God's existence and solve the problem.[6]

Earlier in her life, Eliot seems to have been confident that she had a solution. Her 1857 novel *Scenes of Clerical Life* had identified 'two conditions for goodness: something to love and something to reverence', and had suggested that religiously charged labour could often fulfil the second criterion.[7] But by the middle of the 1870s she had become less certain. In that, she was not alone: the 1870s were a period of dramatic change in British moral philosophy. Sidgwick's massive treatise *The Methods of Ethics* systematised the utilitarian project, but did so at the cost of pointing out its missing foundation. In the wake of Darwin's evolutionary account of morality in *The Descent of Man*, a variety of thinkers sought to develop a moral philosophy on a purely scientific ground. But a rejection of both movements and the rise of British Idealism was signalled by the 1876 publication of F. H. Bradley's *Ethical Studies*.

I will argue that Eliot's late works creatively integrated these competing philosophical currents in a distinct variation on the *Bildungsroman*. Eliot used the narratives of Esther Lyon and Gwendolyn Harleth in particular to explore the nature of egoism and the origins of moral agency. Yet the parable is in some ways contained in the problem itself, for it is in considering the problem of egoism that moral psychology meets meta-ethics. Like Gide's immoralist and Nietzsche's Übermensch, Eliot's egoists are a philosophical challenge embodied in a person, and the story about what happens to them is a story about the nature of ethics.[8]

Let me summarise roughly my understanding of Eliot's theory of egoism. She takes it as a premise that agency requires self-approval; like Plato, she holds that no one willingly pursues something they regard as bad.[9] Thus her egoists at a young age do not think of themselves as immoral, but rather take their own primacy to be reasonable. This attitude is disrupted by a shocking experience of disapproval, which initiates ethical development. In particular, it introduces into the egoist's self the recognition that his or her grounds for self-approval are arbitrary, and thus inspires a search for a better foundation for positive self-evaluation. But that search culminates in recognising the importance of the perspectives of other people, whose own value offers the only meaningful criteria available. Thus egoism turns out to be irrational, insofar as it is incapable of satisfying a basic condition of rational agency – justified self-approval and the integrity that stems from it.[10] And while shame is not exactly beneficial, it turns out to be morally necessary. In a version of what Krista Thomason calls a 'constitutive account' of shame, Eliot identifies the capacity to experience shame as a necessary consequence of the ability to sympathise.[11]

My account of Eliot proceeds in four movements. The first briefly surveys the debate about moral philosophy in England in the 1870s, with an emphasis on the crisis posed by Sidgwick's Dualism. The second considers the very different approach to moral philosophy in

The Descent of Man, and Eliot's curiously direct engagement with Darwinian moral thought in her revision of George Henry Lewes's *Problems of Life and Mind*. The third and fourth consider first *Felix Holt*, as offering in relatively straightforward fashion Eliot's basic view of the foundations of normativity, and then *Daniel Deronda* as the version most aware of possible reservations about it.[12]

Sidgwick's Dualism

In *The Methods of Ethics*, which Derek Parfit called the best account of egoism that philosophers have yet offered, Henry Sidgwick describes the egoist as fundamentally embodying a particular form of rationality.[13] The egoist doesn't deny the existence of norms entirely; he agrees, for instance, that agents are rationally obliged to take the most efficient means towards their goals (*ME*, p. 36). 'We do not all look with simple indifference', Sidgwick remarks, 'on a man who declines to take the right means to attain his own happiness, on no other ground than that he does not care about happiness. Most men would regard such a refusal as irrational' (*ME*, p. 7). As Jerome Schneewind puts it, 'One might even take [this sort of egoistic rationality] to articulate the central strand in the ordinary idea of what it is for someone to act reasonably.'[14] But such an agent 'regards quantity of pleasure and pain to himself as alone important in choosing between alternatives of action' (*ME*, p. 95). 'It cannot be proved', Sidgwick explains, 'that the difference between his own happiness and another's happiness is not *for him* all-important' (*ME*, p. 420, emphasis in original).

Crucial, then, is the distinction between oneself and other people. Sidgwick admits that someone might doubt this point, but thinks that the egoist can plausibly rely on everyday intuitions about psychology:

> It would be contrary to Common Sense to deny that the distinction between any one individual and any other is real and fundamental, and that consequently 'I' am concerned with the quality of my existence as an individual in a sense, fundamentally important, in which I am not concerned with the quality of the existence of other individuals. (*ME*, p. 498)

The normative question arises, in other words, because each of us cares for our own particular experience of existence in a way that others do not.

Sidgwick's premise here might be worthy of challenge on its own, but it becomes more so when compared with another argument, contained in what Schneewind calls 'one of the most interesting passages of the *Methods*'.[15] Sidgwick remarks:

> From the point of view, indeed, of abstract philosophy, I do not see why the Egoistic principle should pass unchallenged any more than the Universalistic. I do not see why the axiom of Prudence should not be questioned, when it conflicts with present inclination, on a ground similar to that on which Egoists refuse to admit the axiom of Rational Benevolence. If the Utilitarian has to answer the question, 'Why should I sacrifice my own happiness for the greater happiness of another?', it must surely be admissible to ask the Egoist, 'Why should I sacrifice a present pleasure for a greater one in the future?' (*ME*, p. 418)

Rational egoism is not quite as axiomatic as it at first appears to be. In moments when I have a desire that conflicts with my overall happiness, it is not obvious why I ought to dismiss the desire. Admittedly, acting on its basis will not maximise my total happiness. But – so the sceptic here remarks – it is not clear how that generates a reason not to do it. As Sidgwick notes, the argument is structurally parallel to the egoist's challenge to the idea of rational benevolence: in the same way that the egoist sees no reason to prefer greater total happiness to his own, so the challenger of the principle of prudence sees no reason to prefer maximisation of his overall happiness to the instant gratification of a given desire.

Sidgwick's response is revealing. Having brought up this insightful challenge, he says that he 'will not press this question now, since [. . .] Common Sense does not think it worthwhile to supply the individual with reasons for seeking his own interest' (*ME*, p. 419). Again, there is a retreat to common sense; Sidgwick thinks it is intuitively obvious that individuals have something called 'their interest', which it is reasonable to pursue even in situations where local inclinations push the agent away from it. Thus there are ultimately two different ways of being rational. Actions that maximise overall or aggregate happiness are rational on the grounds of objectivity, while actions that maximise my own happiness are rational on the grounds of egoism, and the tension between these two norms of rationality – the Dualism of Practical Reason – is insoluble.

Yet we should note that at two crucial moments in the argument – in explaining why individuals have a reason to prefer their own individual happiness over total happiness, and in explaining why they have a reason to prefer the maximisation of happiness over the course of their lives as opposed to following the inclinations they feel at any given moment – Sidgwick falls back on unanalysed common-sense notions about the self. And the two notions are opposed. The response to the universalistic hedonist relies on immediate phenomenology, since it privileges our immediate experience of pleasure as opposed to the inaccessible experience of others. But the second response *denies* the validity of immediate phenomenology, since it suggests the existence of something called one's 'interest', which governs rationality over and above the inclinations one feels at a particular time. This tension between these two common-sense assumptions about the self is precisely the gap that later philosophers have exploited in arguing that morality is just a form of rationality: any account that sufficiently explains why one has a reason to care about one's own interests will also explain why one has a reason to care about the interests of others.[16]

Christine Korsgaard's version of the argument in her *Self-Constitution*, for instance, reiterates the problem of prudence; she considers as an example of imprudence the case of someone who prefers a penny to a dollar.[17] This might seem to be a straightforward case of irrationality, because the penny and dollar are measurable on the same scale, but things are less clear than they seem. Korsgaard writes:

> If I want to buy a piece of penny candy, the instrumental principle [which commands me to take the means to my ends] judges a penny and a dollar to be *equally good* means so far as *that* end is concerned. It is only on the assumption that I ought to pursue or stand ready to pursue more than one of my ends, and also of course that my other ends might cost money, that I am *required* to prefer the dollar to the penny. (*SC*, p. 53)

The seemingly obvious irrationality of preferring pennies to dollars depends upon a background assumption that satisfying more ends is better than satisfying fewer. But this is a 'substantive conception of the good', which is to say that it relies on a non-trivial belief that maximal desire-satisfaction is the *best* thing an agent could do (*SC*, p. 53). It is worth pointing out that it is not just the psychological belief that such action will make the agent happiest, because this claim by itself doesn't generate rational norms. The philosopher defending rational egoism has to hold the further claim that agents *ought* to try to be as happy as possible.

And that claim, Korsgaard thinks, cannot be proven. This is not to deny the fact that preferring pennies to dollars really is a little irrational, though Korsgaard doesn't think philosophers have yet articulated a principle that captures the injunction to prefer 'the achievement of a conjunction of our ends to the achievement of any one of them' (SC, p. 57). Whatever that precise principle turns out to be, though, the source of its normative force is obvious. In her words, 'a formal principle for balancing our various ends and reasons must be a principle for unifying our agency, since that is so exactly why we need it: so that we are not always tripping over ourselves when we pursue our various projects, so that our agency is not incoherent' (SC, p. 58). The point here is that, in explaining how to integrate the pursuits of our ends with each other, the missing principle will necessarily be about how to reconcile the various parts of ourselves, since it is the fact of this partition that gives rise to the problem in the first place.

Unifying one's agency opens up a gap, however, in which it becomes apparent how the respect due to others plays a necessary role. The only way to balance one's projects is to ground them on the basis of reasons, but a reason can only be viable if it can be willed from multiple perspectives – including both the future states of an agent's self and the perspectives of other people. As David Velleman puts the point, 'In order to be a person, you must have an approach to the world that is sufficiently coherent and constant to qualify as a single continuing point-of-view. And part of what gives you a single continuing point-of-view is your acceptance of particular considerations as having the force of reasons whenever they are true.'[18] Agents cannot, in other words, decide that a given consideration gives them a reason to act in one situation and not in another, all other things being equal; to do so is to prevent the self from achieving the unity that allows an agent to make sense of herself. In this appeal to a broader perspective, however, the agent necessarily imagines the perspectives of others. Korsgaard calls this claim the 'publicity of reasons' thesis:

> The reasons that you legislate when you will have to be public, that is, have to have normative force that can be shared by all rational beings, because acting is interacting with yourself – yourself at other times or in other possible situations. You have to make laws for yourself. And unless the laws that you make now bind you at other times and in other situations, and unless the laws that you know you would make at other times and in other situations bind you now, they won't hold you together into a unit after all. (SC, p. 214)

The key point here, which highlights the difference between what philosophers call the 'constitutivist' approach and Sidgwick's, is the notion that action is 'interacting with yourself'. For the laws you make for yourself to actually create you as a self, they have to bind not merely the current you, but also your future selves. However, the only way for a rule to reliably seem compelling to one's future self is for it to seem compelling from a public stance. The egoism that is both entirely selfish and entirely prudential turns out to be impossible – the kind of self-control capable of enforcing prudence is only possible in agents who recognise the force of rules constraining their behaviour towards other people.

Something very like this response to the problem of egoism was present already in the 1870s, in the works of T. H. Green, F. H. Bradley and Edward Caird. As William Mander explains, the Idealists were sceptical that a genuine distinction could be made between an action being good-for-oneself and being good-for-others; as Green in particular emphasised, the distinction between benevolence and reasonable self-love is 'a fiction of philosophers'.[19] Bradley puts the key underlying point pithily: 'The "individual man", the man into whose essence his community with others does not enter, who does not include relation to others in his very being, is, we say, a fiction.'[20] This idea – that selfhood is fundamentally intersubjective – is very much what Korsgaard and Velleman are pushing us to see. Recognising one's dependence on others is the only way to maintain internal self-coherence, and correspondingly the selfishness of egoism produces a chaotic and contradictory mixture of desires. Thus Bradley concludes *Ethical Studies* by contending that 'the bad self is anarchical', since 'evil lusts and appetites are all each for himself, and wage a war of everyone against everyone else who stands in the way'.[21] Korsgaard would agree: part of giving up on moral norms is the abandoning of prudential norms, and so the bad self's own desires war with each other.

In a letter of 13 February 1878, Edith Simcox recounts a discussion of moral philosophy with Eliot: 'the weak point of Utilitarianism, in Sidgwick and others', she writes, 'lay not in their taking human welfare as the standard of right but in their trying to find in it the *moral motive*'.[22] As an alternative, she sympathises with 'the rising school in Oxford which follows Green and Caird to think English philosophy nowhere'. What I want to argue is that Eliot's sympathy for that 'rising school' reflects a fundamental philosophical agreement about the nature of egoism and the most promising account of the sources of normativity.

One key point of agreement is evident from Bradley's suggestion that moral agency begins with and depends upon the experience of an end regarded as intrinsically valuable. 'So far as we are selfish', Bradley writes, 'we do not lose ourselves in anything'; selfishness 'excludes all working for any end which is looked on as what matters, irrespective of our private comfort'.[23] As a number of scholars have noted, Eliot's fiction emphasises the moral importance of the vocation.[24] As her developing protagonists learn, finding meaningful work – tasks that agents can view as mattering in themselves – is an essential step to achieving a coherent life and full moral agency. Of course, this echoes the idea that work is a form of freedom, a claim made famous by Thomas Carlyle.[25] So it is not a surprise to learn that both Eliot and the Idealist thinkers found much to appreciate in Carlyle.[26] Yet Eliot's own particular account of egoism drew as well on a very different line of thought.

Darwin, Eliot and the Moral Sense

Near the end of his 1875 essay 'Right and Wrong: The Scientific Ground of Their Distinction', William Clifford writes: "Now to my mind the simplest and clearest and most profound philosophy that was ever written upon this subject is to be found in the 2nd and 3rd chapters of Mr. Darwin's *Descent of Man.*"[27] Clifford's enthusiasm for Darwin stems, I want to suggest, from a sense that Darwin offered new resources for an account of the sources of normativity. Rather than grounding moral obligation in an Idealist account of the fundamental imbrication of self and society, Darwin turned more humbly to moral feeling as it actually existed. The philosophical impoverishment of this alternative was recognised almost immediately; as a number of writers (though not Clifford) pointed out, a Darwinian ethics could never justify, only explain.[28] But in place of that philosophical justification it promised hardheaded scientific realism. Quoting Kant – 'Duty! Wondrous thought [. . .] whence thy original?' – Darwin argues that while the search for the 'original' of moral duty has been addressed by many thinkers, 'no one has approached it exclusively from the side of natural history'.[29]

That explanation depends on 'the social instincts', which 'lead an animal to take pleasure in the society of its fellows' (*DM*, p. 72). Our 'instinctive sympathy' causes us to value approval from others, along with praise, blame and scorn (*DM*, p. 86). But as we grow and combine these instinctive feelings with 'reason and experience', we can eventually judge ourselves as others would judge us – we 'can appreciate the justice of the judgements' of our fellow men. When this has happened, a kind of experience that originally depended on social feeling appears as something much different; one might say,

'I am the supreme judge of my own conduct, and in the words of Kant, I will not in my own person violate the dignity of humanity' (*DM*, p. 86). To such a person, moral behaviour may thus feel like a distinctively human and personal autonomy – a way of keeping faith to himself above all. But we, understanding the evolutionary source of these feelings, know better. While it may be influenced by 'reason, self-interest, and [. . .] religious feelings', the root of our 'moral sense or conscience' is ultimately the 'social instincts' and 'the approbation of our fellow-men' (*DM*, p. 166).

Thus Darwin's is ultimately a deflationary account of normativity. As he puts it, 'The imperious word *ought* seems merely to imply the consciousness of the existence of a persistent instinct' (*DM*, p. 92). When we fail to satisfy a desire, we feel frustrated; when we feel that desire often, eventually we think it describes something we should do, and thus an instinct becomes a duty. Far from anything divinely inspired, or the sense of a necessary condition for the maintenance of internal coherence, or even a rational obligation implied by our pursuit of happiness, normativity is the banal product of the fact that humans can experience their instincts consciously.

Logically enough, Darwin's account does not offer much by way of resources for addressing the sceptic. He writes:

> If [a man] has no such sympathy, and if his desires leading to bad actions are at the time strong, and when recalled are not overmastered by the persistent social instincts, then he is a bad man, and the sole restraining motive left is the fear of punishment, and the conviction that in the long run it would be best for his own selfish interests to regard the good of others rather than his own. (*DM*, p. 92)

There is nothing one can say to someone who lacks the social instincts. The only solutions Darwin offers are political: one must either make punishment common enough that the fear of it becomes a motivating factor or structure a society in such a way that morality is prudent. This is to give up on answering Korsgaard's normative question; when someone asks why they should act morally when doing so is hard, there is ultimately no answer.

An interesting quirk of intellectual history has made the evidence of George Eliot's engagement with this line of thought particularly clear. As K. K. Collins demonstrated in a groundbreaking essay of 1978, the need for Eliot to take over the process of revising the final volume of *The Problems of Life and Mind* after George Henry Lewes's death in 1878 proved to be a moment of philosophical creativity.[30] For the most part, Eliot's version of the text was unchanged from Lewes's final version, but she significantly revised Lewes's account of the moral sense. And the straightforward Darwinian theory in Lewes's final version becomes something subtly different.

Lewes opens with the claim that the conscience, like the intellect, is a product of evolution and social training. We are not born with a moral awareness any more than we are born able to play music; the development of the moral capacity is the result of education. And we are quite malleable: Lewes quotes Darwin on the society of bees, asserting that 'any action becomes "right" when we have been taught to think it so'.[31] We are vulnerable to social norms in this way because we combine our social instincts with the capacity for reflection and memory, a fact that turns our instincts into 'organised tendencies', which can be so powerful that an individual might eventually 'refuse to do what he thinks to be wrong, though confident that no one else can ever know of the act' (LR, p. 488).[32] But they can also develop in alternating directions; Lewes distinguishes between the Reproductive and the Nutritive emotions, and while the former are inherently sympathetic, the latter are egoistic. The Reproductive impulse eventually becomes the 'desire for Approbation', but the Nutritive comprises our 'aggressive and defensive' impulses, and leads to social manifestations such as war and (intriguingly) 'Trade and Commerce' (LR, p. 491).

As Collins notes, Eliot's revisions push back to a significant extent on Lewes's Darwinian deflation. While Lewes is interested in revealing the animal emotions underlying the internalisation of social disapproval, Eliot stresses the moral transformation that the capacity for such internalisation implies:

> [T]he response to the moral demands of society, whether in the shape of doctrine or of institutions, is little more than the conflict of opposing appetites, the check imposed by egoistic dread on egoistic desire. It is a great progress beyond this brute dread of the stick when the love of approbation attains the ideal force which renders social rule or custom and the respect of fellow-men an habitually felt restraint and guidance. (LR, p. 485)

Eliot's point here is that there is a qualitative distinction between kinds of internalisation. Merely considering the cost of social disapproval against the value of the satisfaction of a censured desire is not much progress; it is simply to impose the check of 'egoistic dread' on egoistic desire. However, when the love of approbation becomes a motivating force in itself, agents perform actions in an importantly selfless way. This is not exactly a point that Darwin would have disagreed with, but the emphasis is different. Where Darwin is interested in showing the animal roots of moral behaviour, Eliot is interested in the transformation given to such behaviour by self-consciousness. In particular, selfish emotions become importantly selfless:

> To the moral sense in this lower stage there is but a faint and confused impression of what constitutes the wrong of wrong-doing [. . .] But in a mind where the educated tracing of hurtful consequences is associated with a sympathetic imagination of their suffering, Remorse has no relation to an external source of punishment for the wrong committed [. . .] The sanction which was once the outside whip has become the inward sympathetic pang. (LR, p. 489)

There is a crucial difference between sorrow that stems from the fear of punishment and sorrow because one senses the hurt of another person. The first is merely another species of egoism, but true remorse is qualitatively different.

Similarly, where Lewes divides the emotions into 'egoistic and sympathetic' categories, Eliot changes the passage to say that 'All emotions in the beginning are egoistic' (LR, p. 491). But as a result of the gradual growth of our awareness, there is a 'continual source of that interest in the experience of others which is the wakener of sympathy', until eventually there is a 'submergence' or 'transference' of egoistic desire into 'sympathetic channels' (LR, p. 491). Collins takes these changes to be driven by a meta-ethical impulse: 'George Eliot can tolerate an ethics historically based upon brute fear and pleasure [. . .] but not one philosophically based upon them' (LR, p. 474). The point is apt: one impact of Eliot's revision is to renew the project of grounding moral norms on the logic of moral psychology.

Thus we can say that there were (at least) three powerful conceptions of the egoist at work in the moral philosophy of the 1870s. Perhaps the most thorough challenge to traditional moral thought lay in Sidgwick's conception of the egoist as a calculating hedonist, unimpressed with the idea that the interests of other people matter. In sympathy with this picture was Darwin's view of the egoist as someone simply lacking common social instincts, an agent that could never be brought to respect morality as such and requiring political management. Against both was the Idealist picture of the egoist as a psychological chaos, lacking the internal coherence that moral principle provided. Like the Idealists, Eliot denied that egoism was a form of rationality and portrayed egoism as a form of incoherence. But her way of explicating the details of what coherent selfhood would look like drew heavily on the theory of the internalisation of social approval so central to the neo-Darwinian approach. To see this, let me turn now to the narrative of moral development in *Felix Holt*.

The Choice Which Gives Unity to Life

Esther Lyon, the heroine of *Felix Holt*, is an instance of a character who recurs throughout Eliot's fiction. Like Hetty Sorrel and Gwendolen Harleth, at the beginning of the novel she is a young, unmarried and pretty egoist. That egoism consists above all in a conviction that her evaluative judgements are the correct ones: 'she had a little code of her own about scents and colours, textures and behaviour [. . .] And she was well satisfied with herself for her fastidious taste, never doubting that hers was the highest standard.'[33] And, not coincidentally, that standard informs Esther of her value: 'her irreproachable nails and delicate wrist' are 'the objects of delighted consciousness to her' (*FH*, p. 77). Thus Esther's self-approval is to some extent reflective; she has a standard and is 'satisfied' with it. Implicitly, though, this is in part because of the positive judgement the standard yields when applied to her.

The novel begins the story of Esther's emergence from egoism with an easily recognisable moment of embarrassment:

> In the act of rising, Felix pushed back his chair too suddenly against the rickety table close by him, and down went the blue-frilled work-basket, flying open, and dispersing on the floor reels, thimble, muslin work, a small sealed bottle of atta of rose, and something heavier than these – a duodecimo volume which fell close to him between the table and the fender [. . .] 'Byron's poems!' he said, in a tone of disgust, while Esther was recovering all the other articles [. . .] 'What, do you stuff your memory with Byron, Miss Lyon?'
>
> She reddened, drew up her long neck, and said, as she returned to her chair again, 'I have a great admiration for Byron.' (*FH*, pp. 68–9)

As a number of writers have noted, shame often occurs when there is a gap between the way we hope to appear and the way we actually do; David Velleman, for instance, argues that shame stems from failures in self-presentation.[34] Predictably, Esther reacts to Felix's criticism by trying to deny that any such slip has occurred: she 'would not have wished [her father] to know anything about the volume of Byron, but she was too proud to show any concern' (*FH*, p. 69). Initially, that is, she compensates for the experience of shame by making the supposedly shameful fact an element in her self-presentation – thus her 'admiration for Byron'.

Yet Felix's judgement persists in her mind. This is not least because Felix, with a surprisingly straightforward moral sadism – 'I should like to come and scold her every day, and make her cry and cut her fine hair off', he thinks – persists in judging her (*FH*, p. 72). Expanding on his criticism of her reading habits, he tells Esther that she cares too much about petty things: 'You don't care to be better than a bird trimming its feathers, and pecking about after what pleases it' (*FH*, p. 123). Instead she should look for deeper concerns: while she need not join her father's church, she should ask herself 'whether life is not as solemn a thing as [her] father takes it to be' (*FH*, p. 123). Understandably, Esther revolts against 'his assumption of superiority' (*FH*, p. 125), mocking his sermonising and telling him that his supposed brave 'truth-telling' is really just rudeness (*FH*, p. 124). However, she is unable to decisively repudiate the criticism. The narrator explains: 'For the first time in her life Esther felt herself seriously shaken in her self-contentment. She knew there was a mind to which she appeared trivial, narrow, selfish' (*FH*, p. 125). It is notable that Esther cannot just shrug off Felix's open rudeness, which is how she has reacted to her father's criticism in the past. There are two reasons why.

The first stems from the nature of shame itself. As Krista Thomason has persuasively argued, the experience of shame does not depend upon agreement on the criteria for shamefulness; we can be ashamed of various elements of our identity even if we do not agree that these are anything to be ashamed of.[35] That's because shame often involves a reduction of ourselves to our non-voluntary identities, to the parts of ourselves that we do not choose to present. Esther need not agree that reading Byron is anything to be ashamed of in order to be ashamed by it; the anxiety stems from the worry that she is nothing but a reader of Byron, nothing but her 'trivial, narrow, selfish' concerns. Thus the tension in her immediate reaction to Felix's sermon: 'She could not change for anything Felix said, but she told herself he was mistaken if he supposed her incapable of generous thoughts', a thought that she immediately makes manifest by getting her father a cup of tea (*FH*, p. 126). Esther is at once interested in denying Felix's reduction of her to merely her selfish aspects and in demonstrating that this reduction is unfair. But there is a second reason why Esther cannot ignore Felix's criticism, one closer to Eliot's specific interest in the moral psychology of shame. Esther is plagued by the fear that Felix's judgements of her might be correct: she has a 'secret consciousness that he was her superior' (*FH*, p. 120), and 'could not bear that Felix should not respect her'. Esther realises slowly but surely that she has no reasons that justify her own 'self-contentment', that her 'little code' of 'scents and colours' is actually arbitrary, and that thus she has no meaningful response to Felix.

The lack of such a principled self-conception appears as well in what initially seem to be unrelated psychological phenomena. Esther suffers, first, from general dissatisfaction and ennui: 'she was not contented with her life: she seemed to herself to be surrounded with ignoble, uninteresting conditions' (*FH*, p. 77). Additionally, her life feels disjointed: 'Her life was a heap of fragments, and so were her thoughts: some great energy was needed to bind them together' (*FH*, p. 173). In Felix's diagnosis, she cares too much about herself: 'you are discontented with the world because you can't get just the small things that suit your pleasure' (*FH*, p. 123). Even Esther's unhappiness is shallow: she is frustrated for the wrong reasons. This is very much what the Idealist theory of egoism predicts. Bradley and Green hold that 'voluptuary' agency is self-defeating, because a form of agency that seeks fulfilment only in satisfying desire can never achieve more than momentary happiness. Thus Esther needs a focus outside of herself that requires 'great energy' to pursue. The energy that will bind up the parts of her life will be exerted not on her but by her.

There are thus three psychological processes at play in Esther's relationship to Felix, and whose interaction demonstrates the essential role that sympathy plays in the ongoing constitution of the self in Eliot's thought. First, Esther is constructing a new basis for justified self-approval; second, she wants something that will address her feelings of boredom and purposelessness; finally, she is integrating the various parts of herself into a coherent whole. These processes are interrelated and mutually constitutive; it is because a project regarded as intrinsically valuable binds together the parts of herself that it offers Esther a new basis for self-approval. Each is intersubjective, depending not on her alone but on the dynamics of Esther's relationship with Felix. This is not just because Esther loves Felix, but because Eliot incarnates in Felix the voice of public reason: 'He was like no one else to her: he had seemed to bring a law' (*FH*, p. 265).

An example will help clarify what I mean. At one point Esther considers listening to Harold Transome give a political speech. She does not generally care about politics, but

[s]he knew that Felix cared earnestly for all public questions, and she supposed that he held it one of her deficiencies not to care about them: well, she would try to learn the secret of this ardour, which was so strong in him that it animated what she thought the dullest form of life. (*FH*, p. 194)

It is not an accident that an attempt to overcome boredom and an attempt to overcome her 'deficiencies' are related, for the fact that she finds politics dull is part of the novel's evidence that she cares too much about herself. Even finding politics interesting would be a step in the right direction. Yet finding something interesting turns out to be a public rather than a private act, for it involves sharing the way someone else sees it, learning the 'secret' behind Felix's 'ardour'. Esther's attempt to care about politics is also and essentially an attempt to sympathise with Felix, to understand his reasons for caring about something that she finds dull.

So, shame finds its moral value as an experience that initiates this process. The narrator is not subtle about this: 'it has been well believed through many ages that the beginning of compunction is the beginning of a new life, that the mind which sees itself blameless may be called dead in trespasses' (*FH*, p. 154). To lack the capacity to feel shame is to be morally dead, and conversely the first experience of shame is moral birth. That is because it is to recognise the perspectives of others as carrying moral weight. Again, Thomason is helpful: the liability to shame is morally essential, she argues, because it demonstrates that one does not take oneself to be the final authority on one's own goodness.[36] Recognising that the opinions of others matter, even if it is only so that one's self-approval can find a firmer basis, is the first step to treating them as if they matter as people. Esther's 'acquaintance with Felix Holt' teaches her 'to doubt the infallibility of her own standard', and that doubt comes along with her mind being 'suddenly enlarged by a vision of passion and struggle, of delight and renunciation, in the lot of beings who had hitherto been a dull enigma to her' (*FH*, p. 252). Thus shame is the source of sympathy, when sympathy is construed as rooted in interest in the experience of others.[37]

That process of changing moral standards and sympathetic growth forms the background to the major dilemma of the novel, Esther's decision about whether to marry Harold Transome or Felix Holt. Clearly both men love her, and Esther believes that she would certainly be happier with Harold. But the happiness would ultimately be meaningless: 'there was a lot where everything seemed easy – but for the fatal absence of those feelings which [. . .] it seemed nothing less than a fall and a degradation to do without' (*FH*, p. 465). The passage continues to a vivid image: 'she saw herself in a silken bondage that arrested all motive, and was nothing better than a well-cushioned despair' (*FH*, p. 465).[38] Precisely because marriage with Harold will be easy, nothing will matter. More than that, the life of ease conduces to the heteronomy that comes with the pursuit of wayward desire.

Felix's principled commitment to political reform, on the other hand, offers the autonomy that comes with the selfless pursuit of a noble goal. As Esther puts it in her testimony at Felix's trial, Felix is only a fanatic 'if it is fanatical to renounce all small selfish motives for the sake of a great and unselfish one' (*FH*, p. 418). Such a pursuit is correspondingly the only way to assemble the fragments of her life, the kind of choice that 'gives unity to life' (*FH*, p. 430). It doesn't even matter if one's pursuit of the goal is ultimately successful; as Felix puts it,

> As long as a man sees and believes in some great good, he'll prefer working towards that in the way he's best for [. . .] I put effects at their minimum, but I'd rather have the minimum of effect, if it's of the sort I care for, than the maximum of effect I don't care for. (*FH*, p. 435)

As usual, Eliot rejects a moral philosophy based on the value of consequences; what matters is the moral psychology underlying selfless action. And – not incidentally – Esther's moral transformation has addressed her sense of shame. When she testifies at Felix's trial, the narrator writes: 'Half a year before, Esther's dread of being ridiculous spread over the surface of her life; but the depth below was sleeping' (*FH*, p. 449). To testify at the trial of a poor, unpopular man she barely knows and who has just led a political riot might have seemed to be idiosyncratic and silly. Yet Esther's belief in Felix and his work have given her a new self-contentment, one that makes it impossible to feel 'ridiculous'. And we are given a sense of something approaching moral equality; although Esther tells Felix, 'I wish to do what you think it will be right to do' (*FH*, p. 474), Felix responds by saying that he will thus 'be forced to be a much better fellow that I ever thought of being' (*FH*, p. 475). In such a way their sympathy with each other will be morally reinforcing to both, and the moral hierarchy between the two – if it has not disappeared – has been transformed into more of a shared set of ideals that both pursue freely.

The Outer Conscience: Sympathy and Self-Constitution in *Daniel Deronda*

Felix Holt gives, then, the broad strokes of an answer to the moral sceptic: there is a kind of fulfilment, freedom and self-coherence that only comes with the pursuit of ends made intrinsically valuable through the awareness of and respect for the reasons of others. While egoism and moral scepticism are certainly possible – the novel's villain, Matthew Jermyn, is 'shame-proof' – they cannot be coherently and deliberately willed (*FH*, p. 403). But it is not hard to poke holes in the novel's theory of moral psychology. Most immediately, Felix's moral sadism is deeply unattractive, all the more so because Esther and the novel believe that her submission to it is morally praiseworthy. It is difficult to agree that Esther's is a life of autonomous freedom when both she and her husband so clearly see it as a form of submission; the incarnation of the moral ideal in a particular person adds to the act of identification with moral principle an element of political power. In what sense, one might ask, is the principle Esther submits to really hers? The novel's conservative politics give this objection an additional edge: when Felix explains that he doesn't think working people should have the right to vote, it is far too easy to conclude that he would also regard his wife's opinions sceptically (*FH*, p. 292). More generally, the novel seems unaware of the dark side of shame; if it can awaken moral transformation, surely it can also inspire crippling self-hatred, bringing about internal division and possibly external violence, instead of coherence and harmony.[39] Finally, one would like to hear more about how exactly the goods of fulfilment and freedom are unavailable to egoists. There certainly seem to be happy sadists who are capable of prudential decision making, yet Eliot's view is required to deny that such agents exist.

These and many more worries seem to have weighed on Eliot in the ten years between the publication of *Felix Holt* (1866) and that of *Daniel Deronda* (1876). *Deronda* is in many ways a reiteration of the moral psychology of *Felix Holt*; once again, a traumatic experience of shame leads a female egoist to develop a capacity for sympathy via a relationship with a male moral exemplar. But Eliot varies in slight ways on almost every element in her theory of moral transformation, and those differences suggest significant philosophical enhancement. To show this, I will offer a brief reading of the novel that aligns with the progression in *Felix Holt*, and then return more closely to its variations.

The famous opening of *Daniel Deronda* – with Gwendolen Harleth gambling away two hundred pounds playing roulette at a German resort, and then kissing her reflection in the mirror – captures as well as any scene in Eliot's work her theory of immature egoism, or what the narrator calls Gwendolen's *'naive* delight in her fortunate self'.[40] Yet like Esther, Gwendolen is usually discontented; as she remarks in the opening scene, 'I am always bored' (*DD*, p. 14). Indeed, this is why she plays roulette; as she tells Daniel later, gambling 'is a refuge from dulness' (*DD*, p. 411).

Gwendolen's naive egoism is interrupted by two moments of public shame. First, Daniel catches her not only gambling, but pawning a necklace to compensate for her losses; Gwendolen experiences Daniel's generosity in returning the necklace as him 'entangling her in helpless humiliation', since no one has 'ever before dared to treat her with irony and contempt' (*DD*, p. 20). Second, she has the misfortune to perform in front of the German music professor Herr Klesmer, whose honest assessment of her music is not complimentary – 'you produce your notes badly, and that music which you sing is beneath you' (*DD*, p. 49). Klesmer's own obvious skill prevents her from repudiating the criticism: 'Gwendolen, in spite of her wounded egoism, had fullness of nature enough to feel the power of this playing' (*DD*, p. 50). Both force Gwendolen out of her self-contentment – Daniel's mere observing of her gambling with an air of moral superiority brings out a 'tingling resentment' (*DD*, p. 10), while Klesmer's performance makes Gwendolen want to stand apart from her own performance, 'to get a superiority over [her own doings] by laughing at them' (*DD*, p. 50).

The gaps thus introduced into her identity transform into moral growth, as Gwendolen comes to care about perspectives outside her own and evaluative standards that do not necessarily confirm her own high value. The process does not happen smoothly; Gwendolyn pushes back psychologically against both men, mocking Klesmer's severity publicly while privately thinking of his 'unconquered' judgement as a 'malign power' (*DD*, pp. 103. 107), and concluding that Daniel thinks 'too much of himself' (*DD*, p. 330). But even these negative responses introduce beneficial self-reflection; as the narrator puts it when Daniel and Gwendolen meet again, 'the struggle of mind attending a conscious error had wakened something like a new soul' (*DD*, p. 332). She has not exactly accepted their judgements of her, but the elimination of the 'crude self-confidence' is itself a major step (*DD*, p. 332).

Gwendolen's subsequent moral growth is mediated above all through her relationship with Daniel. She begins to doubt her previous standard of self-approval, which depended on the attitude of men flirting with her. What good is such admiration, she asks herself, when there is 'some standard in Deronda's mind which measured her into littleness?' (*DD*, p. 418). Yet given this powerful role, Daniel's instructions remain deeply vague:

> 'Then tell me what better I can do', said Gwendolen, insistently.
> 'Many things. Look on other lives besides your own. See what their troubles are and how they are borne. Try to care about something in this vast world besides the gratification of small selfish desires. Try to care for what is best in thought and action – something that is good apart from the accidents of your own lot.' (*DD*, p. 446)

Daniel's point here is that Gwendolen needs to find something she can care about for its own sake, a characterisation of intrinsic value he comes at from several different directions – something valuable for reasons outside selfish desire, or good apart from contingent circumstances, or simply because it is 'the best in thought and action'. And the piece of practical advice he has about how to try to find something to care about in this way is to develop the ability to sympathise – to find things that others care about. Such a project promises autonomy as well, insofar as it will make Gwendolen less vulnerable to the 'puerile stupidity of a dominant impulse' like the one that made her gamble (*DD*, p. 11).

Thus at the end of the novel, Gwendolen has fully internalised Daniel's judgement; he has become an 'outer conscience' for her (*DD*, p. 763). She takes on a new and specific duty, being kind to her family, which Daniel agrees is a 'duty that cannot be doubtful' (*DD*, p. 769). Having developed the ability to sympathise with him, she is 'dislodged from her supremacy in her own world', and thus feelings that could have become jealousy or anger are 'quelled' into 'self-humiliation' (*DD*, p. 804). In a concluding uplift, Gwendolen's final scene shows her promising her mother that everything will be fine (*DD*, p. 807). In a broad way, then, *Daniel Deronda* echoes *Felix Holt*. But a number of philosophically impactful differences between the progression of Esther Lyon and Gwendolen Harleth emerge when they are compared closely.

To begin with something small and concrete, it is worth considering the difference between the initial experiences of shame – between feeling shame because someone inadvertently finds your copy of Byron, feeling shame because someone sees you gambling, and feeling shame because your musical performance isn't as good as someone else's. Thomason makes a helpful set of distinctions for making sense of these different kinds of shame. Even if we agree that a moral capacity such as a liability to feel shame is valuable, this does not necessarily contribute to the value of any particular social practice of shaming, among which Thomason distinguishes three types: the invitation to feel shame, shaming and stigmatising.[41] An invitation to feel shame is importantly private; it is a response to some person's flawed moral action that tries to bring the flaw to their attention. Shaming and stigmatising, on the other hand, are public; their force is not primarily directed towards an attempt to persuade the moral agent in question, but are instead about putting that person's action or identity up for public view and ridicule. Thomason contends that all three responses are ultimately morally flawed, which is to say that while it might be morally admirable to feel shame, it is almost never so to shame someone else. Even an invitation to feel shame carries too much of the arrogance of the shameless agent – 'inviting other people to feel shame for the purposes of self-improvement', Thomason argues, 'undermines our own humility when it comes to our own characters'.[42] The decision to shame furthermore assumes a 'moral executive right: we are responsible for *enforcing* community values as well as upholding them'.[43]

To the modern reader, that seems exactly the problem with Felix Holt. What is striking about his treatment of Esther is, first of all, its publicity – he shames her for reading Byron not when she is alone, but when she is in front of her father. In fact, Felix subsequently appeals to Mr Lyon: 'Ask your father what those old persecuted emigrant Puritans would have done with fine-lady wives' (*FH*, p. 71). The fact that he does not wait for privacy and attempts to enlist Esther's own family against her reveals how little respect he has for Esther, and his openly admitted desire to make her feel ashamed demonstrates how unprepared he is to admit their fundamental equality. Felix's moral arrogance is made all the more prominent by the fact that Esther's slip was inadvertent; all she did was keep a book that Felix disapproves of in her sewing-basket. Keeping these issues in mind makes Felix's decision to go out of his way to visit Esther's house and give her an additional sermon on her moral flaws look comically arrogant (*FH*, p. 121).

The moments of initial shame for Gwendolen are radically different. First, all Daniel does when he sees her gambling is look at her; he says nothing and does nothing, and merely the expression of judgement in his glance is enough to make Gwendolen reckless. Moreover, when he buys and returns the necklace to her, the moment is entirely private: Gwendolen reads the attached note by herself. And then too the note is largely free of moral critique, certainly in contrast to Felix's heavy hand; all Daniel does is say that the necklace is returned to Miss Harleth 'with the hope that she will not again risk the loss of it' (*DD*, p. 18). Klesmer might seem to be a harder case because his comments are not private; they are listening to music after a dinner party. But fundamentally important is the fact that Gwendolen asks for his opinion: 'I should be very much obliged to him for telling me the worst [. . .] I daresay I have been extremely ill taught, in additional to having no talent' (*DD*, p. 49). The fact that Klesmer goes on to agree – 'yes, it is true, you have not been well taught' – instead of politely contradicting her is something quite different from Felix's arrogance.

The claim that this initial contrast between the two novels is significant gains support from a second and related contrast. Like Esther, Gwendolen experiences a second moment of shame at the hands of her exemplars; unlike Esther, this is not because the exemplar in any way seeks it out. Klesmer in particular does as much as he can to keep his opinions about Gwendolen's musical ability to himself; it is only after she seeks his advice on the possibilities of a professional career in music that he decides to share his full assessment of her limitations and the crushing shame that comes with that assessment. But even while Klesmer strikes a tone of superiority in justifying himself by saying, 'I was bound to put the truth, the unvarnished truth before you', he concludes by saying, 'If you take that more courageous resolve I will ask leave to shake hands with you on the strength of our freemasonry, where we are all vowed to the service of art, and to serve her by helping every fellow-servant' (*DD*, p. 260). Here is the humility Felix so clearly lacks; while no false modesty prevents Klesmer from acknowledging his superiority to Gwendolen in musical ability, he knows that ultimately he and Gwendolen are fundamentally equal in their pursuit of a shared ideal, a fact he emphasises in offering to shake her hand. What these differences suggest is that in between *Felix Holt* and *Daniel Deronda*, Eliot had thought about shaming as a moral practice, and concluded that while shame might indeed have moral value, the act of deliberate shaming did not.

One might note, too, the fact that Felix seems to have been divided, becoming Klesmer and Daniel. That fact produces a seemingly odd redundancy in the early parts of Gwendolen's narrative, where Eliot introduces multiple scenes of initiating shame that seem unnecessary for the process of moral transformation she depicts. What philosophical purpose is served by this addition? Or, to put a finer point on it, what is Herr Klesmer doing in this novel? We can get started on an answer to this question by noting a fundamental difference in the forms of shame they induce in Gwendolen. Her shame with regard to gambling is distinctively moral, and arguably prudential; Daniel makes her feel she should not have been so careless with her money. By contrast, the shame that Klesmer induces is specific to music; he makes her recognise that she is not as talented as she thought she was. As it happens, that tracks exactly a distinction that John Rawls makes between 'natural shame' and 'moral shame'.[44] 'Natural shame', Rawls explains, arises 'from the injury to our self-esteem owing to our not having or failing to exercise certain excellences'.[45] But which excellences matter in this way is up to us: 'Those with no musical ability do not strive to be musicians and feel no shame for this lack.'[46] In order for natural shame to be a possibility, a goal requiring a skill in its pursuit must be an element in our self-conception. Conversely, moral shame is more general: it pertains to those excellences that form the necessary conditions for carrying out any life plan effectively.

The distinction matters because of the way it inflects Gwendolen's relationship with the two men and her corresponding moral development. Recall that for Esther, the expansion of her sympathy and the acquisition of specific practical interests were combined; learning to care about politics was fundamentally the same gesture as learning to sympathise with Felix. Here, however, Eliot has split the two processes: Gwendolen's relationship with Klesmer becomes focused on the pursuit of concrete goals, while her relationship with Daniel becomes more and more abstract, involving large questions about moral awareness. Even at the end of the novel, Daniel refuses to give her specific goals, while Klesmer has faded out of Gwendolen's life. I want to suggest that this is not an accident. One reason to question whether Esther's life was a life of freedom was the worry that the goals she took up were not actually goals she had given to herself – the goal of radical political reform via a life in a craftsman's household was much more Felix's project than hers. To address this worry requires the moral exemplar and voice of public reason, then, not to give any specific content to its call for a life of sympathy and autonomy; the sympathetic perspective that Daniel embodies can be a test of the moral value of some specific content, but it cannot yield that content itself. The ambiguity in Daniel's koan-like predictions to Gwendolen – 'You will find your life growing like a plant' (*DD*, p. 769) – stems from the need to negotiate this problem.

If I am correct about Eliot's analysis of the moral issues, it sheds some light on a formal issue that has long worried critics – the relationship between Gwendolen's story and Daniel's story, or the English plot and the Jewish plot. Famously, F. R. Leavis found the Jewish plot confusing and unnecessary, and argued that it should have been removed, presumably with Gwendolen marrying Daniel at the end.[47] Should Eliot have done so, the product would have been a novel much closer to *Felix Holt* – a story in which the heroine's overcoming of egoism was linked to her eventual marriage to a husband embodying concrete political ideals in which she could find clear goals. So Eliot's insistence on keeping Daniel's own acquisition of concrete goals separate from his role in the process of Gwendolen's sympathetic awakening suggests that she saw a limitation in the model that *Felix Holt* exemplified. In that sense, the separation of the Jewish plot is not accidental but essential: for Daniel to have included Gwendolen in his own particular projects would have prevented her from finding her own. Klesmer in turn continues as a central character while Gwendolen is considering a plan of life centred on music, but precisely because his own self is so thoroughly constituted by that set of goals, he cannot be a reliable guide in Gwendolen's pursuit of a broader sympathy. Thus, he moves out of Gwendolen's life – quite literally, marrying someone else and moving to London – at the moment when her moral development reaches a stage through which he cannot help her.

But one might object that *Daniel Deronda* really divided Felix into three figures, not just two. In addition to Daniel and Klesmer, there is also and importantly Grandcourt – another figure who shames Gwendolen, but the only one of the three who actually marries her. Yet Grandcourt's shaming is of another kind entirely: far from inspiring moral reform, Grandcourt uses shame as a means of torture and control. Thus Grandcourt's presence in the novel represents a further objection to the moral psychology in *Felix Holt*, implying that shame is not actually morally beneficial, but a source of self-hatred that moral agents would be better off without.

To briefly recall the plot, the central cause of shame in the relationship between Grandcourt and Gwendolen is the fact that Grandcourt seduced Lydia Glasher, another man's wife, and had four children with her prior to meeting Gwendolen. Refusing to marry Lydia, Grandcourt instead proposes to Gwendolen, but before Gwendolen accepts him Lydia confronts her and demands that Gwendolen turn down the marriage. Gwendolen agrees, but then with some trepidation and an eye towards her mother's precarious finances goes back on her promise. Strikingly, somehow this fact becomes more shameful than Grandcourt's own failures; Gwendolen becomes paralysed by her own broken promise, and 'any endurance seems easier than the mortal humiliation of confessing that she knew all before she married him, and in marrying him had broken her word' (*DD*, p. 424). Yet

Grandcourt is in fact perfectly aware of Gwendolen's moral failure and sees it both as a source of erotic interest and a means of additional control – indeed, the former because of the latter.

As a number of critics have noted, this turns Grandcourt into a dark shadow of Daniel, a figure who calls into question the moral benefits of the self-questioning that Daniel induces.[48] This becomes particularly clear when Grandcourt writes a will naming his illegitimate children as his heirs and has it shown to Gwendolen, thus letting her know that he knows that she knows of his earlier affair (*DD*, p. 595). That is, Grandcourt knows that Gwendolen married him over her better self and in service of financial need, a fact he enjoys displaying to her. It increases her self-disgust: 'Already she was undergoing some hardening effect from feeling that she was under eyes which saw her past actions solely in the light of her lowest motives' (*DD*, p. 602). Yet she cannot resist Grandcourt, both because she feels she has 'no right to complain of her contract', and – more disturbingly – because of Daniel: 'always among the images that drove her back to submission was Deronda' (*DD*, p. 603). Knowing both that Grandcourt thinks she wants to have an affair with Daniel and that Daniel would be horrified if this were her motive, Gwendolen is paralysed, wanting to become closer to Daniel but feeling unable to do so. The shame she feels because Daniel wants her to be a good person and because Grandcourt believes she is not merge into the same experience.

As Martha Nussbaum has argued, the idea that moral reform and growth hinge on self-abasement redirects the energy of the self backwards.[49] One ends up punishing oneself more than helping others, and the self-anger introduces an additional obstacle to actually helping people. This is exactly what happens to Gwendolen: feeling guilty for taking what she feels to be Lydia Glasher's place and money, Gwendolen subsequently directs all that moral energy towards self-punishment, and ends up actually doing nothing to help Lydia. Grandcourt's ability to take advantage of this process, forcing Gwendolen to punish herself further, signals Eliot's awareness of this dimension of shame. And this is why Daniel's advice to Gwendolen combines so many different moral ideas. On the one hand, her remorse is 'the precious sign of a recoverable nature [. . .] It marked her off from the criminals whose only regret is failure in securing their evil wish' (*DD*, p. 697). But on the other, Daniel continually seeks to turn Gwendolen away from the focus on her guilt and point her feelings towards other people and practical good in the world. Recommending that she 'change the bias of her fear', he hopes it can become a tool to 'make consequences passionately present' (*DD*, p. 452). And after Grandcourt's death, when Gwendolen is inclined towards 'scourging' herself (*DD*, p. 767), his concrete recommendations all involve minimising her sense of remorse; he concludes that she is in no way responsible for Grandcourt's death (*DD*, p. 699) and has no duty to decline her inheritance (*DD*, p. 768). The transformation of shame into a capacity for 'penitential, loving purpose' will reveal itself in finding 'unexpected satisfactions' in projects carried out with awareness of the 'newly-opening needs' of others (*DD*, p. 769). Shame is not beneficial in and for itself; instead, it is insofar as a liability to shame is a constitutive feature of sympathy that it proves morally valuable, and moving past the shame into sympathy is essential for full moral agency.

But more important than the challenge posed by Grandcourt's shaming of Gwendolen is the problem posed by Grandcourt himself. The argument developed here has been that, for Eliot, shame is a constitutive feature of sympathy, while in turn sympathy is a necessary feature of autonomy. Only through an acknowledgement of the perspectives of others can an agent develop the ability to regard ends as intrinsically valuable, and only through the acquisition of such ends can agents make their lives into a coherent whole and not simply a collection of conflicting desires. But one might very well question whether sympathy is quite as necessary for unity as Eliot thinks, or – put another way – whether the unity made available by sympathy is quite as valuable as her narratives suggest. Debates in meta-ethics term this the 'schmagency' objection: perhaps it is true that selflessness is necessary for full agency, such writers concede, but then might one not prefer to achieve 'schmagency', which is simply as much unity as is possible without respecting the needs of others?[50] To put the question in Eliot's terms, is there no such thing as 'serene wickedness' – an evil at peace with itself (*DD*, p. 403)? Certainly, it seems naive to deny that such agents are possible.

Eliot's answer to this sceptical challenge has three dimensions, two of which form long-standing principles in her work. First, Eliot consistently represents sympathy as not merely ethically but practically necessary; achieving one's goals often involves understanding the minds of others, and egoists often end up frustrating themselves because they lack this capacity. As the narrator puts it in *Daniel Deronda*, 'There is no escaping the fact that want of sympathy condemns us to a corresponding stupidity' (*DD*, p. 596). Thus, for instance, Matthew Jermyn 'always blundered when he wanted to be delicate or magnanimous' because he inadvertently tries 'to soothe others by praising himself' (*FH*, pp. 114–15) and Tito Melema in *Romola* cannot help but 'overestimate the persuasiveness of his own arguments', because he is 'shut up in the narrowness that hedges in all merely clever, unimpassioned men'.[51] Thus sympathy is in part prudentially necessary, simply because the achievement of our goals depends to a large extent on other people.

Egoism impairs prudence for a second reason too, and in a way that Korsgaard would easily recognise: it prevents agents from making sacrifices for long-term goals. A scene near the end of *Daniel Deronda* offers a contained parable for this idea. Mr Lapidoth, who has lived 'a lazy selfish life' that has eliminated his capacity for 'ruth, compunction, or any unselfish regret', forms a plan to con Daniel Deronda, who is in love with Lapidoth's daughter Mirah. But he finds himself distracted when Daniel happens to leave a ring on a table while visiting the Lapidoths:

> Its value was certainly below the smallest of the imaginary sums that his purpose fluctuated between; but then it was before him as a solid fact, and his desire at once leaped into the thought (not yet an intention) that if he were quietly to pocket that ring and walk away he would have the means of comfortable escape from present restraint [. . .] However he was resolved to go down; but – by no distinct change of resolution, rather by a dominance of desire, like the thirst of the drunkard – it so happened that in passing the table his fingers fell noiselessly on the ring, and he found himself in the passage with the ring in his hand. It followed that he put on his hat and quitted the house. (*DD*, p. 790)

Lapidoth has a clear prudential goal: to extort money from Daniel by threatening Mirah. The amount of money he plans to extort is certainly higher than the value of the ring. Yet when faced with an easy opportunity to steal the ring – even though it means abandoning his plan – Lapidoth is unable to restrain himself. And this is a point Eliot is careful about – it's not that Lapidoth decides to change his plan and grab the easy money; in fact he decides the opposite. But his reflective self-control is no match for his desires and his body, and so he finds himself against himself stealing the ring. The crime is essentially heteronomous.

But Grandcourt presents a tougher challenge. It's not that he entirely lacks the stupidity that comes with a lack of sympathy, or the failure of prudence that comes with a lack of full autonomy. As Eliot suggests at a number of moments, he does not fully grasp what is going in Gwendolen's mind; he believes her to be jealous of Lydia Glasher, not remorseful, and her remorse 'was as much out of his imagination as the other side of the moon' (*DD*, p. 596). Then, too, he is both lazy and abrupt; as his friend and servant Lush thinks at one point, 'there was no telling what might turn up in the slowly-churning chances of his mind' (*DD*, p. 157). But he is in some sense sympathetic and prudent enough; he has enough understanding of Gwendolen's mind to be able to shame her, and enough prudence to escape his debts when an easy opportunity presents itself. And of course, he is utterly without shame, a fact that makes him all the more effective in overriding opposition to his desires from those – like Lydia – who try to shame him. This is the challenge of schmagency: why should one care about autonomy, and thus the requisite sympathy and shame, if we can have a high degree of self-control and all the benefits that come from selfish action?

Christine Korsgaard's own answer to the question of 'serene wickedness' borrows from Plato's account of the various kinds of misguided constitutions for a city. The greatest failed constitution is rule by the 'tyrannical soul': Korsgaard explains: 'In a horrifying imitation of the unity and simplicity that characterise justice [. . .] the tyrannical soul is governed by some nightmarish erotic desire, which subordinates the entire soul to its purposes, leaving the person an absolute slave to a single dominating obsession' (*SC*, pp. 169–70). As opposed to evil as weakness – a person slipping, driven by a wanton appetite – the tyrant imagines evil as single-minded, unconstrained by the moral restrictions that bind the weak.

The philosophical task is to explain how this is not full agency. Korsgaard explains:

> The tyrannical person does not really choose actions [. . .] [because he] doesn't choose *an act for the sake of an end*, the whole package as something worth doing. There's one end [. . .] or act that he is going to pursue or do *no matter what*, and it rules him. And for him that end makes anything worth doing, anything at all, and that's a fact that is settled in advance of reflection [. . .] As I imagine the tyrant, his relation to his obsession is like a psychotic's relation to his delusion: he is prepared to organise everything else around it, even at the expense of a loss of his grip on reality, on the world. (*SC*, p. 172)

The point is that the tyrant is not actually choosing acts to perform, but is rather driven by a single overwhelming desire. Given that this is the case, his actions are not representative of full agency: 'the tyrannised soul can never separate himself from *one* of his impulses' (*SC*, p. 173). Thus, if the tyrant is capable of the limited agency that consists in finding means to his ends, he is not capable of the full agency that would let him consider which ends to have.

In the light of Korsgaard's argument, Grandcourt's interest in Gwendolen takes on a new layer of meaning. It might sound strange at first to say that he is obsessed with her, but we should recall that he follows her to Germany and back without ever saying or even possibly deciding that this is what he is going to do. The narrative leaves it to Lush to explain; when Grandcourt begins complaining about his company at Diplow and announces a desire to go sailing in the Baltic, Lush knows to interpret this as a desire to pursue Gwendolen (*DD*, p. 158). Perhaps more strikingly, for all his desire to exert control, when Grandcourt does make decisions they are usually reactions to Gwendolen's actions. None is more obvious in this light than the cause of his death – his decision to take Gwendolen out by herself in a small sailing boat. The real reason for the decision is not that he enjoys her company, but that he wants to keep Gwendolen from meeting Daniel: 'what he took for certain [. . .] was that Gwendolen was now counting on an interview with Deronda whenever her husband's back was turned' (*DD*, p. 677). The scene reveals how little freedom Grandcourt actually has. While he can appear self-controlled – it was 'true that he had set his mind on this boating, and carried out his purpose' (*DD*, p. 680) – in fact an underlying desire is at work: 'he was ruling that Gwendolen should go with him' (*DD*, p. 681). Defined by his desire to possess and torture Gwendolen, he is driven to act in irrational ways whenever that desire is threatened, a fact that the novel highlights by hinting that taking the small boat out was obviously risky: 'Some suggestions were proffered concerning a possible change in the breeze, but Grandcourt's manner made the speakers understand [. . .] that he knew better than they' (*DD*, p. 681). Thus the limited self-coherence and autonomy that Grandcourt has comes at a high price, as it is only achieved through the obsessive domination of a single desire that overcomes prudential conclusions whenever necessary.

* * *

In sum, then, Eliot's account of the sources of normativity was both sophisticated and dynamic. Finding initial expression in *Felix Holt*, the account matured significantly in *Daniel Deronda*, where Eliot changed significantly her explanation of the moral nature of shame and turned to the hard question of the apparently self-controlled sadistic egoist. My goal in explaining Eliot's view has been to reconstitute her thought in a way that lets her speak from her time to ours, since the problem of the sources of normativity remains just as alive as it was in the nineteenth century. That requires a balancing act between philosophy and the history of ideas, drawing connections between her views and our problems while simultaneously acknowledging the distance between her intellectual world and ours. The hope is to minimise the possibility of an arbitrary connection, a moment where a writer from the past seems to speak deeply to an issue we care about, but which falls apart upon closer examination. As Chapter 3 argued, there is no simple methodological principle that would fully insure a critic against arbitrary anachronism, and I must leave it to the reader to decide whether I successfully negotiate such problems here.

But a related problem might seem more pressing. I have marked clearly points where Eliot drew from or disagreed with her contemporaries, such as Sidgwick, Darwin and Green. But I have much more rarely looked for disagreements between her and later philosophers, such as Christine Korsgaard, Krista Thomason and Martha Nussbaum. Instead, I have used this later group of thinkers as interpretive aids, noting where their ideas clarify Eliot's thinking and where Eliot's ideas seem – to use a loaded word – to anticipate their later developments. An interlocutor might well press on this point: why, exactly, is it worth pointing out when one writer 'anticipates' another? Answering this question requires stepping back to the broader methodological questions of the project, and indeed to the basic question of what it is exactly that literary criticism can do.

Notes

1. George Eliot, 1876–77 Notebook, Warwickshire County Record Office, George Eliot Papers.
2. Mill, *Utilitarianism and Other Essays*, p. 298.
3. Christine Korsgaard, *The Sources of Normativity* (Cambridge: Cambridge University Press, 1996), p. 9.
4. Mill, *Utilitarianism and Other Essays*, p. 308.
5. Henry Sidgwick, *The Methods of Ethics* (Indianapolis: Hackett, 1981), p. 388. Subsequent citations, abbreviated *ME*, are given in parentheses in the text.
6. This phrase is from the dramatic conclusion of the first edition of the *Methods* (Cambridge: Macmillan, 1874), p. 473, and was revised in tone (though not in fundamental philosophical content) in later editions. See Bart Schultz, *Eye of the Universe* (Cambridge: Cambridge University Press, 2009), for a treatment of Sidgwick that links his philosophical argument with this aspect of his life.
7. George Eliot, *Scenes of Clerical Life* (Oxford: Oxford University Press, 2015), p. 251.

8. André Gide, *The Immoralist*, trans. Stanley Appelbaum (New York: Dover, 1996); Friedrich Nietzsche, *Thus Spake Zarathustra*, trans. Walter Kaufman (New York: Modern Library, 1995).
9. As mentioned in the last chapter, this is a key idea in Plato's 'Protagoras', 358d.
10. Miller, *The Burdens of Perfection*, p. 74. As is probably clear, this is in significant disagreement with Miller's claim that Eliot 'would agree with John McDowell' that 'the question "Why should I conform to the dictates of morality?" [. . .] has no answer'. What can happen, McDowell and Miller go on to say, is virtuous habituation – the bringing up of someone in a certain view of the good life. As will become clear, I think this makes Eliot into more of an Aristotelian and less of a Kantian than she really was.
11. Krista Thomason, *Naked: The Dark Side of Shame and Moral Life* (Oxford: Oxford University Press, 2018), p. 12.
12. This aligns with Alexander Welsh's suggestion in a much different context that the novel is Eliot's 'last, marvelous effort to discover [. . .] in consciousness itself, some authority for individual behaviour'. Alexander Welsh, *George Eliot and Blackmail* (Cambridge, MA: Harvard University Press, 1985), p. 329.
13. Derek Parfit, *On What Matters* (New York: Oxford University Press, 2011), p. xii.
14. Jerome Schneewind, *Sidgwick's Ethics and Victorian Moral Philosophy* (Oxford: Clarendon Press, 1977), p. 353.
15. Schneewind, *Sidgwick's Ethics*, p. 367.
16. See Christine Korsgaard, 'The Myth of Egoism', in *The Constitution of Agency* (New York: Oxford University Press, 2008), pp. 69–100.
17. Christine Korsgaard, *Self-Constitution: Agency, Identity, and Integrity* (New York: Oxford University Press, 2009), p. 53. Subsequent citations, abbreviated *SC*, are given in parentheses in the text.
18. David Velleman, *Self to Self* (Cambridge: Cambridge University Press, 2006), p. 22.
19. William Mander, *British Idealism: A History* (Oxford: Oxford University Press, 2011), p. 205.
20. F. H. Bradley, *Ethical Studies* (Oxford: Clarendon Press, 1876), p. 168.
21. Bradley, *Ethical Studies*, p. 304.
22. Edith Simcox, *The George Eliot Letters*, ed. Gordon S. Haight, vol. IX (New Haven: Yale University Press, 1954–78), p. 217. See also *A Monument to the Memory of George Eliot: Edith J. Simcox's Autobiography of a Shirtmaker*, ed. Constance M. Fulmer and Margaret E. Barfield (New York: Garland, 1998), pp. 26–7.
23. Bradley, *Ethical Studies*, p. 275.
24. See, in particular, Alan Mintz, *George Eliot and the Novel of Vocation* (Cambridge, MA: Harvard University Press, 1978). I discuss this scholarship more fully in my article 'Sympathy, Vocation, and Moral Deliberation in George Eliot', *ELH* 85.2 (2018), pp. 501–32.

25. This is, of course, a key claim in both *Past and Present* and *Sartor Resartus*.
26. For a discussion of the Idealists' debt to Carlyle, see Mander, *British Idealism*, pp. 25–7.
27. William Clifford, *The Ethics of Belief and Other Essays*, ed. Timothy J. Madigan (New York: Prometheus, 1999), pp. 61–2.
28. Kwame Anthony Appiah puts the point aptly: 'the dictum of "doing what comes naturally", we can agree, provides no guidance by itself'. Kwame Anthony Appiah, *Experiments in Ethics* (Cambridge, MA: Harvard University Press, 2008), p. 122. Recognition of the problem came, naturally enough, from the religiously minded 'Intuitionist' thinkers who formed the main rival school to Mill's utilitarianism; see, for instance, Lord Selborne's contribution to *A Modern Symposium: The Influence Upon Morality of a Decline in Religious Belief* (Detroit: Rose-Belford, 1878), pp. 191–204.
29. Charles Darwin, *The Descent of Man, And Selection in Relation to Sex* (Princeton: Princeton University Press, 1981), p. 71. Subsequent citations, abbreviated *DM*, are given in parentheses in the text.
30. K. K. Collins, 'G.H. Lewes Revisited: George Eliot and the Moral Sense', *Victorian Studies* 21.4 (1978), pp. 463–92.
31. Collins, 'G.H. Lewes Revisited', p. 485. Subsequent citations, abbreviated *LR*, are given in parentheses in the text.
32. Lewes engages in a bit of light plagiarism in developing this point. His sentence reads: 'Such prevision may be of the highest moral order, so that – to use Kant's fine phrase – "man refuses to violate in his own person the dignity of Humanity" – refuses to do what he thinks to be wrong.' Meanwhile Darwin, in a passage quoted earlier, has this: 'I am the supreme judge of my own conduct, and in the words of Kant, I will not in my own person violate the dignity of humanity' (*DM*, p. 86). But to the contemporary academic, Lewes quoting one source via a more easily accessible second source may be him at his most relatable.
33. George Eliot, *Felix Holt*, ed. Lynda Mugglestone (New York: Penguin, 1995), p. 77. Subsequent citations, abbreviated *FH*, are given in parentheses in the text.
34. Velleman, *Self to Self*, pp. 45–70.
35. Thomason, *Naked*, p. 100.
36. Thomason, *Naked*, p. 149.
37. I allude here to a famous passage from the 'Natural History of German Life', where Eliot writes: 'a picture of human life such as a great artist can give, surprises even the trivial and the selfish into that attention to what is apart from themselves, which may be called the raw material of moral sentiment'. George Eliot, *Essays*, ed. Thomas Pinney (London: Routledge, 1963), p. 270.
38. The word 'bondage' is more literal than it might seem; Harold's first wife – married when he lived in Smyrna, before the events of the novel – was in fact a slave (*FH*, p. 421).

39. As Andrew Miller puts a similar worry, 'Given the patent and gouging costs of such a conception of shame [. . .] what appeal could it possibly have?' (*The Burdens of Perfection*, p. 175). I will argue that its appeal stems from Eliot's attempts to acknowledge and respond to just exactly those 'patent and gouging' costs.
40. George Eliot, *Daniel Deronda*, ed. Terence Cave (New York: Penguin, 2003), p. 18, emphasis in original. Subsequent citations, abbreviated *DD*, are given in parentheses in the text.
41. Thomason, *Naked*, p. 179.
42. Thomason, *Naked*, p. 186.
43. Thomason, *Naked*, p. 203.
44. See John Rawls, *A Theory of Justice* (Cambridge, MA: Harvard University Press, 199), p. 389.
45. Rawls, *A Theory of Justice*, p. 389.
46. Rawls, *A Theory of Justice*, p. 390.
47. See F. R. Leavis, *The Great Tradition* (London: Penguin, 1962), pp. 97–103.
48. Alexander Welsh puts the point aptly: 'if the novel were a game of chess, Deronda would have to be identified as the white mailer' (*George Eliot and Blackmail*, p. 298). But see also Ann Cvetkovich, *Mixed Feelings: Feminism, Mass Culture, and Victorian Sensationalism* (New Brunswick, NJ: Rutgers University Press, 1992).
49. Martha Nussbaum, *Anger and Forgiveness* (Oxford: Oxford University Press, 2016), p. 130.
50. See David Enoch, 'Agency, Shmagency: Why Normativity Won't Come from What Is Constitutive of Action', *Philosophical Review* 115 (2006), pp. 169–98.
51. George Eliot, *Romola*, ed. Dorothea Barrett (New York: Penguin, 1996), p. 282.

Chapter 5

Everyday Aesthetics and the Experience of the Profound

In 'Formalism as the Fear of Ideas', his review of Caroline Levine's *Forms*, Michael Clune takes Levine specifically and literary critics generally to task for merely pointing out moments where literary authors 'anticipate' subsequent developments in various theoretical fields, and for not daring to go further and argue for substantive claims in those fields. He writes:

> We should attend closely to Levine's claim that the nineteenth-century poet anticipates twentieth-century social science. The term *anticipation* appears designed to free the critic from the kind of work that a term like *influence* requires. Whereas a claim of influence necessitates carefully uncovering causal links between a literary work and the various social scientists whose thinking was shaped by it, a claim of anticipation requires merely demonstrating that a certain literary idea resembles a later scientific idea.[1]

Merely noting 'resemblance', Clune goes on to argue, does a disservice to the real power of literary ideas. Citing the example of H. G. Wells's invention of time travel and the influence of the concept on theoretical physics, Clune points out that 'Literature is full of the most astonishing ideas on every imaginable topic', and literary critics interested in interdisciplinary research and connections between literary study and ideas and other fields should not limit themselves to merely noting resemblances – we need to take the next step and look for the open discovery of new ideas.[2]

Clune's point is well taken, but his dismissal of the emphasis on 'anticipation' moves too quickly. As Julie Orlemanski puts it (in a phrase I have quoted once already), 'I am inclined to give more credence to *what we do* in our discipline than to what we say about what we do.'[3] The prevalence of this interpretive technique reveals something about the experience of literature, and it would be too hasty to abandon it in pursuit of more expansive forms of interdisciplinarity. Criticism that notes the way a writer anticipates later theoretical developments reflects at heart the basic impulse to connect the ideas in literature to issues that readers are concerned with now, and is thus simply the latest iteration in a lengthy tradition of reading for the content, even when it calls itself reading for the form. Insisting that such criticism take a further step and seek to innovate in other theoretical fields misunderstands what is really going on in this kind of scholarship. It may seem to be justifying itself in terms of the exterior discipline, but in fact the justification is aesthetic. Such criticism really shows how to find interesting and thus enjoy a given work.

Developing this claim will require returning to the issues in the philosophy of art that Chapter 1 introduced. There, I dealt with the relationship between form and content as an interpretive matter, trying to say what exactly literary content is and what it means to read for it. But as we saw, claims in the philosophy of art turned out to be central to the debate about interpretive method. In particular, formalists such as Cleanth Brooks and A. C. Bradley rested the argument that paraphrase is a heresy on the idea that the unique experience that literature offers is the union between form and content. Thus paraphrasing a work of literature ignored the only thing of real value that the literary text offers. Insisting on the possibilities of paraphrase turned out to be a contention that there is more than one feature of a text and more than one experience it can offer that makes it worth reading and worthy of the title 'literature'. In other words, it is to challenge the formalist account of the literary and emphasise the possibilities of aesthetic pluralism.

This approach will be familiar and tolerable to some more than others. The renewal of aesthetics in literary studies in recent years by a variety of scholars has made familiar the idea that there are alternatives to the Kantian notion of the aesthetic as a distinct realm of disinterested pleasure, a group of approaches usefully grouped under the heading 'everyday aesthetics'.[4] Similarly, the last generation of the philosophy of art has largely given up the formalist account, and scholars such as Noël Carroll and Peter Kivy have significantly enriched the description of the varieties of aesthetic experience; to read philosopher Nick Zangwill's rueful remark that 'Formalism has fallen on hard times' alongside the resurgence of formalism in literary studies is to be struck by the still-significant differences between the fields in the humanities.[5] Although these two approaches have not generally drawn on each other, they are broadly in sympathy, and in what follows I will indicate points of connection.

My own argument is sympathetic with both lines of scholarship, with several changes in emphasis. First, the defences of the aesthetic in literary studies have generally proceeded by showing that the realm of aesthetic experience is not inherently conservative – that there can be, in Isobel Armstrong's concise formulation, a 'radical aesthetic'.[6] They have thus taken the challenge to be met as the need to demonstrate the variety of relationships between aesthetics and political life. While persuasive, this defence concedes too much to formalist definitions of art. First, it concedes the idea that there is something broadly like an 'aesthetic' realm of human experience, an account that will not serve particularly well in explaining the specific pleasure that comes in encountering an exciting idea. If an umbrella term is absolutely necessary – I shall argue in a moment that we should avoid this attempt at distillation as much as possible – something much broader, along the lines of simply imaginative pleasure, would be more useful. Second, the idea that political critiques of the aesthetic are best met by counter-examples misses an important step in the way those critiques got off the ground. Formalist accounts of aesthetic value give artistic experience an ethereal air that in turn enables evaluative scepticism; without that broad sceptical attitude towards the very possibility of aesthetic value, it would have been much more difficult if not impossible to argue that the variety of imaginative pleasures grouped under the category of the 'aesthetic' could somehow as such have a particular political disposition.

As for the philosophers of art, my major revision will be simple but perhaps surprising: I think that they have not recognised the interpretive practices of their own discipline. In particular, I think that methods in the history of philosophy reveal interesting answers to several key questions in the debate about how to read for the ideas in literature. We saw this to a certain extent in Chapter 3, where it turned out that one of the best reasons for combining historical and rational reconstruction of a philosophical text was that it was a good way to find its ideas interesting. And I shall return to this archive again, since methods in the history of philosophy offer a valuable resource for assessing whether it matters that literary texts often don't provide arguments for the claims they make.

Since the argument will thus move over a wide range of issues and into several different scholarly debates, it will be useful to outline its steps. The first will briefly consider Immanuel Kant's *Critique of Judgement*, the key source for the formalist account of aesthetic experience, in order to consider what supports the aesthetic formalist gives for her view and how the pluralist might meet them; much of this section will be familiar to those interested in the topic. The second will turn to aesthetic scepticism in literary criticism and its close relationship to the political critique of the aesthetic; I will show that formalism played an under-appreciated role in motivating that scepticism in the first place and that pluralism offers a promising way out. The third will borrow from work in moral philosophy to develop that pluralism, advancing the importance of thick concepts in aesthetics, and the fourth will explicate a particular thick concept and corresponding aesthetic experience: the 'profound'. The fifth and sixth will return to the political critique and particularly its powerful iteration in Sianne Ngai's work, and contend that a pluralist aesthetics is not as vulnerable to the critique as formalist aesthetics have been.

Pluralism vs. Formalism

One feature of this approach to aesthetic evaluation is that there is a certain amount of collapsing of the borders between aesthetic experience and other kinds of pleasure. After all, a work of art can be profound, but so can persons, conversations and articles in theoretical physics. To accept aesthetic pluralism is similarly to think that aesthetic evaluation is rather messy. So it is worth recalling the argument for the distinctiveness of aesthetic experience in the first place, to see what exactly is involved in accepting this messier version. The *locus classicus* for this argument is Immanuel Kant's *Critique of Judgement*.

In the First Moment of the 'Analytic of the Beautiful', Kant is interested in distinguishing three different kinds of 'delight': the 'agreeable', the 'good' and the 'beautiful'.[7] Only the beautiful will please 'disinterestedly'; the good pleases because it requires cognition of an object under a concept – what is that thing? Ah, it's a good *chair* – while the 'agreeable' pleases because it meets the subject's inclination. The main example of the agreeable that Kant seems to have in mind is food; he writes, 'So far as the interest of inclination in the case of the agreeable goes, everyone says: Hunger is the best sauce, and people with a healthy appetite relish everything, so long as it is something they can eat.'[8] So the point seems to be that the agreeable pleasures stem more from oneself – from one's contingent and particular inclinations – than from the object under consideration.

That's why Kant thinks we are prepared to accept a degree of subjectivity in assessments of agreeability that we would never accept in assessments of beauty:

> As regards the agreeable every one concedes that his judgement, which he bases on a private feeling, and in which he declares that an object pleases him, is restricted to himself personally. Thus he does not take it amiss if, when he says that Canary-wine is agreeable, another corrects the expression and reminds him that he ought to say: It is agreeable *to me*. [. . .] But when he puts a thing on a pedestal and calls it beautiful, he demands the same delight from others. He judges not merely for himself, but for all men, and then speaks of beauty as if it were a property of things.[9]

It is this difference that gives rise to the peculiarity of the judgement of beauty: it is at once subjective, depending on one's private reaction for the validity, and universal, seeming to require the assent of others. That is not true in judgements of agreeability, Kant thinks. We all agree that such things stem from desires particular to ourselves; not everyone likes Canary-wine. But the judgement of beauty does not depend on inclination in this way. The peculiarity of judgements of beauty, which depend on our subjective perspective but which we think hold true for everyone, stems from the seeming disinterestedness of such judgements. They aren't connected to any particular desire we have, and can seem universal. Given the existence of this peculiar kind of experience, we then ask what conditions of the work of art make it possible. Clearly it cannot be an element of the content, since that would involve cognising the work under a set of concepts. So it must instead be something about its formal structure.

Many of the recent critiques of Kant have taken aim at the idea of disinterested pleasure, trying to show that this is not a necessary claim for the definition of aesthetic experience and thus – importantly – that one need not be committed to the distinctiveness of this kind of pleasure in order to accept the idea of the aesthetic. So, for instance, Joe North defends what he calls 'materialist' and 'instrumental' aesthetics against Kant's 'idealist' approach, turning to I. A. Richards to develop an alternative.[10] Similarly, Isobel Armstrong turns to John Dewey's notion of 'art as experience' in order to show the arbitrariness of the boundaries between ordinary experience and Kant's supposedly distinct aesthetic realm.[11] Alexander Nehamas summarises the broad point of this project well: beauty 'is part of the everyday world of purpose and desire, history and contingency, subjectivity and incompleteness'.[12] And

Gerard Genette, albeit with a rather different goal, puts the objection to Kant's initial distinction clearly:

> In many cases, judgements of agreeableness (of physical pleasure) are also accompanied by projections of this sort: contrary to what Kant affirms, we very frequently find ourselves saying that a wine, whether from the Canaries or elsewhere, is 'good', without considering it necessary or relevant to relativise matters by adding a proviso like 'at least as far as I am concerned'.[13]

In other words, one ought not to concede so quickly that it is only judgements of beauty that carry the particular properties that Kant is interested in. And a little reflection supports Genette's point: for Kant's view to be accurate, it would have to be the case that the only time food tasted pleasant was when we were hungry. This, fairly clearly, is not actually the case. Sometimes, we seem to take a disinterested pleasure in eating, and perhaps in many other activities, and correspondingly posit that the things are good in themselves and not because of our inclinations regarding them. This suggests that it is possible to have disinterested and interested pleasures at the same time in the same thing; I can enjoy a glass of something both because it I am thirsty and because it tastes good.

Now, if it is true that it is possible to take disinterested pleasure in things other than beautiful objects, and if the disinterested pleasure one takes in works of art might take a different form than the special experience of the contemplation of beautiful form, then aesthetic experience and what Kant calls the 'agreeable' are less distinct and more intermingled than he suggests. Noël Carroll puts the point flatly, pushing us to move past the idea of disinterestedness into the idea of something like rapt absorption: 'Disinterest is not a fruitful notion with which to attempt to characterise the preoccupied attention we lavish on artworks'.[14] And as Sianne Ngai has powerfully argued, that might be the more persuasive way to think about aesthetic experience anyway:

> The fact that so many intelligent commentators have written as if the specificity of aesthetic experience did in fact hinge on its existing in a pure form [. . .] underscores the disadvantages (which I am hardly the first to note) of an aesthetic theory modelled exclusively or even primarily on beauty [. . .] Although theorists continue to attribute the specificity of aesthetic experience to the presence of a single, exceptional emotion – what Nelson Goodman sarcastically refers to as 'aesthetic phlogiston' – most of our aesthetic experiences are based on some combination of ordinary ones.[15]

Ngai's point is that we ought to rethink the importance of impure aesthetics; her categories of the 'cute', the 'interesting' and the 'zany' all involve the evaluating aesthetic agent combining ordinary experiences and aesthetic experiences, and doing so without anything so abstract or 'pure' as an ideal of beauty. As she notes at the end of the passage, most of our everyday aesthetic experience will be closer to this impure variety than to Kant's disinterested experience of beautiful form. Indeed, one might think – as Goodman does – that this disinterested purity is almost mythical, a 'phlogiston' that exists more in the mind of philosophers than it does in the experiences of people actually enjoying art.

The defences of the aesthetic, though, too often end up reiterating the importance of form. Having undermined Kant's basic argument and thus made way for a move past the traditional assumption that it is only artistic form that can give rise to aesthetic experience, the arguments end up accepting this premise and arguing that forms are simply more capacious and various than Kant recognised. Armstrong's account of Dewey is a useful example of this strategy: 'The demonization of Kant in *Art as Experience*', she writes,

> comes about because of Dewey's need to investigate the sensuous. It makes him look at situations we do not include within the aesthetic, and argue that ordinary experience is in continuity with aesthetic production. He begins with skin, the epidermis, because it participates indeterminately in self and world.[16]

So far so good; Armstrong via Dewey is collapsing the pleasures of erotic desire (associated with skin) into the experience of art, a point Nehamas agrees with in narrating his mixture of erotic and artistic attractions to Manet's painting *Olympia*.[17] But then form reappears:

> For the quickening of arousal is a primary condition of the aesthetic because it precipitates an active shaping of form. Adjusting to ever-changing relations with the environment necessitates, calls out, an ordering principle which initiates form [. . .] without aesthetic form the organism dies of an inability to shape experience.[18]

The biological claim seems implausible, and probably there is some distance between Dewey and Armstrong here. But more important is the line that asserts that arousal is aesthetic *because* it is connected to the 'shaping of form'. To insist that formal structures are sufficient conditions for the aesthetic, such that any experience connected to the 'shaping of form' can be shown to be an aesthetic experience, pushes us back into the Kantian structure that alternative approaches offered to move beyond.

This reiteration of form occurs because Armstrong is interested in defending the aesthetic as such. And fair enough: undoubtedly many of the critiques of the aesthetic are unfair and merit reconsideration, and probably Dewey's aesthetics are indeed much more compatible both with radical politics and with a recognition of the varieties of aesthetic experience. But so long as there is a continued attempt to grasp all those varieties under the umbrella of form, we will fail to grasp the moments when readers react to artistic content, and thus fail to explain the wide variety of reasons readers have for engaging literature and art more generally.[19] Noël Carroll is helpful:

> If we say that something is an artwork if and only if it is intended to afford aesthetic experience *and* we do not stipulate that the object of aesthetic experience is artistic form, many of the previous objections to formalism fall by the wayside, since contemplating the representational content of artworks, including its political content, can count, on the generic aesthetic theory, as aesthetic experience, so long as the experience is valued for its own sake. Whereas dwelling on the moral observations in a novel by Henry James does not count as aesthetic experience for the formalist, a proponent of what I'm calling the generic aesthetic theory will accept it as such, so long as the reader finds the experience intrinsically valuable.[20]

The problem with traditional neo-Kantian aesthetics is not just that it imagines disinterested pleasure as a distinct realm. It's that it cannot do justice to the variety of ways in which works of art draw our attention or create what Rita Felski has come to call 'attachment'.[21] So if we want to insist on hanging on to the word 'aesthetic', we are better off breaking its relation to form and simply using it as the name for experiences the reader finds intrinsically valuable.[22] And we see an additional reason for redefinition when we realise that the reduction of the very broad experience of rapt absorption in art to the much more specific notion of 'aesthetic experience' created via formal complexity played a central role in the rise of aesthetic scepticism in the first place.

Aesthetic Formalism and Aesthetic Scepticism

Famously, John Guillory laid out the disintegration of the aesthetic justification for literary study in *Cultural Capital*. As he explains, the political demands for representation of minority groups characteristic of liberal pluralism led to a demand for cultural representation on college syllabi. This initially involved the inclusion of minority texts in the standard syllabi of the Western canon, and subsequently a search for alternative canons. Guillory writes:

> In the second phase of canonical critique, the curriculum became representative in another sense, by reflecting the *actual* division of the social order into dominant and dominated social groups, each now represented by its own syllabus of works. In this context of representation, the 'values' according to which works were canonised could themselves be called into question or declared to be simply incommensurable with the 'values' embodied by subordinate cultures.[23]

So, the political demand for representation gave way to a philosophical critique: the desire to open the canon to marginalised groups led to a reconsideration of the values that had given rise to the canon in the first place, and a corresponding desire to imagine alternative values.

What is striking here, as Guillory notes, is the collapse of the values expressed by the various canonical texts with the broader concept of aesthetic value or aesthetic justification. The argument that led to this reconsideration involved a searching scepticism about the possibility of a purely aesthetic evaluation. If a text was deemed aesthetically valuable, it could only be because it served the broader interests of a dominant class. Barbara Herrnstein-Smith puts the argument clearly:

> What is commonly referred to as 'the test of time' [. . .] is not, as the figure implies, an impersonal and impartial mechanism [. . .] the texts that survive will tend to be those that appear to reflect and reinforce establishment ideologies [. . .] [T]hey would not be found to please long and well if they were seen radically to undercut establishment interests.[24]

As Herrnstein-Smith goes on to argue, every act of evaluation reflects the judgement of a community, including assessments of aesthetic value. So, any given claim that a text has aesthetic value reflects not an 'impersonal and impartial' judgement, but rather the assertion of a given community's broader values. Thus the critic must see through the claim to objectivity to the political assertion underneath.

Of course, the idea of a political function as such plays a central role in Marxist critiques of the aesthetic, made famous by Raymond

Williams and Terry Eagleton.[25] An essay from Tony Bennett, in which he argues that the aesthetic *as such* serves the interest of the dominant class, offers a concise example of this kind of argument:

> Aesthetic discourse [. . .] is the form taken by discourses of value which are hegemonic in ambition and, correspondingly, universalist in their prescriptive ambit and which have, as their zone of application, those practices nominated as artistic. The position of universal valuing subject which is necessary to such discourse [. . .] can be refused to but not by the individual.[26]

The point here is that the very notion of a distinct aesthetic 'discourse' and experience imagines a sort of essential person – in Bennett's terms, 'a universal valuing subject'. To say that a piece of art is good, full stop, is to say that it ought to be good for everyone; this naturally implies that anyone who thinks it is not good is in some way failing to be a person: individuals cannot refuse the discourse as not pertaining to themselves. But since, per Herrnstein-Smith, we know that claims about aesthetic value are really the assertion of the values of a particular community, it becomes possible to recognise the 'hegemonic' ambition of such claims for what they are – a 'socially specific' discourse claiming universality.

Now, others have challenged this account in a variety of sophisticated ways. But what I want to note is the way the argument gets off the ground by unifying all our evaluative judgements of art into a single realm called aesthetic discourse, and then undermining the justification of the former by revealing some set of problems with the latter. That unification requires impoverishing the varieties of aesthetic experience, in a way that makes it possible to doubt judgements based on them. Herrnstein-Smith offers an especially clear diagnosis of the argument. At one point in her critique of the aesthetic, she writes:

> 'Aesthetic' comes to be roughly equivalent to 'relating certain cognitive/sensory experiences, these being the ones elicited by objects that have certain formal properties, these being the ones that identify objects as artworks, these being the kinds of works that elicit certain cognitive/sensory experiences, these being. . .' and so forth around again [. . .] Since the core examples cited will always be drawn from the Western academic canon [. . .] it is no surprise that 'essentially aesthetic experiences' and 'essential aesthetic value' always turn out to be located in all the old familiar places and masterpieces.[27]

Herrnstein-Smith's point here is that the traditional definitions of the aesthetic are viciously circular. One derives the standard definitions of aesthetic feelings and 'formal properties' from the experience of reading certain works that one knows to be beautiful, but it turns out that the only support given for the claim that these texts are beautiful is the fact that they have the formal features standardly defined as 'aesthetic'. Since the only criterion for the formal features derives from the set of standard works and the only criterion for the set of works is the set of standard formal features, the argument is circular. And, as she implies with the phrase 'Western academic canon', this circularity gives rise to the suspicion that the real criteria for the selection of canonical works are political, and that cultural objects become 'aesthetically valuable' just insofar as they are useful tools for social manipulation by some dominant class.

What is important to note about this argument is that it depends on the logical gap between formal properties and aesthetic value. In other words, it is because of the need for a (supposedly) independent criterion of value – that is, a criterion other than the list of works – that the aesthetic value of some formal property comes into question. But that ignores the possibility that the proper identification of a property might support *itself* as valuable, and thus offer on its own an independent criterion for picking out texts worthy of attention. In other words, if one stays with the specific property – if one does not make the unifying, commensurating, formalist move – then the circularity does not appear.

I take this intuition to be in line with Guillory's own slightly buried view. One of the main arguments of *Cultural Capital* was the contention that the problem of aesthetic relativism did not arise from aesthetic experience as such, but rather from the very specific discourse of aesthetic value. He writes:

> The concept of value, then, must be referred to that totality, even though the latter is, strictly speaking, unimaginable *as a totality*; it is a totality of conflict and not of consensus. [The discourse of value] must deny not so much the reality of conflict as the *constitutive* nature of conflict.[28]

What Guillory means here, in part, is that the discourse of value arises from the need to assess and rank multiple but incompatible things. It is the conflict between such things, whether they are art objects or commodities or actions (I shall say more about these last in a moment), that creates the need to set them in a clear relation to each other by assigning each a greater or lesser amount of value.

Thus, the problem of relativism in literary criticism was in a surprising but important way generated by syllabi, as the mechanics of the classroom forced critics to rank works by choosing some and not others to teach.

The critique of the aesthetic that Herrnstein-Smith relies upon assumes that aesthetic evaluation as such is one and the same with the discourse of aesthetic value. But, as Guillory argues, there is no reason to accept this claim:

> Smith's discursive orientation allows her to assert throughout her study the historical situatedness of values and evaluation without raising as a distinctly different question the situatedness of the discourse of value [. . .] Within this problematic, evaluation is assumed to be a transhistorical feature of human social organization – which it no doubt is – *but so is the discourse of value*, or what Smith calls 'axiology.' The latter assumption is not correct.[29]

There is an intriguingly unstated point here that Guillory does not go on to spell out. The argument proceeds by showing the historical conditions for the 'discourse of value', which for Guillory arise at the end of the eighteenth century. But lying implicit is the notion of a kind of aesthetic evaluation that does not depend on the ranking intrinsic to the notion of aesthetic value. What might this kind of evaluation look like?

Aesthetic Evaluation without Aesthetic Value

We might start with one observation that Guillory makes about the discourse of value. He writes:

> The universalization of the 'universal equivalent' of exchange value is the historical condition not of judgement in general but of the modern discourse of value, the discourse of universal commensuration, the commensurability of every object with every other. In fact it is only the money-form which permits such commensuration, as it is entirely possible to conceive of different kinds of 'good', of objects which need never be placed on the same scale of value, which need never be compared at all.[30]

In other words, the issue is commensurability, or the insistence on translating the 'goodness' of a thing into an abstract value, so as to be able to compare it to the goodness of another thing. This, for

Guillory, is a historically specific form of evaluation, one brought about by the rise of a particular economic formation. It is 'entirely possible' for other forms of evaluation to exist, and they need not depend on commensurability or comparison at all. Such forms of evaluation would not require the translation or abstraction implicit in the notion of 'aesthetic value'. One need not necessarily accept the historical claim – it seems quite possible that comparative evaluation predates the eighteenth century – to take the philosophical insight that a non-commensurable aesthetics might not be subject to the same objections.

A very similar argument has developed in moral philosophy, in the neo-Aristotelian movement now called 'virtue' ethics. Martha Nussbaum writes of Aristotle's view:

> The student of [it] will have, and/or acquire, a good understanding of what courage, friendship, generosity, and many other values are; he will understand how, in our beliefs and practices, they differ from and are non-interchangeable with one another. He will then be in a position to see that to effect the commensurability of the values is to do away with them as they currently are, creating some new value that is not identical to any of them. The question will then be whether his single-valued world can possibly have the richness and inclusiveness of the current world [. . .] This, in turn, looks likely to be an impoverished world.[31]

Something very like this kind of impoverishment seems to be what Guillory is describing in the creation of 'aesthetic value'. All of the specific reasons why artistic works are enjoyable get translated into a new value, 'not identical with any' particular reason. However, in this translation, much of what made the specific reasons compelling disappears. Against this view, Nussbaum and Aristotle recommend an ethics of 'incommensurability', a pluralistic ethics, one that refuses to weigh (for instance) courage and generosity against each other. Thus, an aesthetics of incommensurability would be one that stayed with the specific reasons why a work is compelling.

This way of thinking about conceptual terms received an important development in the anthropological work of Clifford Geertz, who – citing Gilbert Ryle – distinguished between 'thick' and 'thin' descriptions of a culture.[32] Thin descriptions of an event capture the physical movements of those participating, but thick descriptions move past this into an understanding of the context behind them, rendering them intelligible. As Geertz puts it, 'Culture is not a power, something to which social events, behaviours, institutions, or processes can be causally attributed; it is a context, something within which they can be intelligibly – that is, thickly – described.'[33] Bernard Williams then drew on these terms in moral philosophy, writing, 'Thin ethical concepts are concepts like "good", "right", and "wrong". "Abortion is wrong", if anybody makes so unqualified a claim, is an ethical statement that deploys a thin, in fact the thinnest, ethical concept.'[34] These compare with 'ethical statements deploying concepts such as "cruel", "brutal", "dishonest", 'treacherous", or which describe people as chaste, kind-hearted, or whatever. Such statements, in my terms, deploy thick ethical concepts.'[35] What matters here, as Nussbaum suggested, is the richness that such concepts offer for the evaluative stance. And one such concept might be the deep, the thought-provoking or the 'profound'. To show that a novel from George Eliot is profound is just to show that we have reason to read it, that the experience it affords is one worth having. No further argument demonstrating the value of being profound is necessary; indeed, to try to reduce the profound to some concept of value is to eliminate the specificity that makes it compelling.[36]

Accordingly, one need not appeal to the bare notion of 'aesthetic value', and thus there is no reason to start down the circular logic that Herrnstein-Smith traces. One could, of course, redefine 'aesthetic value' to mean just the evaluative content in the thick concepts, but it's important to keep in mind that 'value' is not in this case the ontologically separate, abstract, universal and metaphysically dubious entity that Herrnstein-Smith rejects and Guillory historicises; indeed, it is not even neatly separable from the descriptive content in the concept. Under this redefinition, the 'aesthetic value' of a work that is profound is just another way of saying that others will enjoy engaging the ideas it invites them to regard, that it is capable of evoking their interest, absorption and excitement.

Let me give a brief description of how an aesthetic evaluation through thick concepts works. One of the first arguments along these lines was Frank Sibley's, whose 1959 paper is one origin point for contemporary thinking about thick aesthetic concepts.[37] The main thrust of Sibley's argument is to distinguish between 'aesthetic' and 'non-aesthetic properties': a line might be delicate and flowing, but it might also be black and curved. These two sets of properties might suggest that it is possible to draw clear connections between them – to say that an object with some specific set of non-aesthetic properties will necessarily also have certain corresponding aesthetic properties. However, Sibley contends, the relationship is not so straightforward: 'aesthetic concepts are not condition-governed even in this way. There are no sufficient conditions, no non-aesthetic features such that the presence of some set or number of them will beyond question justify or warrant the application of an aesthetic term.'[38]

However, despite the lack of a clear and necessary link, the relationship between aesthetic and non-aesthetic properties might nevertheless admit of some explanation. In 'A Sensible Subjectivism', David Wiggins writes: 'Amusement for instance is a reaction we have to characterise by reference to its proper object, via something perceived as funny (or incongruous or comical or whatever). There is no object-independent and property-independent, "purely phenomenological" or "purely introspective" account of amusement.'[39] Wiggins's point here is that the feeling of amusement cannot be defined independently of either the feeling or the object that inspires it; we cannot say what the word 'funny' means without reference to the kinds of things that inspire it, nor (perhaps obviously) without an explanation of the subjective nature of the reaction. But this does not mean that conversation and debate about the issue is useless: 'We can do a little better than saying that the funny is that which makes people laugh.'[40] More substantially, 'When we dispute whether x is really funny, there is a whole wealth of considerations and explanations we can adduce, and by no means all of them have to be given in terms simply synonymous or interdefinable with "funny".'[41] The point here is that the application of a thick concept involves a sensitivity to facts about an object, and those facts and their connections to the thick evaluative concept can be the subject of explication and debate – which is to say, of literary criticism.

The Profound as a Thick Concept

Suppose, then, that one goal of literary criticism is to explicate judgements involving thick aesthetic concepts, hoping to produce consensus about what Wiggins calls the 'considerations and explanations' involved in the experience of particular works. Presumably, though, agreement on the features that make a particular work elegant or funny matters primarily insofar as it might enable someone to have an aesthetic experience that they would not otherwise have. As Stuart Hampshire puts it in a phrase that Sibley liked, 'if one has been brought to see what there is to be seen in the object, the purpose of discussion is achieved [. . .] The point is to bring people to see these features.'[42] Nick McAdoo explains that for Sibley, artistic criticism was a kind of persuasion: it was a way of guiding viewers towards a certain experience of the work of art.[43] Criticism on this model is a way of pointing, calling certain features of a text to a reader's attention in the hope that a new way of seeing it would become available.[44]

But the idea that this is even possible might at first seem to be a non-starter. A brief analysis of a scene from Oscar Wilde's play *The Importance of Being Earnest* will help make the point.

> Lady Bracknell: Now to minor matters. Are your parents living?
> Jack: I have lost both my parents.
> Lady Bracknell: To lose one parent, Mr. Worthing, may be regarded as a misfortune; to lose both looks like carelessness.[45]

One reason why Lady Bracknell's line is funny is its surprising comparison of two different definitions of the word 'loss'; Wilde brings together the loss of tragedy with losses caused by everyday forgetfulness. It's an instance of the rhetorical technique of zeugma or syllepsis, of the same sort one sees in Charles Dickens's line that a woman 'went straight home in a flood of tears and a sedan-chair': the listener or reader expects one thing on the basis of the first use of the word, and is subsequently surprised and (ideally) amused by the second.[46]

I take this brief explication to describe the sort of considerations that Wiggins has in mind as underlying the application of thick concepts in aesthetics. Certainly the condition is not sufficient for humour. Not all combinations of two different senses of a word's meaning in a single sentence are funny, and picking up which combinations will be funny inescapably involves evaluative norms. Nor is the condition necessary, as there are certainly other ways to be witty. But it is nevertheless a real explanation, insofar as it does not simply repeat the word 'funny' but instead describes some of the features that combine to produce its humour. What is more, this concept plays a real and obvious role in aesthetic deliberation. If someone asks whether she should read *The Importance of Being Earnest*, the response 'Yes, it's funny' is reasonable and meaningful. Because 'humour' is a thick evaluative concept, the fact that a text is humorous provides, all by itself, a reason to read it.

But would the explication by itself help someone who didn't find the line funny in the first place laugh at it? The answer is quite obviously no. Certainly one could probably get to a stage where confused readers might be able to see why someone else had found it funny, and maybe even have a shadow of laughter after they 'got' the joke, but having a similar aesthetic reaction to that of readers who laughed the first time they heard the lines seems obviously off the table. This insight has led a number of thinkers to deny Sibley's basic premise about what criticism can do. Susan Sontag, for instance, claims that interpretation 'takes the sensory experience of the work of art for granted, and proceeds from there'; she thus implies that there is no interpretation that could change the sensory experience of art, as does her call for an 'erotics' instead of a hermeneutics of art.[47]

I share Nehamas's response to this. It is not in fact possible to distinguish between an interpretation and a description of a work of art: every description of a work of art is also a way of experiencing it.[48] Sontag's argument does point to something important about artistic experience, though, which is how often it depends on surprise. The reason jokes can't be explained isn't that it's intrinsically impossible to explain humour, but that once someone tells you the specific facts you need to have in order for the joke to be funny, it's much more difficult to be surprised. And there are a number of other examples of thick concepts where the same will be true; if a film, for instance, is supposed to be exciting and a particular viewer does not find it so, it will not help matters much for a well-intentioned critic to try to explain how it is exciting.

But the experience of reading an interesting, exciting and profound idea can be different; explanation in this regard can genuinely change the experience of a book. Probably this is because the explanation is in such moments itself the culmination of a surprise. Parts of the text that seemed confusing or irrelevant suddenly connect up and take on new importance when given a clear explanation. I suspect this is one reason why critique rarely changes the popularity of the books it targets.[49] In revealing the deep problems hinted at in marginal details of the texts that they consider, critics make a given work seem to be 'about' something important, creating an experience akin to that of the profound. Such an aesthetic experience is more impactful than the actual logic of the argument.

What is it to experience an idea as profound? Here a second difference between the profound and other thick concepts emerges. If, generally speaking, texts are funny because their writers intend them to be so, the intention to say something profound seems often inversely related to actually doing so. In a delightfully savage reading of Paul de Man's analysis of Archie Bunker, Toril Moi writes:

> But let us grant de Man his point, which seems to be that when we ask a rhetorical question, we aren't usually asking a question. This is fair enough, but hardly news. As I read on, I realise that de Man is inviting me to feel a kind of dizzying intellectual exhilaration at the implications of this insight.[50]

Dizzying intellectual exhilaration, indeed – a thing worth having, certainly. But like many aesthetic effects, it loses its impact when it becomes clear that the effect is the goal and that there is a deliberate strategy to produce it. To know that a writer is trying to dazzle me philosophically usually makes me sceptical. Instead, the profound supervenes on attempts to tell the truth about important questions (or at any rate attempts that seem to do so). This returns us to the argument from the end of Chapter 3, where it emerged that the impulse towards rational reconstruction stemmed from the fact that readers encounter new ideas not merely as gestures connected to particular individuals but as possible truths for their own consideration. We can see now that the two are related: the experience of finding an idea exciting and interesting is the same as finding a connection between it and some problem that one is currently thinking about.

It is tempting to go a step further and simply say that it is not just attempts to tell the truth that make a text profound – it is actual truths. When a text conveys accurate information, especially about an important issue, this can be a component of its artistic value. This is Richard Gaskin's view; he holds that it is, of course, not decisive for aesthetic value, but other things being equal, false claims detract from a work's merit and true claims add to it.[51] Putting the claim about truth this way fits too with an opposing view, connected to what philosophers of literature have called the 'no-argument' problem.[52] Since literary works do not offer support for their claims, Lamarque and Olsen suggest, it seems odd to assess them in those terms; arguments and poems being different things, it is strange to call a poem's lack of an argument an artistic failure. What this has in common with Gaskin's view is the idea that whether an idea in a text matters as an idea depends above all on whether it is true.

But this is not at all an assumption recognised in interpretive scholarship in the history of philosophy, which contains numerous examples of writers regarding the texts they interpret in a much different way, carefully and even lovingly reconstructing works whose arguments they believe to be fundamentally false.[53] Descartes's *Meditations* offers a quintessential example in this regard. Essentially, all of the major claims in the book are false: the mind does not relate to the brain in the way Descartes imagines, knowledge of the external world cannot be arrived at in the way he suggests, and if some divine entity exists, that existence has not been demonstrated by Descartes's proofs. But these facts have not interrupted the scholarship on Descartes. And, as anyone who has taught the book knows, it is a great book to read and to talk about. That is because it is deeply profound: it identifies important questions and offers creative attempts to address them.[54] Certainly it would be better in a philosophical sense if its claims were true; at least, Descartes would have thought so. But I am not convinced that this would make it more profound. As an aesthetic experience, it hinges on the importance of the questions involved and the creativity of the answer given, not on what other accounts of the questions ultimately determine to be the best answer.

We see a similar strategy in a particular genre of literary criticism – interpretations that work by showing how a set of texts on an esoteric question of little interest in fact address more general issues of contemporary relevance. To pick one example, English literature before the twentieth century was deeply concerned with doctrinal disputes and fine-grained differences between Protestantism and Catholicism. Both John Milton and Edmund Spenser, to pick two famous examples, were seriously concerned with this issue. But critics writing on these authors often do not simply parse these doctrinal positions; instead, they show how they are relevant to a question that we (or some portion of 'we') take seriously now. Thus, for instance, Julia Lupton reads Milton's 'Samson Agonistes' as a reflection upon acts of religious terror; Samson's act of pulling down the pillars of the temple is a 'death by – and *to* – public space'.[55] The value of this reading depends upon regarding religious terrorism as a serious issue worth understanding, and Lupton's reading works through a rational reconstruction that shows how Milton's poem addresses the issue. We can treat this as a contribution to political theory, but at least as much as this Lupton is pointing out a way to enjoy 'Samson Agonistes' – to return to Rorty's phrase, helping the dead author put his act together for a new audience.

The Political Critique Redux

But of course, there is a problem. One might see the way a thick concept such as the profound or the funny combines facts and values as not really addressing the problem that the aesthetician needed to solve. While it might be true that to call something funny is both to describe and to praise it, the concept by itself offers no obvious reason to think that this particular descriptive fact ought to be combined with this particular evaluation and affective response. In this way, aesthetics through thick concepts might seem to be not so much a way of addressing the problem of aesthetic evaluation as a way of hiding it.

This is precisely what Gerard Genette thinks. He writes that

> aesthetic adjectives [...] smuggle their axiological character past us under a descriptive character [...] Aesthetic, semi-descriptive, or semi-judgemental predicates, by means of which one judges under cover of describing, are also, in the domain they operate in, persuasive or valorising descriptions that bridge the abyss between fact and value without becoming too conspicuous.[56]

For Genette, then, the inextricable link between description and evaluation in thick aesthetic concepts is precisely the problem with them. Inconspicuously, as if they were merely describing a work of art, they import an evaluative stance.

Because of this feature, they are 'powerful tools of objectification', and play a key role in what Genette calls the 'aesthetic illusion'. He writes:

> The aesthetic illusion consists in objectifying this value itself ('this red tulip is beautiful'); objectification treats the effect (the value) as if it were a property of the object, and, consequently, the subjective appraisal as if it were an objective 'evaluation'. Evaluation, in the proper, legitimate sense of the word, is a judgement based on objective criteria, as when an expert values an object in light of its condition and prevailing market rates. Aesthetic appreciation, for its part, takes itself for, and gives itself out as, the evaluation that it is and cannot be, as soon as (and to the extent that) it illusorily objectifies its causes.[57]

In other words, to react to something aesthetically is to pretend that a fact about oneself is actually a fact about the object. I laugh at a story, but I don't think that this means 'I laugh at things like this'; rather, I think 'This story is funny.' Genette calls this the 'constitutive illusion' of aesthetics, insofar as what is actually a study in human psychology and anthropology appears as a study of certain special objects. It is thus not actually a form of 'legitimate' evaluation, which can only be based on 'objective criteria'. And on this view, thick concepts might actually be the guiltiest evaluations of all, insofar as they disguise their objectifying nature by hiding the way they link fact and value. Of course, this resonates with the Marxist critique of the aesthetic that we traced earlier.

There is a parallel problem with the use of thick concepts in moral philosophy. One powerful argument in support of the objection that Genette and others are making is simply the fact that our thick concepts admit of variation. One way we know that aesthetic evaluations say more about the evaluating person than they do about the evaluated object is simply that there has been change; the same objects praised or condemned at different places and times, and different evaluating concepts given greater or lesser emphasis. There are synchronic variations, as different cultures and societies use and care about different thick concepts, and diachronic variations, as which concepts a society cares about have changed over time. Indeed, this might be even more apparent in ethics than it is in aesthetics; Bernard Williams gives the example of 'chastity' as a thick concept that many moral agents would today reject as capable of giving reasons for action.[58] Nor should one understate the extent to which there is variation and disagreement within a culture. Williams offers another example: 'There was a marvellous moment in one of Oscar Wilde's trials when counsel read to Wilde a passage from one of his works and asked, "Mr. Wilde, don't you think that's obscene?" Wilde replied, "'Obscene' is not a word of mine."'[59] The point, of course, is that Wilde was not disputing whether his actions were obscene, but rather the validity of the thick concept entirely.

When viewed this way, one might think that thick aesthetic concepts are therefore less interesting as a philosophical resource and more revealing as a kind of history. In the same way that one might write a revealing history of the rise and fall of the virtue of 'chastity', a history that tried to understand why a given concept might matter in one place and time and not in another, one might write a history of the changes in thick aesthetic concepts and of the corresponding processes of objectification. And this summarises briefly what Sianne Ngai's recent work has done. The concepts in which she is interested – the 'cute', 'interesting' and 'zany' – are important primarily because of what their current prominence tells us about the nature of late capitalist society. As she puts it, 'My wager in this book is that finding a way to grasp this historically specific configuration, if not exactly "system" of aesthetic categories, will be similarly salutary for getting a handle on postmodernism'.[60] She explains further:

> [Contemporary] zaniness, cuteness, and interestingness are, at the deepest level, about performance, commodities and information. At the same time, by calling forth specific powers of feeling, knowing, and acting in relation to these ordinary, if by no means uncomplicated, 'objects', they play to and help complete the formation of a historically specific kind of aesthetic subject: 'us'.[61]

In other words, it is essential for Ngai not to rest on the position 'this picture is interesting, and therefore I have reason to like it'. Rather, one must recognise that which concepts matter to a given 'aesthetic agent', so to speak, and which affective experiences they create and correspond to, are a matter of radical historical contingency. There is an 'us' that is importantly different from previous us-es, and the concepts that they used – indeed, their aesthetic experiences, their 'feeling, knowing and acting' – are not the same as the experiences that we have. Thus, the critic interested in aesthetic categories must put herself outside of them, recognising the changes between thick concepts as more important and revealing than the stance within a thick concept itself.

Naming the Feature: A Response

This is a powerful objection and a deep problem, and I don't think it is possible to overcome it entirely. But keeping in mind that this is really a version of the objection that Herrnstein-Smith was making earlier, I want to argue that an elaborated version of the same response I gave there can mitigate much of the objection's force. To see this, consider that aesthetic scepticism can be motivated by several different kinds of disagreement about artistic judgement. First, what one might call 'intra-concept' conflict involves a dispute about which artworks instantiate a given concept. Two people might both share the concept 'funny', but disagree about which works are funny. On the other hand, 'inter-concept' conflict involves a situation where one aesthetic agent has a concept and corresponding experience that the other does not; one might imagine a conflict between someone who has the concept 'cute' and someone else who doesn't. Additionally, we can distinguish between 'explicable' and 'inexplicable' conflict, both at the intra-conceptual and inter-conceptual level. In other words, we can ask why it is that a person experiences something as funny while another does not, and why it is that a person has a concept such as the 'funny' while another does not. That matters, because if a conflict is explicable, then the apparent tension between two aesthetic experiences reveals itself as not fundamental. One might take the taste of food as an example. As it happens, I love coriander, but to a friend of mine it tastes like soap. And she is not alone; a recent study has found that a significant portion of the world's population experiences coriander as having a soap-like taste, and suggests a genetic basis for it.[62] What the analysis of the cause of the discrepancy points to is evidence of what it would take to resolve this tension. One could give the coriander-tastes-like-soap experience to another person with a genetic modification, or vice versa.

Now, this might seem to posit and depend upon a norm. The majority for whom coriander tastes pleasant are the standard against which coriander's soap-like taste is deemed abnormal. And this then would suggest that an argument follows about who is right – which thick concepts an aesthetic agent should have, and which objects correctly instantiate them; as we saw Tony Bennett put it earlier, the evaluation thus depends upon a sort of 'universal valuing subject'. Does coriander 'really' taste like soap? Is *The Importance of Being Earnest* 'really' funny? Whose experience is the right one? Which aesthetic concepts and corresponding experiences should one prefer to have?

Moral philosophy has gone to great lengths to try to answer this question, to try to show that some concepts are truth-sensitive while others are not.[63] Perhaps this is the right strategy for ethics, but here aesthetics should split off. 'Which aesthetic experiences should one prefer' is a trick question; the right answer is all of them. One needs to be wary of the distorting effects of dilemmas. Having to decide whether the concept of the 'funny' accurately describes the truth of some text ignores the fact that it describes an experience worth having. Someone who finds Tayari Jones, Gao Xinjian, Rumi and Sophocles insightful – each in their own way – will have a richer, fuller aesthetic life than someone who dismisses any of them. There is no call to designate a text as 'more insightful' or as 'really insightful', and one should resist the impulse towards aesthetic ranking that requires it.

It is in this way that the emptiness of Genette's objection becomes apparent, with a reminder of the power of the fact that the thick concept names the feature that justifies the evaluation. Perhaps it is true that thick concepts such as the funny smuggle evaluation in under an attitude of description. But the evaluation is not the less accurate for that fact. It is as if he had argued that people who thought coriander tasted good were mistaken, because nothing about the structure of the plant necessarily leads to the taste they experience. Of course, there's a sense in which this is true, but that truth has no impact on the rationality of the person who decides to eat it. Similarly, if it is true that a work of art makes someone laugh, then it is funny, and worth reading insofar as it enables that experience. And arguing about whether the work is funny overlooks the fact that one's aesthetic life would be richer if one could see it that way. The value of explaining a conflict is not justificatory, as if one person's experience of a text was right and another's wrong. To return to Sibley's theory of criticism, the value of an explanation is practical, so that someone who has found a work of art profound can help someone else see it that way too. And this theoretical goal of aesthetic openness is worth keeping in mind even in cases of contradiction. To return to my earlier example, suppose that there was a person who happened to fall into the group to whom coriander tastes like soap. To fit it more closely to the kind of problem Genette has in mind, suppose as well that this person doesn't mind it – in fact, she enjoys the taste of soap. And suppose finally that there is an injection that would give her the ability to taste coriander the way the majority of the world does.

It takes a better person than me to avoid the pun: should she want to take the shot with an aesthetic? Yes, but only if it will be an addition, rather than a change. The way the rest of the world tastes coriander is not preferable to the way she does, but in an ideal world one would be able to taste both: one would have access to both kinds of experience. Regrettably, this seems to be impossible; we cannot taste coriander both as soap and not as soap. But the aesthetic openness I am developing here is not required to discriminate between such experiences, beyond the basic recognition that someone somewhere has considered the experience worth having. The need to discriminate is forced upon us by the limits of time, attention and lifespan, not by the nature of aesthetics as such.

Both Genette and Herrnstein-Smith make much of the condescension in traditional aesthetics. Genette attacks what he calls the argument from maturity, pointing out that the belief in a process of aesthetic maturation can 'be established only with reference to the superiority of the ("difficult") works he appreciates in his mature years (which age is that?) over the ("easy") works he appreciated when he was an adolescent; the supposed proof thus clearly depends on the very circumstances it is supposed to prove'.[64] Similarly, Herrnstein-Smith diagnoses what she calls the 'developmental fallacy', pointing out that 'even if it were the case that people throughout the world uniformly and universally preferred "X" at age five, "Y" at age 25, and "Z" at age fifty, that *array* of common differences would not be evidence of the objective *superiority* of any particular point on it'.[65] But both of these arguments rely on the assumption that aesthetic evaluation must consist in a comparative ranking. If we abandon that assumption, then it becomes clear that there is a version of the argument from maturity that is not vulnerable to this objection. The point of expanding one's aesthetic capacity and one's range of aesthetic concepts isn't that these are better than those one had as a child; rather, it's simply that they are an addition.[66]

It is one of the small tragedies of life that it does not seem possible to embrace completely the varieties of artistic experience. It is difficult to maintain the ability to laugh at the things one found funny as a child, to wonder at the things one found profound then, and to similarly be able to laugh and wonder at texts commonly interesting to adults. In other words, one has to sacrifice the aesthetic experience of a child in order to gain the experience of an adult. But one need not fall into the self-deceiving trap of thinking that the aesthetic experience of the adult is superior, or the sceptical trap of thinking that there is no legitimate form of aesthetic evaluation because neither is more valuable than the other. Rather, *both* are valuable – both are experiences worth having – and, to the extent that it is possible, aesthetic agents have reason to pursue both.

How far, exactly, can one stretch this point, embracing the wide variety of thick concepts on the grounds that there is no good reason to insist on choosing one or the other? As it happens, Victorian aesthetics offers useful examples for this kind of worry. Matthew Sussman has recently pointed out that Victorian criticism often drew on concepts that we today primarily think of as ethical.[67] Thus, in one of Sussman's examples, Abraham Hayward praises *Vanity Fair* for its 'masculine good sense'.[68] The view I have elaborated here would seem to require a willingness to share in this aesthetic experience, but one might very well balk at the gender politics involved in this judgement, this aesthetic experience and this subjectivity.

And putting the point this way suggests a bigger problem. Despite their apparent neutrality, concepts such as the 'funny' and the 'profound' are not entirely innocent; to have such concepts and to care about the experiences they name is to be the kind of person who cares about such things (I can imagine Ngai responding with an argument like this). The separation between ethics and aesthetics breaks down when one realises that having the experience requires that one become a certain kind of person. It's for this reason that Wayne Booth insisted that the engagement or 'coduction' with a text combined aesthetic and ethical evaluation; he saw that they were not really separable. Booth writes: 'In discovering that we know something about the quality of this poem – that at least some of its parts are well chosen for their task – we already discover something about the ethos of the poet: he shows the integrity of the devoted craftsman.'[69] The poem that invites judgement under a certain aesthetic criterion – formal unity – invites the reader to share in an ethos of integrity that is not exactly ethically neutral.

One might nevertheless distinguish thick aesthetic concepts on something like a continuum of ethical norms; perhaps a concept such as the 'elegant' imposes less on the ethos of the reader than does the 'profound' or 'masculine good sense'. Yet to push the response too far in this direction is to fall back into Kantian disinterestedness. If an aesthetic concept is entirely distinct from the particularities of our identity, in such a way that we can adopt it, its evaluations and the experience it names without any other changes to our life and our subjectivity, then it begins to seem that such thick aesthetics are not really different from formalism in its more traditional iterations. So, there is a dilemma: either admit that there's no real distinction between the thick concepts in ethics and those in aesthetics, or admit that there's no real distinction between aesthetics by thick concepts and aesthetic formalism.

But this, it seems to me, is less a decisive problem for the view than an opportunity for a path forward. Part of the problem is that the vocabulary we have for thick concepts as applied to literature is so impoverished; research that combined anthropological and historical study with literary criticism might collect and organise the broad vocabulary that readers have used to name the experiences that justified the reading of a given book. And both horns of the dilemma are worth exploring: it is worth figuring out both how one's life would change with the embrace of a given thick concept, and how various concepts might be integrated with each other in a way that imposed minimally on one's broader ethos.

If there is a broader overall ideal, then, it is simply an aesthetic cosmopolitanism – a willingness to try new things, and an openness to appreciating what it is that artworks have to offer. And it is perhaps on this point that my account diverges most sharply from that offered by Ngai and Herrnstein-Smith. Both writers are committed to the claim that one's aesthetic evaluations are in some sense given, not a matter of choice. In Herrnstein-Smith's view this is a source of inevitable conflict: 'institutions of evaluative authority' establish the illusion of consensus and help suppress divergent tastes when they appear.[70] One's tastes and preferences reflect the community-wide illusion of an evaluative truth. Similarly, as we saw earlier, Ngai's aesthetic categories 'help complete the formation of a historically specific kind of aesthetic subject: "us"'.[71] These claims overlook the stance of agency: the kinds of aesthetic subjects that we become are to a limited extent up to us. The fact that our aesthetic concepts change over the course of our lives is evidence that any given configuration is not permanent. We can always listen to the promise that happiness might lie elsewhere.

Notes

1. Clune, 'Formalism as the Fear of Ideas', p. 1194.
2. Clune, 'Formalism as the Fear of Ideas', p. 1198.
3. Julie Orlemanski, 'Scales of Reading', *Exemplaria: Medieval, Early Modern, Theory* 26.2–3 (2014), pp. 215–33 (p. 227).
4. I am indebted to Joseph North for his summary of this trend, which includes scholars such as George Levine, Elaine Scarry, Rei Terada and Winifred Fluck (*Literary Criticism: A Concise Political History*, p. 128). See also Yuriko Saito, 'Aesthetics of the Everyday', in *The Stanford Encyclopedia of Philosophy*, ed. Edward N. Zalta, available at <http://plato.stanford.edu> (last accessed 18 December 2019) for an effective introduction to the field. Rita Felski, 'Everyday Aesthetics', in Jeffrey Williams and Heather Steffen (eds), *The Critical Pulse: Thirty-Six Credos by Contemporary Critics* (New York: Columbia University Press, 2012), pp. 193–201, is also helpful.
5. Nick Zangwill, 'Feasible Aesthetic Formalism', *Nous* 33.4 (1999), p. 610.
6. Isobel Armstrong, *The Radical Aesthetic* (New York: Wiley-Blackwell, 2000), p. 21.
7. Immanuel Kant, *The Critique of Judgement*, trans. James Creed Meredith (Oxford: Clarendon Press, 1952), p. 48.
8. Kant, *The Critique of Judgement*, p. 49.
9. Kant, *The Critique of Judgement*, pp. 51–2.
10. North, *Literary Criticism: A Concise Political History*, p. 15.
11. Armstrong, *The Radical Aesthetic*, p. 163.
12. Alexander Nehamas, *Only a Promise of Happiness* (Princeton: Princeton University Press, 2007), p. 35.
13. Gerard Genette, *The Aesthetic Relation*, trans. G. M. Goshgarian (Ithaca: Cornell University Press, 1999).
14. Carroll, *Beyond Aesthetics*, p. 34.
15. Sianne Ngai, *Our Aesthetic Categories: Zany, Cute, Interesting* (Cambridge, MA: Harvard University Press, 2012), p. 45.
16. Armstrong, *The Radical Aesthetic*, p. 163.
17. Armstrong, *The Radical Aesthetic*, p. 163; Nehamas, *Only a Promise of Happiness*, p. 18.
18. Armstrong, *The Radical Aesthetic*, p. 164.
19. Interestingly, Armstrong's recent work acknowledges more of a cognitive role in aesthetic experience. She writes that 'to think seeing necessarily arouses that sensory immediacy, and the intellectual power that simultaneously recreates sensation, which is the fundamental experience of the aesthetic'. Isobel Armstrong, *Novel Politics* (Oxford: Oxford University Press, 2016), p. 217.
20. Carroll, *Beyond Aesthetics*, p. 46.
21. Rita Felski, *Hooked: Art and Attachment* (Chicago: University of Chicago Press, 2020).

22. Even this definition of the concept might not be broad enough, since – as Carroll goes on to argue – surely there are many moments where we find works of art instrumentally as well as intrinsically valuable (*Beyond Aesthetics*, p. 46).
23. Guillory, *Cultural Capital*, p. 19.
24. Barbara Herrnstein-Smith, *Contingencies of Value: Alternative Persepectives for Critical Theory* (Cambridge, MA: Harvard University Press, 1988), p. 51.
25. See Raymond Williams, *Marxism and Literature* (Oxford: Oxford University Press, 1977), and Terry Eagleton, *The Ideology of the Aesthetic* (New York: Wiley, 1991).
26. Tony Bennett, 'Really Useless "Knowledge": A Political Critique of the Aesthetic', *Thesis Eleven* 12 (1985), pp. 28–52 (p. 36).
27. Herrnstein-Smith, *Contingencies of Value*, p. 35.
28. Guillory, *Cultural Capital*, p. 282.
29. Guillory, *Cultural Capital*, p. 283.
30. Guillory, *Cultural Capital*, p. 323.
31. Nussbaum, *The Fragility of Goodness*, p. 296.
32. Clifford Geertz, 'Thick Description: Toward an Interpretive Theory of Culture', in *The Interpretation of Cultures* (New York: Basic Books, 1973), pp. 3–30.
33. Geertz, 'Thick Description', p. 14.
34. Bernard Williams, 'Truth in Ethics', *Ratio* 8.3 (1995), pp. 227–42. Such concepts are central as well in *Ethics and the Limits of Philosophy*.
35. Williams, 'Truth in Ethics', pp. 234–5.
36. It is perhaps worth pointing out that something similar is true about the claim that reading the text produces pleasure or happiness. If pleasure is taken to be something over and above the experience of humour, or perhaps an essential element within it, such that humour 'causes' or 'creates' pleasure, then there is a threat that it can be just as abstracting as 'value'. On the view that I am developing here, it is true that profundity and humour are pleasurable only in the sense that we enjoy them: there is no central core of 'pleasure' to either experience that could be distilled and compared.
37. Frank Sibley, 'Aesthetic Concepts', *The Philosophical Review* 68.4 (1959), pp. 421–50 (p. 424).
38. Sibley, 'Aesthetic Concepts', p. 426.
39. David Wiggins, 'A Sensible Subjectivism', in Russ Shafer-Landau and Terence Cuneo (eds), *Foundations of Ethics: An Anthology* (New York: Blackwell, 2007), pp. 145–56 (p. 149).
40. Wiggins, 'A Sensible Subjectivism', p. 149.
41. Wiggins, 'A Sensible Subjectivism', p. 149.
42. Stuart Hampshire, 'Logic and Appreciation', in *Aesthetics and Language* (London: Blackwell, 1967), pp. 161–70.
43. Nick McAdoo, 'Sibley and the Art of Persuasion', in Emily Brady and Jerrold Levinson (eds), *Aesthetic Concepts: Essays after Sibley* (New York: Oxford University Press, 2001), p. 36.

44. Although I don't think we agree on the details, this is broadly a version of what Nathan Hensley has called 'curatorial reading'; see 'Curatorial Reading and Endless War', *Victorian Studies* 56.1 (2013), pp. 59–83.
45. Oscar Wilde, *The Importance of Being Earnest and Other Plays*, ed. Peter Raby (Oxford: Oxford University Press, 2008), p. 266, I.524.
46. Charles Dickens, *The Pickwick Papers* (New York: CreateSpace Independent Publishing Platform, 2015), p. 364. I thank my colleague Dragan Ilic for pointing out the role that zeugma plays in this passage.
47. Susan Sontag, 'Against Interpretation', in *Against Interpretation* (New York: Picador, 2001), pp. 3–14 (p. 13).
48. Nehamas, *Only a Promise of Happiness*, pp. 122–3.
49. See Felski, *The Limits of Critique*, p. 63.
50. Moi, *Revolution of the Ordinary*, p. 144.
51. 'What we surely can say, however, is that truth is a *pro tanto* marker of merit, and falsehood a *pro tanto* defect, in a work of literature' (*LTL*, p. 135).
52. Mikkonen summarises the point well. He thinks of it as a subset of the 'triviality' argument, which holds that truth content is irrelevant to works of literature because the truths they convey are banal; see *The Cognitive Value of Philosophical Fiction*, p. 63. For a quintessential statement of the position, see Jerome Stolnitz, 'On the Cognitive Triviality of Art', in Eileen John and Dominic McIver-Lopes (eds), *The Philosophy of Literature: Contemporary and Classic Readings* (New York: Blackwell, 2004), pp. 317–23.
53. Other readers will have their own favourite examples of this kind of argument; mine is an essay of Christine Korsgaard's which argues that Kant's belief that revolutionaries should receive the death penalty revealed a hidden sympathy with them. See Christine Korsgaard, 'Kant on the Right of Revolution', in *The Constitution of Agency*, p. 256.
54. As mentioned in Chapter 1, this is in sympathy with Lamarque and Olsen's attitude, if not their overall position – the role they give to 'humanly interesting content' is very much in line with my emphasis on important questions.
55. Julia Lupton, *Citizen Saints: Shakespeare and Political Theology* (Chicago: University of Chicago Press, 2005), p. 197.
56. Genette, *The Aesthetic Relation*, pp. 92–3.
57. Genette, *The Aesthetic Relation*, p. 92.
58. Williams, 'Truth in Ethics'.
59. Williams, 'Truth in Ethics', p. 237.
60. Ngai, *Our Aesthetic Categories*, pp. 51–2.
61. Ngai, *Our Aesthetic Categories*, p. 233.
62. See Ewen Callander, 'Soapy Taste of Coriander Linked to Genetic Variants', *Nature.com*, 12 September 2012, for a summary of the study by N. Eriksson et al., available at <http://www.nature.com/news/soapy-taste-of-coriander-linked-to-genetic-variants-1.11398> (last accessed 16 June 2015).

63. Certainly this was the debate surrounding Bernard Williams's use of the concepts; see Mark Jenkins, *Bernard Williams* (New York: Acumen, 2006), pp. 133–48, for an explanation of this debate.
64. Genette, *The Aesthetic Relation*, p. 108.
65. Herrnstein-Smith, *Contingencies of Value*, p. 80.
66. Genette may have impulses in this direction already. He writes: 'To put it frankly, it seems to me that aesthetic maturity, if there is such a thing, begins with the recognition of pluralities' (*The Aesthetic Relation*, p. 110).
67. Matthew Sussman, 'Stylistic Virtue in Nineteenth-Century Criticism', *Victorian Studies* 56.2 (2014), pp. 225–49.
68. Sussman, 'Stylistic Virtue in Nineteenth-Century Criticism', p. 225.
69. Booth, *The Company We Keep*, p. 108.
70. Herrnstein-Smith, *Contingencies of Value*, p. 40.
71. Ngai, *Our Aesthetic Categories*, p. 233.

Chapter 6

Robert Browning, Augusta Webster and the Role of Morality

Throughout this study, we have been concerned with stories as means of expression. I have sought to demonstrate that narratives, like other literary texts, can be communicative tools and ways of developing complex ideas, and that this fact is central to understanding the variety of aesthetic effects they create. But I want to end by considering the limits of this claim. After all, there are certainly moments when the introduction of a narrative element serves to impede communication and not to facilitate it.

Many critics have, for instance, regarded the narrative elements in Robert Browning's poetry as interesting precisely because they prevent straightforward communication. In the ironic effects created in his famous dramatic monologues, it is essential that the reader regard the ideas in Browning's poems not as sincere attempts to articulate a position but as behaviour that reveals the speaker's character – the real topic of the poem. So when for example the speaker in 'My Last Duchess' says his wife was 'too soon made glad / too easily impressed', we will certainly misunderstand the poem if we treat this as a psychological diagnosis advanced sincerely and which the reader is meant to contemplate.[1] Browning does not mean us to consider whether it is actually possible to be impressed too easily. The point of the poem is rather to use such ideas to characterise the speaker, who has had his wife murdered, and demonstrate the way he has understood and justified his actions.

Such a displaced relation to ideas is characteristic of much of Browning's art, a fact noted by the contemporaries who often urged him to write poetry in his own voice.[2] In fact such friends connected Browning's early unpopularity with his insistence on the 'dramatic lyric' and refusal of the tradition of distilling philosophical truth in the Romantic lyric.[3] In that sense refusing to read for the content and recognising Browning's use of ideas as a tool of characterisation is historically sensitive, a way of grasping what the innovative poetic techniques in Browning's work meant in his environment.

Yet reflecting on Browning might lead an interlocutor to a deeper objection. After all one might say that Browning is certainly still interested in philosophical ideas: 'My Last Duchess' might be thought of as a diagnosis of insanity and cruelty. Those ideas are simply not the ideas overtly expressed in the poem. Thus the interpretive methods described in this book, with their emphasis on the rational reconstruction of overt claims, have a deeper problem. Not only do they fail to account for aesthetic effects other than those created by profound philosophical ideas, they cannot even deal with the more sophisticated ways literary texts use such ideas. Once we make the example poetry and not prose, one might argue, the limitations of the idea of rationally reconstructing a literary text become apparent.

My goal in this chapter is to address these worries, using a dual strategy. Considering Browning's 'Bishop Blougram's Apology', I will argue that rational reconstruction is capable of the subtlety necessary to account for moments of insincerity and irony in the engagement with philosophical ideas; even texts that do not openly articulate their key claims can yield them to an appropriately nuanced paraphrase. At the same time, I want to concede that it is certainly possible for texts to refuse this method, and to deny readers the sense of a clearly asserted claim they might contemplate. I will, however, argue that there is no reason to make this refusal definitive of literature or even poetry as such. In fact it is not even essential to the form of the dramatic monologue. A comparison between Browning and his contemporary Augusta Webster reveals that it is perfectly possible to use dramatic monologues as a means of communication and not as a threat to it, and that Browning's strategy reflects not some culmination or perfect distillation of the technique but instead his own personal and idiosyncratic decision about which artistic effects to create.

Browning and Ideas

In some ways it is ironic that Browning's poetry presents such challenges to the idea of reading for the content, for an earlier generation of readers valued him precisely for his philosophical theology. At the end of the nineteenth century, texts such as Sir Henry Jones's *Browning as a Philosophical and Religious Teacher* (1891) and A. C. Pigou's *Robert Browning as a Religious Teacher* (1901) approached the poet straightforwardly as a thinker.[4] Their works thus exemplify one of the core contentions of this study: there is a long history of literary criticism valuing literary works for their content. Jones's preface is revealing in just this light; while conceding to the formalist that it is wrong to neglect 'the artistic aspect', he argues that there is 'an advantage in attempting to estimate the value of what he has said, apart from the form in which he has said it'.[5] Surprisingly to our ears, Jones thinks Browning's works clearly call for this method: 'of all modern poets', he writes, 'Browning is the one who most obviously invites and justifies such a method of treatment'.

This has not been the attitude of Browning's more recent interpreters. In the wake of deconstruction, critics such as Alan Sinfield, Herbert Tucker and Isobel Armstrong have generally agreed that Browning's dramatic monologues are interesting and important precisely because they refuse to be easily paraphrased.[6] Tucker goes so far as to compare the paraphrasing reader to Browning's murderous Duke: 'In haste to determine *the* meaning of the poem, a reader like the Duke risks losing touch with the *activity* of meaning [. . .] the ducal reader puts the poem to death.'[7] To read for the ideas is not an option among several a reader might take; it is instead a betrayal of the very thing that makes the poem worthy of attention. Complicating matters somewhat, this is also a debate about which period in Browning's long career is most important. Tucker concedes with some slightly polemical phrasing that Browning's late poetry 'degenerates into dogma', and Jones concedes that the 'dramatic element' in Browning's early work makes it difficult to 'say with certainty, "Here I catch the poet."'[8] Thus a methodological debate about how to interpret the poems stems from and corresponds to a broader debate about which experiences of the variety on offer in reading Browning's poetry make it worthwhile.

The conflict between Browning the thinker and Browning the ironist is particularly visible in 'Bishop Blougram's Apology' and in the lengthy body of criticism on the poem, a line of scholarship that might be tedious except for its extensive engagement with the difficulties involved in reading for the ideas in a complex literary text. To briefly recall some details, the poem narrates the after-dinner conversation between the wealthy Catholic Bishop Blougram and the sceptical agnostic journalist Gigadibs. Some 970 of the poem's 1014 lines are spoken by Blougram – the reader infers Gigadibs's questions and objections only from Blougram's responses – but the poem ends with a brief and crucial incursion from a narrator, who explains that a few days after the conversation Gigadibs quit his job and moved to Australia.

The arguments that Blougram deploys in the conversation are wide-ranging, defending traditional Christianity in many and occasionally surprising ways. As F. E. L. Priestley argued in an influential 1946 article, the poem is best understood as series of reductios.[9] Blougram proceeds by initially adopting his opponent's premises and revealing their absurdity, as for instance in a creative version of Pascal's Wager. Granting for the sake of argument that he is an atheist, he argues that he would in such a state be troubled by the 'The Grand Perhaps' of religious belief, just as he is now troubled by the threat of scepticism, and thus atheism offers no more internal peace than his current state.[10] He turns as well to political justifications, referring to the need to value the 'chain of faith' for holding 'the rough purblind mass we seek to rule' (BBA, ll. 754–6), and alludes openly to a series of leading nineteenth-century philosophers, including John Newman, David Strauss and Friedrich Schelling. But perhaps the most interesting of Blougram's arguments for the contemporary reader involve his questioning of the role of morality in human life.

Late in the poem, Blougram turns Gigadibs's (implied) accusation of hypocrisy and dishonesty back on him. Even if one grants that Blougram has failed to live up to his Christian commitments, the same is no less true of Gigadibs, who continues to follow moral principles that could never survive the kind of scepticism he is applying to Blougram's faith. Attempts to found such principles on scientific grounds are comically inadequate: 'Philosophers deduce you chastity / Or shame, just from the fact that at the first / Whoso embraced a woman in the field [. . .] saw the use of going out of sight / In wood or cave to prosecute his loves' (BBA, ll. 825–32). Yet Gigadibs does not take the failure of such intellectual efforts as seriously as logic would have him. He has set himself the goal of integrity above all, of a 'grand simple life' that permits him to be 'whole and sole [him]self' (BBA, ll. 82, 58). But there is a self-division and cowardice; in Blougram's words: 'I live my life here: yours you dare not live' (BBA, l. 852). Should one accept Gigadibs's scepticism as a premise, then there are two equally unattractive conclusions: either a nihilistic and amoral scepticism, or an intellectual duplicity at least as hypocritical as that of which Blougram is accused.

Blougram's own alternative is to develop a morality that adjusts Christian principles to the realities of the world without abandoning them. In a line that has drawn a good deal of criticism from Christian readers of the poem, Blougram claims that 'My business is not to remake myself / But make the absolute best of what God made' (BBA, ll. 354–5).[11] He denies in other words that Christianity requires self-alienation or radical self-transformation. Rather than hating himself and feeling compelled to change everything, Blougram takes his duty to consist of finding morally permissible ways to express himself, including even desires that we might find unsavoury.[12] As the poem's extended metaphor puts it, 'We mortals cross the ocean of this world / Each in his average cabin of a life' (BBA, ll. 100–1). Gigadibs in Blougram's diagnosis is trying to furnish that cabin elaborately, with a piano and a marble bath, yet this overly strict moral code will lead only to hypocrisy and inaction. A morality that can actually be lived, Blougram contends, requires accommodation to the conditions of the world.

One might connect this easily to Bernard Williams's critique of 'the morality system', or what he more provocatively termed 'the peculiar institution' of morality.[13] As he puts the challenge, 'There cannot be any very interesting, tidy, or self-contained theory of what morality is, nor, despite the vigorous activities of some present practitioners, can there be an ethical theory, which, together with some degree of empirical fact, will yield a decision procedure for moral reasoning.'[14] In Blougram's diagnosis, Gigadibs is just such a practitioner of simplistic moral philosophy, who misses the much broader variety of ethical obligations and their imbrication with prudential goals and practical interests. Since such goals and interests are the root of caring about anything in the first place, it is self-defeating to insist that a man care about impartial morality over them.[15] Correspondingly a pursuit of moral integrity that makes no accommodation for practical interests and dispositional facts about the person supposed to possess it will inevitably frustrate itself.

Thus Blougram's position is both philosophically creative and provocative, and admits easily of a rational reconstruction. One could connect Blougram's challenge to broader debates about moral scepticism, evolution and the foundations of ethics, and the role of ideal moral theory in everyday deliberation, and thus engage the poem via sympathetic interpretations of the connections between these issues and Blougram's arguments. Yet there are deep questions about how readers should regard the relationship between Browning, Blougram and Blougram's views. Even Blougram himself doesn't take his ideas all that seriously; the narrator tells us in the interjection at the end of the poem that Blougram 'believed, say, half he spoke', with the rest being 'some accidental arbitrary thoughts' (BBA, ll. 980, 984). And the poem makes it deeply ambiguous whether Gigadibs's actions reflect an acceptance of Blougram's arguments or a rejection of them. After explaining his emigration to Australia, the narrator tells us that

'By this time he has tested his first plough / And studied his last chapter of St. John' (BBA, ll. 1013–14). The question here is whether the emphasis falls on 'St. John' or 'last'; does this mean that Gigadibs has started reading the Bible or that he has stopped?[16] And finally, one might very reasonably think that the self-justifying nature of Blougram's arguments is the key to understanding them. As in 'My Last Duchess', philosophical and psychological claims matter not in themselves, but insofar as they reflect the nature of the speaker, a power-hungry voluptuary who has gained a disturbing amount of social prominence. Blougram's praise of hypocrisy might seem to give the game away here, defending his moral failures precisely by admitting them.

Certainly this was how early reactions understood Browning's overall point. G. K. Chesterton, for instance, thought the poem was obviously ironic, a satirisation of worldly clergymen and a demonstration of their moral failures.[17] That understanding predominated until the 1946 article by Priestley, which argued that in fact Blougram's arguments are persuasive, a creative defence of his own nuanced religious views against the crude scepticism of the naive Gigadibs.[18] In the wake of Priestley's essay, critics recovered Blougram as a much more sympathetic figure, even – in the eyes of one critic – a poet himself, a 'freed, passionate, newly empowered man'.[19] Of course, that recovery has itself been challenged; recently Jonathan Loesberg has found Blougram 'fairly unproblematically unsympathetic'.[20] Naturally enough critics have looked for compromise views, as in Philip Drew's 1970 contention that the poem first reveals the flaws in Gigadibs's agnosticism only to demonstrate also the fallacies in Blougram's moral and religious compromises.[21] This interpretive history should thus give pause to any critic who thinks that reading the poem should primarily involve the philosophical analysis of Blougram's arguments.

Yet the force of this objection can be overstated. Three points are salient. First, as Loesberg admits in a footnote, 'no one can entirely escape from' beginning with an evaluation of Blougram's argument.[22] In that sense a basic rational reconstruction is an essential interpretive step, since one cannot figure out where or how Blougram's views reflect on his character without first articulating what those views are. Even the tensions and points of omission in the arguments, potentially revealing of key aspects of his character, are discernible only after an attempt to assemble them coherently. Second, many of the ambiguities introduced by the levels of mediation between Browning, Blougram and Blougram's arguments can be accounted for easily and interestingly by such a reconstruction. If the poem is, for instance, a study in self-deception and self-justification, this is not impossible for a philosophical reading to acknowledge. On such a reading, one might emphasise Blougram's contempt for simplicity, and consider how an insistence on complexity and flexibility enables him to avoid confronting his betrayal of his principles.

Third, to insist that because the poem situates its arguments in an ambiguous context a reader is not justified in reading the poem primarily to agree or disagree with them is to insist that the poem's aesthetic coherence is the most important thing about it, a claim that (as we have seen) one might reasonably deny. Why not decide that what one cares about are Blougram's arguments, and not what Browning or even Blougram thinks about them? Historians of philosophy, after all, do this all the time, pulling an argument from a section of a work by Aristotle or John Locke without feeling any need to insist on fitting their interpretation into an account of the larger whole. To excerpt the poem in this way might offend the formalist, but the formalists do not have a monopoly on artistic appreciation.

It is certainly true, however, that excerpting is necessary. While the arguments are undeniably in the poem, so are the various layers of qualification and irony. The poem does not invite one to treat Blougram's views coherently, not least because Blougram does not. One might well decide to ignore that fact, but such a dismissal risks the sort of wayward anachronism considered in Chapter 3; to start with a dismissal of the author's intention in the poem – in this case, even including a dismissal of the speaker's intention – ends with a dismissal of the text itself. If one is not interested in the nuanced positioning of Blougram's arguments, then the sense in which one is actually reacting to the poem becomes much less clear.

Thus I want to concede in part to Tucker, Armstrong, Loesberg and the many other readers who hold that Browning's poetry cannot be read straightforwardly for its ideas. A rational reconstruction is a necessary but crucially not sufficient way of coming to grips with a poem like 'Bishop Blougram's Apology'. Even when it offers ideas that reward rational reconstruction, the kind of sincere attempt to address issues of general import that rewards anachronistic reading is missing, an absence that forces the reader back to the text's ambiguities and to the search for other possible interpretations of the poem. Blougram may well have something profound to say, but conveying that profundity is not the point of 'Bishop Blougram's Apology'.

Augusta Webster's Poetics of Clarity

Yet this kind of ambiguity is not definitive in any way of art, literature, poetry or even the dramatic monologue. It is instead the result of Browning's decision to pursue particular aesthetic effects and to work with philosophical ideas in a distinct way. That decision and its alternatives become clear if we look at the poetry and drama of Browning's contemporary, Augusta Webster. As Joshua Taft has noted in a revealing article, Webster offered a deliberate poetics of straightforwardness in contrast to Browning's. As he puts it, 'Webster's poetry embodies this literalism in a style that pursues clarity just as Browning aims for difficulty.'[23] This does not involve a rejection of formal or more precisely stylistic concerns. Rather, Taft argues, Webster 'values clarity and communicability as a stylistic achievement, a difficult but rewarding process of selecting just the right words to make writing and its exchange of ideas as comfortable as it can be'.[24]

The nature of literary communication is one of the key themes in Webster's brief essay 'Poets and Personal Pronouns'. On the one hand, Webster insists that the 'I' in a poem is not the biographical author, as naive readers seem to expect. 'Some people so thoroughly believe this', she writes, 'that they will despise a man as a hypocrite because, after having written and printed "I am the bridegroom of despair" or "no wine but the wine of death for me"', the poet 'goes out to dinners and behaves like anybody else'.[25] The search for biographical correlates to literary characters or literary events, she goes on, reflects a mistake about what poetic construction is, and in that sense readers had better come to see a divide between the literal author and the text. But on the other hand, this divide is necessary not because poets do not try to say something directly to their readers, but because of the nature of what they have to communicate. Poets do not speak simply in their own voice precisely because they are philosophers; they attempt to capture universal experience and to represent it in a way that readers recognise themselves. 'We look to the poet for feelings, thoughts, actions if need be', Webster argues, 'as the manifest expression of what our very selves must have felt and thought and done if we had been those he puts before us and in their cases.'[26] And it is the need to solicit this nod of recognition from the reader that makes the poetic 'I' so misleading; as Webster concludes, the poetic 'we' comes closer as a shorthand for the stance of the poet in the poem.

In keeping with this approach, Webster certainly uses the dramatic monologue as a form of distancing from herself, but it is a distancing that clarifies rather than obfuscates. The speaker's identity does not qualify or undermine the ideas expressed over the course of the poem but instead enriches them. One way of putting this is to say that it is a version of the form in which that form becomes content, something a paraphrase can capture, instead of a recalcitrance that refuses paraphrase. In particular, Webster is fascinated by the experience and aftermath of moral dilemmas, and she uses the identities of her speakers to enhance the philosophical dimensions of the problems involved.

We see this clearly in Webster's dramatic dialogue 'Pilate', a depiction of a conversation between the Roman judge and his wife Procla at some point after Christ's execution. In Webster's hands, Procla is the voice of regret and doubt; as the poem opens, Pilate is responding to her (implied) critique of his decision, claiming that she (like most women, in his view) is too married to the narrow application of principles in a limited world, and does not recognise the flexibility sometimes made necessary by larger events:

> And so she'll make her roads
> Run straight to little points within the hedge,
> And never thinks there may be curves to take
> To reach great points outside.[27]

Webster gives Procla a curt and insightful reply:

> *Procla.* And does that mean
> A woman thinks a judge is to be just,
> And a man thinks a judge is to resolve
> What policy were spoiled if he were just? (P, ll. 13–16)

Procla thus calls out both Pilate's arrogance and his moral laxity; Pilate has given up the idea of ruling solely with a concern for justice in favour of a broader political role, letting attempts to maintain or improve policy affect judicial rulings. And Pilate concedes the point in his response: 'a man, ruler as I am / Must look beyond the moment, must allay / Justice with prudence' (P, ll. 17–19). This goes so far in Pilate's imagination as to permit the punishment of the innocent: 'Innocence is much / To save a man, but is not everything / Where a whole province is at stake for Rome' (P, ll. 19–20). For Pilate, the need to address prudential concerns is a hard fact that judges must accept and act on.

Thus in the opening lines of the poem, Webster invokes an old problem in moral philosophy and the utilitarian tradition: the balance between rights and consequentialist concerns. To describe the problem as it is usually put, there is a certain kind of trial that will pose a dilemma for a utilitarian judge.[28] Suppose that there is a man on trial whom the judge knows beyond a shadow of a doubt to be innocent. Yet the judge also knows that the broader populace is so convinced of this man's guilt that there will be extensive rioting if he is found innocent, rioting that will certainly lead to extensive destruction and the deaths of at least a few people, who are also presumably innocent.

What should such a judge do? It is unhelpful in such a case to note, as John Stuart Mill does, that rights are usually codifications of principles that maximise overall utility; undoubtedly it is true generally that a justice system that finds innocent people innocent and guilty people guilty will promote overall welfare more than a system that does the opposite, but the question is why one ought to care about rights in the exceptional cases where this is not true.[29] Nor is it helpful to argue, as rule utilitarians do, that promoting a belief in a fair judicial system is itself useful, since the judge certainly need not reveal that he believes himself to have convicted an innocent man. Only the results of the trial will be public, not the decision procedure used to yield them.

Webster's Pilate, superficially self-confident, is ultimately torn about this question. He defends himself at first by insisting on the negative consequences his judgement of Christ has averted, 'hundreds crucified; rapine and fire [. . .] Half our Jews dead, the other half grown dumb / For utter fear' (P, ll. 43, 46–7). But then Procla makes a telling point: if it is true that 'the past is past' and should simply be forgotten, still a man 'may find good from sorrow for ill deeds' (P, l. 69). In other words, the question shifts from whether Pilate did what he had to do to whether he ought to feel sorry for what he did do. At first, Pilate scoffs at this argument: 'What good? Will sorrow lengthen a man's days / Or give him wealth or triumphs?' (P, l. 70–1). He elaborates on this point when his wife presses him on the question of Christ's divinity and the immortality of the soul: 'Let us take life as softly as we can', he tells her, 'and not nurse sorrow' (P, 159–61). A resolute materialist, Pilate concludes that one ought to embrace life as it is.

But after she leaves, Pilate reveals a different side of himself: 'Indeed these several days I have not lost / The sense of shame that shook me when he looked / With quiet eyes at me, standing condemned / By my allowance' (P, ll. 207–10). He tries to persuade himself that he is guiltless, that there was nothing more he could have done to hold back the Jewish mob, and that his superiors in Rome would have condemned him if he had incited a riot. Then too he reflects that after all the man is dead now and the point is moot. Yet he cannot shake the thought of Christ on the cross and the wrongness of his execution, and ends by thinking that although 'To weep past evil is a vainer thing / That to shake drops of dew upon the fire', he would nevertheless 'give this right hand [. . .] to purchase that redemption' (P, ll. 374–5, 371–3). Webster's Pilate is a practical man who does not wish to dwell on the past, who indeed thinks such dwelling is useless and conceited. Moreover and importantly, he does not believe in Christ's divinity or a supernatural world of any sort. Nevertheless he believes that he has done wrong, and that a moral purification would be necessary if it were possible.

This then is a complex moral reaction. Webster's Pilate does not believe he should have acted differently, but nevertheless feels that he has done something wrong. Moral philosophy for much of its recent history would have regarded this as incoherent, and that to believe that an action was wrong was simply and necessarily to believe that one should have done something else.[30] Indeed one can still occasionally find this generalisation about moral philosophy from those outside the field.[31]

Yet as a significant amount of recent work has acknowledged, to deny the existence of genuine moral dilemmas overlooks one of the major insights of tragedy. Sometimes moral agents have the ethical bad luck to be placed in a situation where they do something wrong no matter what they do.[32] The wrongness of a given action in such a situation is not eliminated by the fact that it was the least bad of a variety of options; the killer of the innocent does not become morally blameless simply because he averted a riot. In Ruth Marcus's vivid phrase, there is a moral residue.[33]

What is the nature of this residue or remainder? Most narrowly, it can be understood simply as a descriptive claim about the likelihood of regret, the fact that such agents will probably wish that it had not been necessary for them to act as they did, and that the situation had somehow been avoided.[34] Indeed, some argue, this regret may be simply the input of instinctive processes that are entirely irrational from a normative perspective.[35] More broadly, it can function as a call for moral creativity, finding ways to redress the violated obligation via apologies or other forms of restitution. But most deeply, it can be understood as a deep violation of one's character and a bar to complete integrity. Goodness is fragile, in Martha Nussbaum's illuminating formulation, and sometimes what one does alters one's moral nature. The mark of an evil action does not disappear simply by not thinking about it.

Webster's poem 'Medea in Athens' approaches Browning's style in showing us a moral agent living in the wake of this kind of self-violation. Webster gives us an older and happily remarried Medea, reflecting on her life and in particular the murder of her children. Confronting Jason's ghost, she remains wholehearted in her hatred of him, but is less self-possessed in thinking of her children. The end of the poem reads thus:

> Yes, 'twas best so: my sons, we are avenged.
> Thou, mock me not. What if I have ill dreams,
> Seeing them loathe me, fly from me in dread,
> When I would feed my hungry mouth with kisses?
> What if I moan in tossing fever-thirsts,
> Crying for them whom I shall have no more,
> Here nor among the dead, who never more,
> Here nor among the dead, will smile to me
> With young lips prattling 'Mother, mother dear'?
> What if I turn sick when the women pass
> That lead their boys; and hate a child's young face?
> What if –
> Go, go; thou mind'st me of our sons;
> And then I hate thee worse; go to thy grave
> By which none weeps. I have forgotten thee.[36]

Medea narrates the kind of suffering one might expect from someone who has violated a core moral value, or what Lisa Tessman calls a value that has been 'sacralised', conceived as an obligation whose violation is unthinkable.[37] She does not precisely regret her actions, telling us again that it is for the 'best' that she has acted as she has. But she sleeps poorly and is disturbed by mothers and their children, and is struck by recurring memories of her sons. And more than that, the final lines of the poem enact the self-division: she does not wish to remember her children and must thus avoid all reminders. Murdering her children has eliminated forever the possibility of coherent moral character; to betray an identity-structuring commitment as Medea has is a kind of death.

Yet this last might seem to take things too far. Medea is, after all, still alive. To think that evil action might mar one's character suggests that one of the main reasons for acting well is something like moral purity, understood here as the maintenance of integrity. And that can paradoxically begin to seem like selfishness; to care too much about moral purity is ultimately to forget this world and the needs of the people in it. Thomas Nagel puts the point well: 'what gives one man a right to put the purity of his soul or the cleanliness of his hands above the lives or welfare of large numbers of other people?'[38] It is worth noting that Webster's Pilate is in this respect better than the one given in the Book of Matthew, who washed his hands of the situation rather than confront his own responsibility and involvement in the matter. While Webster's Pilate has washed his hands in a literal sense, he has certainly not done so in the deeper and psychological dimension; he recognises and accepts the inevitable moral consequences of his position in the world. Perhaps tragic dilemmas do indeed permanently mar one's character, but that might be superior to a shallow moral cleanliness.

What is hard about this particular objection is that it seems in principle impossible to weigh the various options in the deliberative process against each other in a way that captures the reasons motivating them. The reasons motivating us to care about moral integrity might seem to be of a piece with those we have for caring about the well-being of other people, but that there is a disjunct becomes clear whenever one attempts to imagine comparing them. Integrity does not seem to be the kind of thing that can be weighed against other desirable states of affairs, and moreover if an action is in fact the option that contributes most to the welfare of others, then to a consequentialist it cannot by definition be a violation of one's moral integrity.

Webster is certainly not a consequentialist, yet she has some sympathy for the idea that virtue ethics are too committed to ideas of moral purity. In her work, a theory of moral deliberation that finds a way to weigh personal moral integrity alongside other options appears necessary but difficult to articulate, and her dramatic monologues show her characters finding ways to conceptualise this peculiar sort of moral dilemma. If 'Pilate' introduces it in a near-textbook thought experiment, her poem 'A Castaway' takes it up via perhaps the most vexed figure in Victorian moral thought – the prostitute. What is striking about the poem is the way it uses a sceptical investigation of Victorian moral attitudes about sexual purity to suggest broader worries about the role that characterological concerns should play in practical deliberation. As Amanda Anderson has noted, the image of the fallen woman in Victorian culture was a vexed one because an acknowledgement of the determinative forces of social identity threw into question psychological assumptions about the possibility of self-determination.[39] Webster's poem, which narrates the thoughts of a sex worker named Eulalie as she flips through her diary, engages these problems directly, ultimately offering a qualified defence of the importance of moral character alongside both a spirited attack on the shallow purity of empty virtue and a rueful acknowledgement that moral fulfilment can be dependent on non-moral attitudes. The core of that defence is symbolised in the speaker's preoccupation with her diary, which symbolises her dissatisfaction with herself and her corresponding lack of self-coherence. Yet the whole is governed by a certain lightness, as if moral integrity is not quite all it is cracked up to be.

The poem opens with the speaker musing over the girl she used to be, as revealed in the opening pages of the diary. She studied French and learned to sing, and aspired only to have tea with the clergyman. Such a figure seems impossible to reconcile with the person the speaker is now: 'And now it seems a jest to talk of me / As if I could be one with her, of me / Who am . . . me'.[40] As the poem progresses, the speaker reveals that she has tried and failed to reconnect with her former self; she went to a women's 'Refuge', but found she could not stay more than a week (C, l. 239). Such an attempt reflected naivety, she concludes, about the characterological consequences of her decisions: 'A wild whim that, to fancy I could change / My new self for my old because I wished!' (C, ll. 206–7). Now she knows better: ''Tis a sick fancy' (C, l. 212). Why exactly it is impossible is complex; partly, it's because she can no longer be happy with a life of quiet domesticity. 'How could I henceforth be content', she asks, with any life that lacks 'a hot merry fever?' At the same time, she also thinks that material substance and companionship might have been sufficient: the Refuge kept her 'so much alone' and 'famishing'. But it is a moot point now, as her old self is like an old home that no longer has a place for her.

And to a large extent she is comfortable with that fact and accepting of her profession. 'I have looked coolly on my what and why', she explains, 'And I accept myself' (C, l. 137). After all, her profession is just as honourable if not more so than many others; lawyers, doctors, preachers and others regularly practise forms of dishonesty and hypocrisy. Such 'virtuous worthy men' may actually be worse, since they 'feed on the world's follies, vices, wants' while receiving moral encouragement and thus maintain a duplicity she at least can avoid (C, ll. 92–3). Then, too, she argues for a consequentialist account of the moral dimension of her work: no one is actually hurt by it.

A possible objection to the view – what about the wives of the men she sleeps with? – leads Eulalie into her first philosophical reflection on the nature of moral purity. She is contemptuous of the objection's underlying premise, since the husbands these married women are in fear of losing are not particularly valuable, nothing 'worth crying for or keeping' (C, l. 101). And at the same time, she thinks it would be easy to prevent such problems if such women cared to do so: ''tis not such a mighty task / To pin an idiot to your apron-string' (C, l. 106). That they do not reveals the selfish laziness at their core: ''tis an easier life to let them go / And whimper at it for morality' (C, ll. 111–12). In Eulalie's subsequent diagnosis, such women are committed to a meaningless self-satisfaction; proud of never kissing anyone other than their husband, they refuse to admit that no one else wants to kiss them. The purity of such 'glass-case saints' is thus irrelevant, because unearned, and their scorn for beautiful sex workers like herself can and should be ignored (C, l. 128).[41] Their path may take in 'church and chapel', but it is just 'A roundabout and decent way to hell' (C, ll. 145–6). A pure and blameless life attained through the escape of hard decisions or the good luck of avoiding them does not merit moral praise, and correspondingly impure lives do not merit moral critique when they result from the same. Having confronted such a decision herself, Eulalie tells herself that she can safely ignore the opinions of those who have not.

Yet alongside this defence Eulalie enacts self-dissatisfaction.[42] This appears early in the poem, in her consideration of whether or not she is 'modest' (C, l. 47). She is not drunk in the streets, after all, and doesn't stand on street corners. However, as she forces herself to admit, 'I flout myself' (C, l. 58). This dissatisfaction with her profession appears again in Eulalie's complex reaction to her own beauty. At first it is a source of pride; it is what allows her to feel herself 'a woman still', one with pride and even 'modesty' (C, l. 43). But it is a source of anxiety too, since it makes her vulnerable to age; to be 'Old', 'the cruellest word that ever woman learns', will render her 'forgotten and solitary' (C, ll. 178–80). To have a career dependent on her beauty forces her to identify with a transient and contingent part of herself. That is why Eulalie is eventually so contemptuous of love and men; she has been loved several times but never cared for, which is why she remarks, 'I hate men' (C, l. 258). She wants someone to care for her, not merely to love her. And the professional requirement to 'flout' herself continually violates that goal.

Eulalie's reflections thus alternate between two reactions to her moral character. Generally the scorn she receives is misguided and hypocritical, but she also thinks it contains an element of accurate moral perception. Near the opening of the poem she burns a religious pamphlet and mocks its judgement of prostitutes who paint their cheeks; Eulalie dryly remarks, 'I always wear them pale' (C, l. 161). But subsequently her critique turns to the limits of female opportunity, her brother having received in a month a sum that would have bought her 'teachers for a year' (C, l. 503). These two responses align in a critique of patriarchal society but differ on the moral status of prostitution: on the first it is a career like any other, while on the second its existence is an evil that demonstrates the failure of the social order.[43] And over the course of the poem, the second critique ultimately supplants the first, and the confidently beautiful Eulalie of the poem's opening transforms into the anguished and ashamed protagonist of a tragedy. That change in emphasis should not be read as a mere replacement, however; rather, it suggests a gradual acknowledgement of what one might call the social preconditions of moral integrity.

This is the tension at the turning point of the poem, the passage where Eulalie reveals that she has had a son who died. The father seems to have been her pimp: 'His father would not then have let me go.' And Eulalie takes the birth and death of her son to mark a Rubicon in the moral trajectory of her character:

> Some ways can be trodden back,
> But never our way, we who one wild day
> Have given goodbye to what in our deep hearts
> The lowest woman still holds best in life,
> Good name – good name though given by the world
> That mouths and garbles with its decent prate
> And wraps it in respectable grave shams
> And patches conscience partly by the rule
> Of what one's neighbour thinks, but something more
> By what his eyes are sharp enough to see.
> How could I scorn it with its Pharisees
> If it could not scorn me: but yet, but yet –
> Oh God, if I could look it in the face! (C, ll. 439–51)

Eulalie here preserves her sense that social norms and the judgements that follow from them are full of hypocrisy; the 'decent prate' of the world is a grave sham. And the people who live by such norms are often contemptible, needing to supplement their own moral judgement with public opinion.[44] Nevertheless such social acceptance has a root in moral truth: the idea of a 'good name' matters even though it is 'given by the world'. And Eulalie recognises this core of moral truth precisely insofar as she knows she has failed it; she would love to be able to scorn the idea of a good name as mere gossip, but she cannot. Thus Eulalie's lack of a good name and her inability to look her life 'in the face' turn out to be interrelated.

This merges into Eulalie's reflections on the role that moral bad luck has played in her life. Near the end of the poem, she echoes a famous idea from Plato's *Republic*: Cephalus's argument that the most valuable feature of wealth is that it enables moral life, since it makes it easier to avoid the necessity of cheating or deceiving others.[45] In Eulalie's rueful formulation:

> Money's the root of evil do they say?
> Money is virtue, strength: money to me
> Would then have been repentance: could I live
> Upon my idiot's pride? (C, ll. 594–7)

As Eulalie explains, she has been forced into a hard choice by her poverty: either prostitution or starvation. While 'those who need not sin have safer souls', to make this the core of a moral sermon ignores the grim reality of those with 'bodies to save' (C, ll. 167–8). In such situations money reveals itself as a moral necessity and moral pride as a luxury, one Eulalie believes she would have better without. This, however, introduces an element of wavering and an alternative stance – if Eulalie believes in part that she has nothing to be ashamed of and that she can justifiably ignore moral condemnation, she also believes that she has indeed done and continues to do something necessary but wrong, something she cannot be proud of. The condemnation of others may not matter, but her own self-judgement is neither so easily nor reliably dismissed.

The transition from self-assurance to anxiety appears finally in her relationship to the diary. At first it is pleasant; she enjoys remembering the girl she used to be. But quickly the diary becomes a source of anxiety – 'that silly diary', which brings back 'the old vexing echoes' (C, l. 190) And the fact that she cannot quite accept herself appears in her unwillingness to remember who she used to be: 'I hate the useless memories', she thinks, and that she had 'Best take Now kindly' (C, ll. 193–4). By the end of the poem, after she has remembered both the way her brother abandoned her and his subsequent marriage to an heiress, she is on the verge of sobbing, and thankful that someone appears to talk with her; the final line of 'A Castaway' is 'one gets so moped alone' (C, l. 630). To be forced to dwell too much with herself is to recognise the gaps between the person she was, the person she wanted and wants to be, and the person she is, and the extent to which self-contentment is only possible by ignoring those gaps. Reconciling them – that is, becoming a person she could wholeheartedly approve of – is beyond her control. Correspondingly, the socially fraught concept of purity turns out to contain a core of truth. Eulalie conveys this through the revelation of the way her current state is in part the result of her own actions, and thus something for which she could be said to be responsible. Near the poem's end, she tells us, 'I see clear now and know one has one's life / In hand at first to spend or spare or give [. . .] and if you spend or give that is your choice / And if you let it slip, that's your choice too' (C, ll. 553–61). The act corresponding to this abstraction seems to be her decision at some earlier point to send money back to her brother after first begging for it. That surge of pride and independence, Eulalie thinks, is precisely the reason she finds it so difficult to maintain pride and independence now.

The nature of a tragic dilemma and the role that concern for character can and should play in it is finally at the centre of Webster's 1882 closet drama *In A Day*. Set in Greece shortly after its conquest by Rome, the play narrates the last day in the life of a wealthy Greek man named Myron. Through no fault of his own, Myron is charged with treason, and thus put into a situation where he has to choose between concern for his moral character and concern for others. If he pleads innocence, he will be able to challenge the charge and publicly maintain his honesty. However, his slaves will be tortured and interrogated as part of the investigation, and sold into the hands of crueller people if he is subsequently found guilty. This matters rather more than it might to a similar man, because his slaves are his real friends and family, and in fact he has started the process of freeing them that very day. One slave in particular, Klydone, is a woman who loves him and whom he intends to marry after she is freed. Pleading guilty will allow him to avoid all these consequences; no one will torture his slaves, who will be allowed to leave; eventually an offer is made that he too will be allowed to leave, banished in return for a guilty plea. But he will have to let the public falsehood stand.

The play's creativity in depicting the arguments for and against either option is striking. At first, Myron's slaves insist that he protest his innocence and let them be tortured. Klydone's father, the slave Olymnios, makes a consequentialist argument:

> Myron, thy death that brings thee little ill
> Breeds many ills for many: there's my reason.
> Thy harmless wealth will be crime's instrument;
> Thy lordships tyrannies; thy dues extortions;
> Thy slaves, thy clients, friends that hang on thee,
> All that had good in thee, are left despoiled.[46]

Klydone agrees, and adds that surely she should have the right to decide what happens:

> Ah, think; take heed for us; be the choice ours:
> Better some present pain than that long loss. (*ID*, p. 56)

Myron argues that he cannot permit others to suffer for him: 'Nay, love, thou wooest me to a shameless deed' (*ID*, p. 56). But Olymnios argues that this gets things backwards:

> Were't but for thee,
> But for the brute's poor greediness of life,
> Thus were the deed a shameless. Not so now.
> 'Twere a diviner courage than to die
> To front the shame and sorrow. (*ID*, p. 56)

Olymnios puts the point gracefully, but he is essentially accusing Myron of selfishness, of caring more about his moral character than the possibility of actually helping people. The courageous act in this moment is not to save his slaves from suffering, but rather to bear the shame of letting them suffer for him, understanding that it is both what they choose and what will lead to better results overall for them in the long run. In other words once one shifts the perspective from Myron's examination of his own character to the welfare of his slaves, what would originally be a shameless act becomes a selfless one, and certain virtues – namely, honesty and justified pride – reveal themselves to be, in this situation at least, self-regarding scruples.

But Myron is not persuaded. He instead decides to claim that he is innocent while making plans for Olymnios, Klydone and the other slaves to escape, and to be able to claim money owed to him: in this way, the only person who will suffer consequences is himself. It's at this point in the play that Myron's friend Euphranor appears with an offer from the proconsul Lavinius: Myron will be permitted to live and to leave with his slaves so long as he confesses publicly. That offer distils the dilemma, for now his slaves will be safe no matter what he does. Now the question is simple: would Myron rather live, but be banished and deemed guilty, or die? One might think the answer is simple – existing being preferable to not existing on balance – but Myron begins to look for reasons to turn the deal down. When Euphranor, himself a Greek patriot and revolutionary against the Romans – in other words, a man actually guilty of the treason that Myron is accused of – goes on to say that he would take the deal in an instant, Myron's response is revealing. For Myron is surprisingly open about his non-moral reasons for preferring the overtly moral stance of proclaiming his innocence:

> Thou has thy purpose like an inward sun
> That floods all darkness with a summer hope;
> But I, it was my world that shone on me,
> What shall I do in the dusk? No; best end now.
> A lifelong stranger on unnatural hills
> [. . .] And there's penury to add;
> Cross, timid, counting, chaffering penury.
> No. Tell him no. I am too much a coward. (*ID*, p. 63)

The speech here gives the lie to his earlier protestations that he could never do something so 'shameless' as let his slaves be tortured for him, by revealing the selfishness and laziness that can underlie a supposed concern for one's moral character. To Myron, it is quite literally easier to stand on principle and die than contemplate the novel life of poverty and hardship that banishment will require. Characteristic of so much Victorian moral psychology, the problem is that Myron doesn't have a project structuring his life: without a 'purpose' that 'floods all darkness with a summer hope', Myron can see no reason why he should voluntarily endure the suffering the prosecutor offers. Yet we should note that there is a kind of honesty here, too. A coward, perhaps, but not a hypocrite.

Still, Klydone's interjection after this speech – 'He said he loved me' – underlines this critique (*ID*, p. 64). Myron is thinking too much of himself and forgetting his duties to those he loves and who love him. And Myron's subsequent response does not bode well for the future of their relationship; when Euphranor tells Myron that Klydone is braver than he is, Myron essentially calls her naive:

> In sooth she is
> But 'tis a singing lark meant for the plains,
> That, since it can soar high in the smooth air,
> Thinks it could house in the vulture's barren crags. (*ID*, p. 65)

Klydone, understandably, is not amused:

> Wilt never be in earnest, even now?
> No lark art thou, but a slight butterfly,
> That folds its wings and ends at the first chills. (*ID*, p. 65)

Myron, less condescending, reiterates his lack of courage:

> I am. So be content and let me cease;
> A kinder fate than grunting desolate winds. (*ID*, p. 65)

Myron's refusal to take Klydone seriously reiterates his refusal to let her be tortured for him; he does not believe in her strength. It goes unstated, but it seems also possible that he does not believe that she – a young and beautiful woman – really does love him. Certainly Klydone's response is to try to persuade Myron that he can trust her, and that a poor life with a wife will be just as satisfying as his rich but solitary one has previously been: 'love me more / Trust me to fill thy life as thou dost mine' (*ID*, p. 66). Yet Myron cannot; he asks Olymnios if she can bear it, and then – when Olymnios answer unequivocally that she can – he announces that he is going to take a nap, without answering Klydone's final, urgent request and clarifying whether he intends to plead guilty or innocent.

In a twist, though, Myron turns out to be right about Klydone's weakness. She decides to take matters into her own hands and submits herself for torture while Myron is sleeping, believing that she can resist and swear throughout that Myron is innocent. However, she turns out to be wrong about herself, and under torture confesses falsely that Myron has committed treason. Olymnios is harsh, calling her afterwards 'a wincing mindless babe / A crouching thing distraught by pain, and faithless' (*ID*, p. 74). But Myron, waking up from his nap to find himself condemned to death, is generous: 'Dear, thou has done thy best / How couldst thou bear past nature?' (*ID*, p. 75). Indeed, he tells her, he only loves her more now.

These two reactions to Klydone are reiterated in a more dramatic way at the play's close. Condemned to death by poison, Myron urges Klydone to live and to marry someone else, and thus he tries to help her forget her failure. But Olymnios is less sympathetic:

> *Myr.* Let her not brood upon my death too much.
> And most of all persuade her from remorse [. . .]
> *Olymn.* No, Myron, self-blame's a shrewd counsellor;
> I will not help Klydone from that good.
> *Myr.* She is such a woman as some griefs could kill.
> *Olymn.* Better to die by an ennobling grief
> Than to live cheerful in too low content. (*ID*, p. 91)

Thus the issues of character and consequence recur: Myron is primarily concerned for Klydone's physical welfare, urging her father to help her forget him. But Olymnios cares only for her moral character. Indeed he happily bites the bullet involved in the strong version of this thesis, asserting that it can be better to die than to become comfortable with certain moral failures. That in fact he may not quite believe this is revealed a moment later; when the two men learn that Klydone has committed suicide, Olymnios ducks into an adjoining room and kills himself too. Myron's own death is peaceful, fading away as he listens to a song about the inextricability of joy and grief.

And so the play ends up revealing flaws in the moral outlooks of each of the three main characters. Klydone's self-confidence, courage and dedication turn out to cover a fatal inability to be honest with herself and with those who depend upon her. She is not as strong as she thinks she is, and that mistake leads to both her own death and that of the men she loves. Olymnios's stoic concern for moral character above all certainly leads to his own death, but more importantly contributes to that of his daughter; indeed if we recognise that he has been her moral exemplar and tutor, one might fault his strictness for contributing to her inability to be honest with herself. Meanwhile Myron, whose moral laziness and indecisiveness seemed undeniably selfish, reappears in this final act as newly generous. Perhaps unpardonably tolerant of his own weaknesses, he is equally and admirably forgiving of Klydone's, and more aware than Olymnios is of the potentially fatal effects of shame. In that sense Webster leaves us with a newfound respect for Myron's honesty; if he is not a moral hero, and if he is too dependent on material comforts, he does at least know it, and makes no attempt to hold others to a higher standard than he holds himself.

In A Day reverses the argumentative trajectory of 'A Castaway': 'A Castaway' begins by denying the importance of moral character and ends up conceding its importance to a certain extent, while *In A Day* opens with the essential primacy of moral character and ends up conceding its limits. But both texts ultimately arrive at similar points: one's character should indeed be a matter of concern, but it is not the only element worthy of ethical consideration, and non-moral elements such as one's own personal welfare may be and should be an element in practical deliberation alongside moral factors. Myron and Eulalie are radically different in most respects, but they share a fundamental honesty in recognising the importance of wealth; surely Myron agrees that 'money is virtue'. Yet neither goes so far as to dismiss the basic insight that Pilate came to: that it is indeed possible to flaw one's life irreparably. Webster does not fully explain how one might arbitrate these concerns – concerns for other people, concerns for one's own character and concerns for one's practical welfare – but rather highlights a primary tool for dealing with them well: Pilate, Eulalie, Myron and even Medea are all fundamentally honest, and above all honest with themselves.

Thinking in Poetry

In her 2004 book *Poets Thinking*, Helen Vendler opens with a brief anecdote about what seems like an interesting experiment; at the 1983 English Institute, three scholars outside literary studies – a philosopher, a political scientist and an anthropologist – were asked to offer presentations on Alexander Pope's *An Essay on Man*.[47] Vendler was apparently disgusted by the results; 'the scandal', she remarks, was that these scholars 'had only one way of thinking about a poem: they translated it into its conceptual paraphrase, and proceeded to dismiss the paraphrase on the grounds of its intellectual irrelevance to modern thought'.[48] They had ignored the key premise that paraphrase is a heresy: 'poems are not their paraphrases, because the paraphrase does not represent the thinking process as it strives toward ultimate precision, but rather reduces the poem to summarised thought'.[49] That Vendler is beating up a straw man is obvious; presumably the three scholars did not think that the poem was its paraphrase. In fact, probably no one has ever thought or said that poems were their paraphrases, and it is yet again revealing of the power of formalism that it has to make up its enemies.

What has perhaps been implied is the more limited claim that paraphrases can capture some of what makes a poem interesting: namely, its intellectual content. And in this sense, the basic procedure of the scholars that Vendler mentions, which apparently involved a historically inflected reconstruction of the ideas in Pope's poem and a subsequent engagement with them on the basis of present concerns, seems reasonable enough. But Vendler disagrees with this more limited claim, too. Analysing *An Essay on Man*, she writes that no paraphrase could ever capture the poem's thought, because the poem is an enactment of a process of thinking that loses its vitality when summarised and clarified. 'As leaden "ideas" rephrase themselves in his witty and exquisitely literary brain', she writes, 'Pope creates a cinematic flow of living thought, instead of presenting [. . .] thought embalmed.'[50] So paraphrases miss not merely the traditional aesthetic qualities of the poem, but even its more philosophical and theoretical dimensions.

I do not understand this metaphor, and I think the fact that Vendler has to fall back on metaphor is instructive. The notion that one form of written expression of ideas is 'living thought' while others are 'embalmed' seems incoherent at first blush; it's true that some writers are boring while others are exciting, but this has as much to do with what they are saying as how. The implicit phenomenological claim will moreover seem strange to anyone who has ever enjoyed reading philosophy or literary criticism. It's true that there can be something exciting about watching a complex text dance around an idea, but clarity and clear progression can be exciting, too. Much depends on how interesting the idea is. And upon second glance the notion that Pope's ironically expressed claims are somehow alive in a way that sincere claims are not looks like aestheticist snobbery. Vendler claims a monopoly on what thinking really is: 'It is as if the poet wants to say, "This is what thinking really is like: have you ever known it?"'[51] One might imagine a poet such as Webster replying dryly, 'I am not quite sure that you know what you are talking about.' Vendler's claim seems finally to be forced upon her source material. She asks rhetorically, 'What delights the poet, then, in the exposition of an idea?' and answers, 'I am afraid the answer is quasi-intelligibility, together with the two answers Pope gave – memorableness and concision.'[52] It is striking first of all that Vendler has to add a wholly separate category to the two reasonably clear points that Pope makes, and present it as if all three aligned neatly (they don't). More than that, however, the slippage from Pope to 'the poet' is telling: even if we grant that Pope was interested in only being partially understood, this fact leads no credence at all to the idea that poetry as such depends on ambiguity and a refusal of straightforward expression.

This is one of the points that the poet Mary Karr makes in her 1991 polemic 'Against Decoration'. Overtly challenging Vendler's emphasis on the 'intricacy of form' in contemporary poetry, Karr denies that complexity is interesting for its own sake, and calls for a return to communication and clarity.[53] In a bracing passage, Karr writes:

> Deconstruction has permitted poets to be weak communicators. I'm thinking specifically of the glib meaninglessness in poets like Ashbery and his heirs, the language poets. It's ironic, though, that theories invented to collapse distinctions between form and content now provide writers with permission to ignore the referents of words, thereby elevating form to a communicative end in itself [. . .] the linguistic and decorative experience of a poem should not outweigh the human or synthetic meanings.[54]

Karr, a distinguished poet in her own right, here gives the lie to Vendler's attempt to monopolise the nature of poetry. Certainly it is possible to write poems that refuse clear expression and frustrate attempts at paraphrase. But this is no more essential to poetry as such than any other poetic strategy.

Poems that care about content as much as form, that seek to communicate as clearly as possible, have just as much right to the title 'poetry' as any other. And such is one way to capture the difference between Augusta Webster and Robert Browning, for Webster is a poet thoroughly interested in communicating, in using varying perspectives not as obfuscatory screens but as ways of analysing difficult ideas. Karr's evisceration of her formalist rivals 'glib meaninglessness' offers at the level of poetic practice the theoretical point this book has developed: to say something interesting is an artistic achievement in its own right.

Notes

1. Robert Browning, 'My Last Duchess', in Collins and Rundle (eds), *The Broadview Anthology of Victorian Poetry and Poetic Theory*, p. 224.
2. This objection was put most famously by his wife Elizabeth Barrett Browning, who in a letter of 25 May 1846 wrote, 'I do not think that, with all that music in you [. . .] you should not teach what you have learnt, in the directest and most impressive way, the mask thrown off.' Quoted in Alan Sinfield, *Dramatic Monologue* (New York: Methuen, 1977), p. 58.
3. As Stefanie Markovits has brought out in a recent book, Browning was very much not alone. The mixture of narrative techniques with poetic modes was both a popular strategy in the Victorian period and a source of scorn to critics who regarded such combinations as a betrayal of the purity of lyric poetry. Stefanie Markovits, *The Victorian Verse-Novel: Aspiring to Life* (Oxford: Oxford University Press, 2017), p. 16.
4. A. C. Pigou, *Robert Browning as a Religious Teacher* (London: Clay and Sons, 1901); Sir Henry Jones, *Browning as a Philosophical and Religious Teacher* (London: Macmillan, 1902).
5. Jones, *Browning as a Philosophical and Religious Teacher*, p. viii.
6. Isobel Armstrong, *Victorian Poetry: Poetry, Poetics, Politics* (London: Routledge, 1993); Herbert Tucker, *Browning's Beginnings: The Art of Disclosure* (Minneapolis: University of Minnesota Press, 1980); Sinfield, *Dramatic Monologue*.
7. Tucker, *Browning's Beginnings*, p. 182.
8. Tucker, *Browning's Beginnings*, p. 187; Jones, *Browning as a Philosophical and Religious Teacher*, p. 11.

9. F. E. L. Priestley, 'Blougram's Apologetics', in Boyd Litzinger and K. L. Knickerbocker (eds), *The Browning Critics* (Lexington: University of Kentucky Press, 1965), pp. 167–80.
10. Robert Browning, 'Bishop Blougram's Apology', in Collins and Rundle (eds), *The Broadview Anthology of Victorian Poetry and Poetic Theory*, pp. 263–77 (l. 190). Subsequent citations, abbreviated BBA, are given in parentheses in the text by line number.
11. See, for instance, David Ewbank, who writes with some asperity that 'it must be remarked that Blougram's apology is based on a premise of which the Catholic faith could not approve', a fact that 'would appear to be too obvious to require explicit statement', except that non-Catholic critics fail to recognise it. David Ewbank, 'Bishop Blougram's Argument', *Victorian Poetry* 10.3 (1972), p. 263.
12. Blougram admits to 'power in me and will to dominate / Which I must exercise, they hurt me else', as well as a preference for the 'dainties' of life (BBA, ll. 322–3, 328).
13. See Bernard Williams, *Moral Luck* (Cambridge: Cambridge University Press, 1982), p. ix; also Bernard Williams, *Ethics and the Limits of Philosophy* (New York: Routledge, 2012).
14. See Williams, *Moral Luck*, p. ix.
15. For a discussion of this aspect of Williams's thought, see Mark Jenkins, *Bernard Williams* (Chesham: Acumen, 2006), p. 58.
16. Thomas Fish puts the problem well: 'Which last chapter of John – the gospel, one of the epistles, or the Revelation? And does studying "his last" suggest the beginning or ending of a spiritual quest ... or neither?' Thomas Fish, 'Be "Whole And Sole Yourself": The Quest for Selfhood in "Bishop Blougram's Apology"', *South Atlantic Review* 56.1 (1991), p. 32. On the 'beginning' side of the debate, one can include Priestley, Arnold Shapiro, Philip Drew in 1970 (*The Poetry of Browning: A Critical Introduction* [New York: Methuen, 1970]) and Hoxie Fairchild, who goes so far as to call it a 'giveaway', an irony-breaking moment that reveals Browning's real attitude towards his speaker ('Browning the Simple-Hearted', in Litzinger and Knickerbocker [eds], *The Browning Critics*, p. 222). On the 'ending' side, one can include, among others, R. G. Collins, Jonathan Loesberg and Philip Drew in 1975, who writes that he previously took the line to mean that Gigadibs 'had studied the Gospels to the very end', but that after all 'it might mean that Gigadibs had taken Blougram's advice and stopped bothering his head any more with the sort of theological puzzles posed by St. John'. Philip Drew, 'Browning and Philosophy', in Isobel Armstrong (ed.), *Robert Browning* (Athens: Ohio University Press, 1975), pp. 106–7.
17. See G. K. Chesterton, *Robert Browning* (London: Macmillan, 1903), ch. 8.
18. See Priestley, 'Blougram's Apologetics', pp. 139–47.
19. Margaret Faurot, '"Bishop Blougram's Apology": The Making of the Poet-Shepherd', *Victorian Poetry* 31.1 (1993), pp. 1–18 (p. 10). See

also Julia Markus, 'Bishop Blougram and the Literary Men', *Victorian Studies* 21.2 (1978), pp. 171–95.
20. Jonathan Loesberg, 'Browning Believing: "A Death in the Desert" and the Status of Belief', *Victorian Literature and Culture* 38 (2010), pp. 209–38 (p. 217). See also R. G. Collins, who argues that Priestley mistakes the end of the poem, which really shows Gigadibs deciding to make money. R. G. Collins, 'Browning's Practical Prelate: The Lesson of "Bishop Blougram's Apology"', *Victorian Poetry* 13.1 (1975), pp. 1–20.
21. Drew, *The Poetry of Browning*, p. 125.
22. Loesberg, 'Browning Believing', p. 234.
23. Joshua Taft, 'Scepticism and the Dramatic Monologue: Webster against Browning', *Victorian Poetry* 53.4 (2015), pp. 401–21 (p. 403).
24. Taft, 'Scepticism and the Dramatic Monologue', p. 406.
25. Augusta Webster, 'Poets and Personal Pronouns', in *Augusta Webster: Portraits and Other Poems*, ed. Christine Sutphin (Peterborough, ON: Broadview, 2000), p. 369.
26. Webster, 'Poets and Personal Pronouns', p. 367.
27. Augusta Webster, 'Pilate', in *Augusta Webster: Portraits and Other Poems*, ed. Sutphin, pp. 149–60 (ll. 10–13). Subsequent citations, abbreviated P, are given in parentheses in the text by line number.
28. See, for instance, H. J. McCloskey, 'A Non-Utilitarian Approach to Punishment', *Inquiry: An Interdisciplinary Journal of Philosophy* 8 (1965), pp. 249–63.
29. Mill, *Utilitarianism and Other Essays*, p. 333.
30. Terrance McConnell, in his entry on 'Moral Dilemmas' in *The Stanford Encyclopedia of Philosophy*, explains that admitting the possibility of such dilemmas undermines several bedrock assumptions about what ethical theories should do, for instance the belief that such theories should be 'action-guiding' (*The Stanford Encyclopedia of Philosophy*, ed. Edward N. Zalta, <http://plato.stanford.edu> [last accessed 18 December 2019]). And in two monographs, Lisa Tessman has developed significantly the claim that moral dilemmas are an intrinsic element of human moral experiences and thus inevitable; see Lisa Tessman, *Moral Failure: On the Impossible Demands of Morality* (Oxford: Oxford University Press, 2014) and *When Doing the Right Thing is Impossible* (Oxford: Oxford University Press, 2017).
31. Gary Saul Morson, 'Review of *Dostoevsky the Thinker*', *Notre Dame Philosophical Review*s 9 (2002), available at <http://ndpr.nd.edu/news/23116-dostoevsky-the-thinker> (last accessed 1 February 2014).
32. Lisa Tessman cites Bernard Williams's famous 1965 paper 'Ethical Consistency' as the source for contemporary considerations of moral remainder; see 'Ethical Consistency', *Proceedings of the Aristotelian Society* 39 (1965), pp. 103–38. A subsequent paper by Williams and a response from Thomas Nagel reinvigorated the analysis of moral luck and moral dilemmas a generation ago; see Bernard Williams, *Making Sense of Humanity* (Cambridge: Cambridge University Press, 1995), and

Thomas Nagel, *Mortal Questions* (Cambridge: Cambridge University Press, 1979).
33. Ruth Marcus, 'Moral Dilemmas and Consistency', *The Journal of Philosophy* 77.3 (1980), pp. 121–36.
34. There is a rich and increasing body of empirical literature on 'moral distress' in medical practitioners; see E. G. Epstein and S. Delgado, 'Understanding and Addressing Moral Distress', *OJIN: The Online Journal of Issues in Nursing* 15.3 (2010), DOI: 10.3912/OJIN.Vol15No03Man01.
35. For a discussion of this research, see Tessman, *Moral Failure*, ch. 2.
36. Augusta Webster, 'Medea in Athens', in *Augusta Webster: Portraits and Other Poems*, ed. Sutphin, pp. 169–78 (p. 178).
37. Tessman, *On the Impossible Demands of Morality*, p. 94.
38. Thomas Nagel, 'War and Massacre', *Philosophy and Public Affairs* 1.2 (1972), p. 132.
39. Amanda Anderson, *Tainted Souls and Painted Faces: The Rhetoric of Fallenness in Victorian Culture* (Ithaca: Cornell University Press, 1993), p. 18.
40. Augusta Webster, 'A Castaway', in *Augusta Webster: Portraits and Other Poems*, ed. Sutphin, pp. 192–213 (ll. 24–6). Subsequent citations, abbreviated C, are given in parentheses in the text by line number.
41. Indeed, Eulalie speculates, it may be that they only care about integrity because they envy and want to denigrate 'impure' women like her.
42. My reading here is in keeping with Christine Sutphin's. Sutphin writes: 'I think it would be wrong to conclude, as Susan Brown does, that Eulalie "accept[s her]self." Certainly, she says this and it may in part be accurate, but this statement is early in the monologue, and what emerges over its course is Eulalie's profound ambivalence.' Indeed: I am arguing that this ambivalence stems from a broader problem about the role that questions about integrity and character should play in deliberation. Christine Sutphin, 'Human Tigresses, Fractious Angels, and Nursery Saints: Augusta Webster's "A Castaway" and Victorian Discourses on Prostitution and Women's Sexuality', *Victorian Poetry* 38.4 (2000), pp. 511–32 (p. 520).
43. This is, of course, a tension duplicated in many analyses of prostitution, in the Victorian era and since. More broadly, the tension reflects two alternative views of what feminist analysis should look like, as either an acknowledgement of surprising forms of female agency or a recovery of the hidden victims of history. See Judith Walkowitz, *Prostitution and Victorian Society: Women, Class, and the State* (Cambridge: Cambridge University Press, 1982), for a discussion of Victorian prostitutes with an eye towards these issues.
44. As Anderson notes, the tendency in the rhetoric of fallenness is to regard the trajectory as irrevocable once it has begun. What is interesting about Eulalie's analysis is that the problem is not her nature per se, but the way her self-coherence is dependent on public attitudes, and thus a loss of reputation carries moral costs.

45. Plato, *The Republic*, trans. G. M. A. Grube, rev. C. D. C. Reeve (Indianapolis: Hackett, 1992), p. 5.
46. Augusta Webster, *In A Day* (London: Kegan et al., 1882), p. 55. Electronic copy made available via the Hathi Trust. Subsequent citations, abbreviated *ID*, are given in parentheses in the text.
47. Helen Vendler, *Poets Thinking: Pope, Whitman, Dickinson, Yeats* (Cambridge, MA: Harvard University Press, 2004), p. 10.
48. Vendler, *Poets Thinking*, p. 11.
49. Vendler, *Poets Thinking*, p. 6.
50. Vendler, *Poets Thinking*, p. 27.
51. Vendler, *Poets Thinking*, p. 27.
52. Vendler, *Poets Thinking*, p. 25.
53. Mary Karr, 'Against Decoration', in *Viper Rum* (New York: Penguin, 2001), pp. 49–72 (p. 50).
54. Karr, 'Against Decoration', p. 71.

Epilogue: Between Immersion and Critique – Thoughtful Reading

Let's take a step back. In the introduction, I sought to demonstrate some of the ways in which formalism has become instinctive in literary criticism, using several different genealogies. The first briefly surveyed some current thinkers, including Franco Moretti, Caroline Levine, Jonathan Kramnick and Anahid Nersessian, who assert that formalism is constitutive of literary study and a distillation of the best elements of its scholarly history. The second looked at how formalism had emerged as a contrast to methods based on reading for the content and ideas of literary texts, considering first a trajectory up to the New Criticism and Cleanth Brooks's diagnosis of the heresy of paraphrase and subsequently an arc away from it, one through Fredric Jameson and Jacques Derrida that maintained the suspicion of literary content. And the third looked at the scholarship that formed the 'ethical turn', which similarly refused to read for the moral thought in literature, preferring to emphasise the ethical effects of form. All the while, though, there has been a sort of normal science of literary criticism that largely refused the insistence on form and was willing to let its scholarship rest with attempts to bring authors into conversation with issues that the critics cared about. That school of criticism has never received the dignity of a formal title, and I concluded by suggesting that it deserved one. Moreover, I argued, the moral thought in Victorian narratives offered a useful example in this regard, since it is a literary tradition deeply concerned with communicating an important message, and subsequent traditions in moral philosophy offer useful resources for clarifying the ideas such authors had.

Chapter 1 then introduced one of the key claims of the book: that implicit claims about the relative value of different aesthetic experiences are the real basis for overt claims about interpretive method, even when those methods deny any form of aesthetic justification. As Kendall Walton's 'guernicas' thought experiment implies, this is in fact true of the form/content distinction itself: the very same element of a text can be thought of as either form or content depending on the background of the reader who encounters it. Uncovering further details of the presumed reader who can see forms instead of content, the idea of formalism as an attitude – as opposed to a particular school of thought or interpretive approach – emerged. Showing the contempt this attitude has for reading for the content, distilled particularly in the notion of the 'heresy of paraphrase', I turned to the analytic philosophy of literature. Even though this tradition contains its own deeply committed formalists, it respects the notion that reading for the message of a literary text is a thing that a reasonable reader might want to do, and thus can contribute to the elaboration of a method based on reading for the content. Defining literary content as everything in a text that could be captured by a paraphrase, the chapter moved to Richard Gaskin's notion of an 'ultimate' paraphrase, and argued that its criterion on maximal concision in a paraphrase reflected a formalist commitment that one need not accept. Paraphrases can be as multifarious as the contexts in which a literary text could speak, and an ultimate paraphrase is better thought of as an impossibly large set containing all those possibilities. Texts inspire such diverse paraphrases, the chapter concluded, via invitations to allegory, which ask readers to look beyond the specific events narrated in a story for broader and deeper connections.

Chapter 2 sought to illustrate a way of reading for the content that would follow the method elaborated over the course of Chapter 1. It sought to turn Anthony Trollope's use of the marriage plot and the romantic triangle, standard formal devices in a great deal of fiction, from forms into contents. It did so by connecting the events of the plot with a particular philosophical problem: akrasia, or weakness of the will. Often the problem in a Trollope novel is that the hero is akratic, and thus the events of the story allegorically turn into an analysis of the problem – what causes it, what consequences it has, and how one emerges from it. Trollope's works turned out to offer a sophisticated theory of the variants of irrationality, including self-deception, conscious akrasia and a peculiar but interesting state of rational akrasia, one that both existed in a productive tension with various theories in nineteenth-century moral thought and that speaks fruitfully to current debates in moral psychology.

Chapter 3 took up directly the problem that Chapter 2 had ended with, the issue of the use of ideas from contemporary thinkers in interpreting writing from the past. It elaborated its approach by tracing versions of the problem through a number of different debates in the humanities; initially the question of whether *Plan 9 from Outer Space* is in fact a revolutionary modernist film, then a debate about 'presentism' in Shakespeare studies, next Shoshana Felman's elaboration of the distinction between the implication and application of a theory in psychoanalysis, and finally a debate in the history of ideas in the wake of Quentin Skinner's work. Using in particular Richard Rorty's distinction between the rational and historical reconstruction of a text, whereby the latter limited itself to what a thinker could have recognised as her view while the former was willing to move both to the strongest possible version and to the version that spoke most interestingly to present debates, I suggested that a surprisingly important justification for the combination of the two interpretive moods was aesthetic – that rational and historical reconstruction showed the best way to enjoy a book with philosophical claims. Indeed, the call to rational reconstruction cannot be avoided, because it stems from the way readers encounter new ideas as possible truths. The chapter concluded by reviewing a group of interpretations of Walt Whitman, showing how readings that appear to disagree with each other are in fact varying rational reconstructions.

Chapter 4 then demonstrated the combination of historical and rational reconstruction that Chapter 3 defended. It opened by reconstituting the debates about the foundations of moral obligation in England in the 1870s, which saw three significantly different approaches to the problem – Sidgwick's utilitarian account, Darwin's evolutionary approach and the neo-Hegelian/Idealist treatment of F. H. Bradley and T. H. Green – in open disagreement with each other. I argued that George Eliot's thinking about the role of shame in moral development showed her engagement with these questions, and that the comparison between *Felix Holt* and *Daniel Deronda* in particular showed her thinking through the details of such an account. Eliot ultimately offered a view in which the experience of shame marked the first registration of an awareness of the importance of other people, since it was only via an acknowledgement and incorporation of the perspectives of others into the formation of one's reasons and goals that the kind of self-approval necessary for integrity could become possible. The chapter concluded by turning to Henleigh Grandcourt, who as an open egoist who nevertheless maintains a semblance of self-control represents a difficult challenge to Eliot's account. Noting how the presence of the character marked the philosophical development of Eliot's thought, I contended that various behavioural tics bore allegorical depth, as Eliot's suggestion of the kinds of failures no egoistic agent could ever eliminate.

Chapter 5 returned to the key question introduced in Chapter 1, namely, the problems with limiting the analysis of aesthetic experience to that offered by the formalist account. Rehearsing both Immanuel Kant's attempt to distinguish the disinterested pleasure of beauty from other forms of pleasure and recent critiques of this view, I argued that objections to Kant's view had done significant work in questioning the existence of this particular feeling, but had returned puzzlingly committed to formalist assumptions in regarding the aesthetic as a unified field. Turning to work on thick concepts in moral philosophy, which combine description and evaluation, the chapter argued that such concepts both promised to better capture the varieties of the experiences of art and offered a better response to the evaluative scepticism that lay behind and supported political critiques of the aesthetic. I then concluded that the gap between thick concepts in the evaluation of art versus those in moral philosophy in fact worked to the advantage of the artistic concepts, since they admitted of an openness that ethical concepts could not quite achieve.

Chapter 6, finally, gave concrete detail to these claims by comparing the analysis of morality in Robert Browning and Augusta Webster. Both authors are obviously interested in moral life and in the tension between moral claims and other factors in practical deliberation. But Browning's early dialogues explore this problem through a series of speakers who deliberately invite ironic treatment. Such a pose makes it difficult to tell how to regard an idea – whether it is a claim that Browning means to assert, or whether it is flawed in a way that reveals the character of the speaker, an interpretive tension vividly demonstrated by the arguments in 'Bishop Blougram's Apology'. Such difficulty ultimately suggests that Browning is not interested in using poetry to communicate, but instead in using ideas in the poem to create a different sort of artistic experience. Augusta Webster, in contrast, uses the speakers in her dramatic monologues to clarify the specific nature of the problem she is thinking about – offering Pontius Pilate to consider the tension between the goal of promoting maximum welfare and the concerns of justice, and a prostitute to consider the tension between the empty integrity of a privileged life and the necessary moral compromises that come with needing to make a living. The chapter concluded by contrasting Helen Vendler's continued scepticism of paraphrase with Mary Karr's recommendation that contemporary poetry end its investment in mere 'decoration'.

I hope thus to have theorised and demonstrated a new form of criticism. It challenges many of the basic assumptions of current methods, but is itself responsive to and is indeed primarily a self-conscious iteration of long-standing practices in the field. My theorisation, defence and demonstration has mixed a variety of argumentative strategies, sometimes challenging theoretical premises outright, sometimes showing how the intuitions that motivate a practice can be redeployed in an alternative, and sometimes comparing existing practices and pulling out principles from them. Whether that defence has been successful is obviously not for me to say, but I very much hope that this is not the end of the conversation. I would hope for a new rise in scholarship, carried out by readers who are experts in various other disciplines and intellectual formations, helping to connect us to the ideas in literature and thus bring new texts into our lives. Moreover, I would hope for a broader study of thick concepts in aesthetics; Frank Sibley apparently kept long lists of such concepts, adding new ones whenever he encountered them, and I would hope that literary critics could continue that pattern, enhancing our understanding of the reasons for reading literature via a mixture of anthropology, philosophy and criticism. But those are as yet merely hopes.

What remains then is to say just a bit more about the peculiar kind of reading practice I have described and attempted to carry out. It is based on a series of compromises. It emphasises overt statements in literature but uses them to draw out ideas that are allegorically suggested. It admits the importance of historical reconstruction and the threat of arbitrary connections, but insists on the need for rational reconstruction as a response to the allegorical impulse. And it identifies the 'profound' as a term for the peculiar experience of reading a book that makes genuine claims about an important problem, but where one may not be persuaded that the claims are entirely true. The gap between 'possibly true' and 'actually true' is central to the excitement and interest constitutive of the encounter with a profound idea; it evokes thinking, something not quite agreement and not quite disagreement.

The best term I have for this kind of reading is that it is thoughtful. If immersion in a text involves being caught up in the excitement it can offer, while 'critique' names a reading practice that involves standing back and defamiliarising the experience of a book, thoughtfulness sits in between the two. It is very similar to the kind of reading that Cristina Bruns has described, which hinges on the 'interdependence of the immersive and reflective or distancing modes of literary reading'.[1] It does move regularly to the allegorical level, asking not merely what is happening in a book but what it means; however, it does so when invited to by the text, thinking of the ideas in the text as another one of the experiences it creates and not as an uncovering of something it denies or hides. And it does not deny the historical origins of a text, but acknowledges them in a way that enhances instead of marginalising its intellectual content.

One could say more about this set of distinctions, and try to parse the combination of closeness to and distance from the text involved in reading thoughtfully. And it would be worthwhile to work through the various meanings of the word 'thoughtful', and its particular combination of affective and intellectual response, and consider the possibilities for thoughtful reading more generally. But what I hope to have accomplished here is to demonstrate that some texts in particular call for and reward it. Certainly for me, a substantive part of what it means to engage with a text such as *Middlemarch* is to think about the ideas it offers. This book stems, in the last analysis, from a desire to do justice to that feeling.

Note

1. Cristina Bruns, *Why Literature? The Value of Literary Reading and What It Means for Teaching* (New York: Continuum, 2011), p. 66.

Index

References to notes are indicated by n.

Adler, Mortimer, 126
aestheticism, 4–13, 15, 26–7, 41, 174–6
  and conflict, 194–7
  and evaluation, 184–7
  and Kant, 176–80
  and philosophy, 55, 57, 58
  and scepticism, 180–4
  and thick concepts, 187–94, 197–8
Agamben, Giorgio, 50
agreeability, 176–8
akrasia, 76–8, 80–9, 121, 126, 233
  conscious, 89–94
  rational, 95–100
Albright, Daniel, 41
allegory, 65–8, 128–9
Altieri, Charles, 48
American literature, 19–20
anachronism, 110–12, 113–14, 117–25, 129, 133
Anderson, Amanda, 25, 79–80, 215
animals, 148, 150, 151
anti-cognitivism, 5, 6–10, 15
apRoberts, Ruth, *The Moral Trollope*, 78–9, 80
Arac, Jonathan, 116
Aravamudan, Srinivas, 'The Return of Anachronism', 129
Aristotle, 13, 24, 101, 124, 209, 185
Armstrong, Isobel, 175, 177, 179–80, 205, 209
Arnold, Matthew, 18–19
  'Dover Beach', 61–2, 63
Arpaly, Nomy, 102, 103
  'On Acting Rationally Against One's Best Judgement', 95–6
Arsić, Branka, 50
art, 23–5, 41, 42–3, 54–5, 181–2
Attridge, Derek, 48, 49, 70n28–9

Austen, Jane, *Pride and Prejudice*, 2, 22, 55–6, 66, 70n15
Austin, J. L., 120

Bacon, Francis, 110–11
Balzac, Honoré de, 19
Barthes, Roland, 10, 65
Beardsley, Monroe, 54, 55
beauty, 24–5, 176–8, 235
Bell-Viada, Gene, 10
Bellis, Peter, 130
Bennett, Jane, 'The Solar Judgement of Walt Whitman', 131–2
Bennett, Tony, 182, 195
Bentham, Jeremy, 81, 104n16
Bergson, Henri, 19
Best, Stephen, 26–7, 28, 38n125
Bevir, Mark, 121, 124
Bildungsroman, 142
Blake, William, 20, 21
Boas, George, 19
Booth, Wayne, 15, 16–17, 197
  The Company We Keep, 34n66, 202
Bradley, A. C., 51–2, 53, 174
Bradley, F. H., 234
  Ethical Studies, 142, 147–8
Brooks, Cleanth, 51–2, 53, 174, 232
  Understanding Fiction, 8–9
  The Well-Wrought Urn, 8, 18, 19
Browning, Robert, 203–9, 210, 227
  'Bishop Blougram's Apology', 204, 205–9, 235
  'My Last Duchess', 203, 204, 205, 208
Bruns, Cristina, 236

Caird, Edward, 147
capitalism, 18–19
Carlyle, Thomas, 148
Carroll, Lewis, 122, 125

Carroll, Noël, 53–4, 55, 56–7, 108, 174
  and aesthetics, 178, 180
  Philosophy of Art: A Contemporary Introduction, 41
Catholicism, 191
Cavell, Stanley, 14, 34n66
character, 6, 7, 72n44, 203–4
Charnes, Linda, 109
Chesterton, G. K., 208
Christianity, 191, 206–8, 211–13
Christie, Agatha, 43
Church, Margaret, 'Thomas Wolfe Dark Time', 19, 20
Cicero, 87
cities, 20, 21
Clifford, William, 'Right and Wrong: The Scientific Ground of Their Distinction', 148
close reading, 11
clues, 43, 44
Clune, Michael, 24
  'Formalism as the Fear of Ideas', 37n111, 173
coduction, 15
Cohen, Stephen, 112
Coleridge, Samuel Taylor, 18–19
Collins, K. K., 149, 150, 151
Columbus, Christopher, 123, 124
Conan Doyle, Arthur, 43
conflict, 194–6
Conrad, Joseph, 116
consciousness, 13
content, 2–3, 28–9, 233
  and definition, 39–40
  and Eliot, 68
  and intellectual, 4–5, 9
  and paraphrase, 63–4
  and philosophy, 57–8, 59–60
  and poetry, 51–2, 61–3
  and reading, 18–25
  and surface reading, 25–9
  and works, 40–6
Crash (film), 17
Culler, Jonathan, 54
culture, 185–6, 193
cuteness, 193–4

Dames, Nicholas, 72n49
Danto, Arthur, 53, 54
Darwin, Charles, 150, 151, 234
  The Descent of Man, 142, 143, 148–9
Davidson, Donald, 81, 82–3, 91
De Grazia, Margreta, 109
De Man, Paul, 10, 54, 65, 189
deception *see* self-deception

deconstruction, 27–8, 56, 205, 226
Defoe, Daniel, 120
Deleuze, Gilles, 50
Deresiewicz, William, 48
Derrida, Jacques, 10, 11, 13, 14, 232
Descartes, René, *Meditations*, 190–1
desire, 90, 91, 148–9
detective fiction, 43, 44, 48
Dewey, John, 177, 179, 180
Dickens, Charles, 188
  Oliver Twist, 24
Dickie, George, 54
didacticism, 5–6
Diggins, John Patrick, 127
dignity, 18–19
Dimock, Wai Chee, 109, 130
disinterest, 176, 177, 178–9, 235
Dollimore, Jonathan, *Radical Tragedy*, 110–11
Dostoevsky, Fyodor, *Crime and Punishment*, 35n79
dramatic monologues, 203, 204, 205, 210–11
Drew, Philip, 208, 228n16
Dualism of practical reason, 142, 143–8

Eagleton, Terry, 54, 63, 182
egoism, 142, 143–8, 234
  and Eliot, 151–5, 157–8, 163, 166
Eliot, George, 9, 142–3, 168–9
  Adam Bede, 14
  Daniel Deronda, 4, 5–6, 143, 157–68, 234
  and egoism, 151–2
  Felix Holt, 143, 152–7, 159–60, 161–3, 234
  and Lewes, 149–51
  Middlemarch, 66, 67–8, 113, 237
  and morality, 147–8
  and the profound, 186
  Romola, 165–6
  Scenes of Clerical Life, 141–2
  and virtue, 140
Eliot, T. S., 31n23
elucidation, 56–7, 64
Empson, William, 65
enjoyment, 48–9
Eskin, Michael, 13–14
ethics, 13–18, 21–2, 25, 47, 232
  and Sidgwick, 141, 142, 143–5
  and thick concepts, 198
  and Trollope, 78–82, 121
  and virtue, 185–6
  see also morality

Euripides, *Hippolytus*, 62
evaluation, 181–7
evolution, 142, 143, 148–9, 234
explication, 68

fan fiction, 70n15
Felman, Shoshana, 114, 234
  'Turning the Screw of Interpretation', 115, 116–18
Felski, Rita, 12–13, 56, 180
  The Limits of Critique, 28, 114, 116, 201n49
feminism, 55–6
fiction, 43–4, 48, 70n15
Fish, Stanley, 46, 54, 56
Fleishman, Avrom, *George Eliot's Intellectual Life*, 9
Fletcher, Angus, 65
Flint, Kate, 97
Foley, Barbara, 50
form, 40–6
  and definition, 39–40
  and Eliot, 68
  and history, 112–14
  see also formalism
formalism, 1–2, 3–4, 9–10, 17–18, 173–6, 232–3
  and aesthetics, 180–4
  and attitude, 46–53
  and content, 26–7, 28–9
  and origins, 23
  and pluralism, 176–80
Forster, E. M., *Aspects of the Novel*, 31n23
Foucault, Michel, 14, 22, 56
Frege, Gottlob, 53, 59
friendship, 15, 16
Frost, Robert, 'Desert Places', 45, 46
Fulmer, Constance, 25
funny *see* humour

Gadamer, Hans-Georg, 128–9
Gajowski, Evelyn, 109, 110
Gallagher, Catherine, 112–13
Gallop, Jane, 10–11
Garber, Marjorie, 109
  The Use and Abuse of Literature, 48
Gaskin, Richard, 56–7, 67, 233
  Language, Truth, and Literature, 54, 59–60, 62, 190
Geertz, Clifford, 185–6
generalisation, 66–8
Genette, Gerard, 10, 178, 192, 195–6

genre fiction, 43–4
gentlemen, 101–2
Gibson, John, 47
Gissing, George
  Demos, 114
  The Nether World, 113
Glendinning, Victoria, 76
Goldman, Alan, *Philosophy and the Novel*, 55–6
Goodlad, Lauren, 132
Grady, Hugh, 109–10, 111
Greek literature, 13
Green, T. H., 147, 234
Greenberg, Clement, 53
Grice, Paul, 57
guernicas, 42–3, 44, 232–3
Guillory, John, *Cultural Capital*, 180–1, 183–5

Haines, Simon, 16
Hale, Dorothy, 7
Hampshire, Stuart, 187
happiness, 144–5
Hardy, Thomas, *Tess of the D'Urbervilles*, 65
Hartman, Geoffrey, 2
Hawkes, Terence, 109–10, 111
Hayward, Abraham, 197
Hegel, G. W. F., 22, 119
Hegelian thread, 13–14
Hensely, Nathan, 47
heresy of paraphrase, 19
Herrnstein-Smith, Barbara, 181, 182–3, 184, 186, 194, 196, 198
high realism, 4
Hinchman, Ted, 99
Hirsch, E. D., 'Transhistorical Intentions and Persistence of Allegory', 128
history, 109, 111–14, 126–9, 132–3
  and ideas, 118–26, 129–32
Holbo, John, 111
Hollander, Rachel, *Narrative Hospitality in Late Victorian Fiction*, 21–2
Horace, 67
Hull, David, 122
humour, 187, 188–9, 191, 192, 194, 195, 197

Idealism, 142, 147, 148, 154
ideas, 4, 5, 6–7, 8–9, 173–4
  and Browning, 203–9
  and history, 118–26, 129–32
  and poetry, 225–6

illusion, 192
imagination, 23–4
interestingness, 193–4
internalism, 91–2, 105n23
interpretation, 56–7, 110, 115–18
  and humour, 188–9
  and truth, 127–8
inventiveness, 48
irony, 28

James, Henry, 7, 8, 17, 24–5, 31n23, 47
  The Art of Fiction, 6
  'Daniel Deronda: A Conversation', 5–6
  The Turn of the Screw, 115–17
Jameson, Fredric, 133, 116, 232
  The Political Unconscious, 12–13, 112–14
Johnson, Gary, *The Vitality of Allegory*, 65
Jones, Karen, 100, 103
Jones, Sir Henry, *Browning as a Philosophical and Religious Teacher*, 204–5
Judaism, 162–3
judgement, 83, 90–1; *see also* rationality
Juvenal, 60

Kafka, Franz
  'Before the Law', 11, 13
  Metamorphosis, 65
  The Trial, 63
Kant, Immanuel, 148, 235
  Critique of Judgement, 175–80
Karr, Mary, 235
  'Against Decoration', 226–7
Kastan, David, *Shakespeare After Theory*, 111–12
Kateb, George, 130
Keats, John, 52, 59
Kincaid, James, 79, 80, 101
Kipling, Rudyard, 4
Kivy, Peter, 51, 174
Korsgaard, Christine, 141, 166, 167–8, 169
  Self-Constitution, 145–7
Kramnick, Jonathan, 2, 232

Lamarque, Peter, 65, 67
  Truth, Fiction, and Literature, 52–4, 58, 62, 63–4
Lamb, Robert, 121
Landy, Joshua, *How to Do Things With Fiction*, 17, 18
language, 53, 54

Latour, Bruno, 27
Lauritzen, Paul, 130
Leavis, F. R., 4, 162–3
Lee, Wendy Anne, 50
Leighton, Angela, 41
Levine, Caroline, 47, 232
  Forms, 1–2, 173
Levine, George, 25
Levinson, Marjorie, 2, 46, 59
  'What is New Formalism?', 30n4, 30n6, 37n120, 70n20
Lewes, George Henry, *The Problems of Life and Mind*, 143, 149–50, 151, 171n32
literary criticism, 1–2, 3–4, 173–4, 232
  and ethics, 13–18
  and philosophy, 54–6
  and Victorian studies, 132, 138n91
  see also New Criticism; post-structuralist criticism; structuralist criticism
literature, 19–20, 52–63, 173–4; *see also* fiction
Locke, John, 119, 209
Loesberg, Jonathan, 208, 209
Lopez, Jennifer, 17
Love, Heather, 24
Lovejoy, Arthur, 118
Lubbock, Percy, *The Craft of Fiction*, 7
Lupton, Julia, 191

McAdoo, Nick, 187
McAlindon, Tom, 110
McCarthy, Mary, 4
McGann, Jerome, 59
McKeon, Michael, 112–13
McMaster, Juliet, 99
Maioli, Roger, 24
Mander, William, 147
Marcus, Ruth, 213
Marcus, Sharon, 26–7, 28, 38n125
marriage, 55–6
  and Eliot, 163–4
  and Trollope, 76, 77–8, 96–100, 102, 103n1, 233
Martinich, Aloysius, 125
Marx, Karl, 118, 121
meaning-mongers, 17, 18
Mele, Alfred, 83–4, 85, 90
Melville, Herman, 'Bartleby, the Scrivener', 50
Mencken, H. L., 19–20
Meredith, George, 6
Mikkonen, Jukka, 64, 67

Mill, John Stuart, 81, 104n16, 212
  Utilitarianism, 140–1
Miller, Andrew, 25
Miller, D. A., 113, 114
Miller, J. Hillis, 10
  The Ethics of Reading, 14
Milton, John, 'Samson Agonistes', 191
mimesis, 65, 66
Minogue, Kenneth, 124
minority groups, 180–1
modernism, 23, 25
Moi, Toril, 23, 48, 56, 189
  Character, 72n44
moral philosophy, 13–18, 76–82
  and culture, 185–6
  and thick concepts, 192–3
  and Trollope, 101–2
  and Webster, 211–13
morality, 4–5, 25, 78–82, 92–3, 232
  and Browning, 206–8
  and Darwin, 148–9
  and dilemmas, 229n30
  and Eliot, 140–3, 147–8, 150–1, 155–6, 158–62, 163–5
  and Lewes, 149–50
  and Webster, 211–25
Moran, Richard, 89, 106n36
Moretti, Franco, 43, 44, 232
  Distant Reading, 1, 2
Morris, William, 18–19
Murdoch, Iris, 34n66
mystery novels, 43, 44
mythology, 43–4

Nagel, Thomas, 67, 214–15
narrative, 4, 5, 10–11
  and Browning, 203–4
  and mystery novels, 43
Nehamas, Alexander, 177, 179, 189
Nersessian, Anahid, 2, 232
New Criticism, 5, 7–11, 18, 19, 232
Newman, John, 206
Newton, Adam Zachary, 15–16
Ngai, Sianne, 176, 178–9, 193–4, 197, 198
non-humans, 20, 21
normativity, 140–1, 148–9, 168–9
North, Joe, 113, 132, 177
novels of ideas, 4
Nussbaum, Martha, 13, 16–17, 47, 169
  and Aristotle, 185
  and Dames, 72n49
  and goodness, 213
  and morality, 164
  and Whitman, 130, 131–2, 138n88

Olsen, Stein Haugom, 65, 67
  Truth, Fiction, and Literature, 52–4, 58, 62, 63–4
Olympia (Manet), 179
Orlemanski, Julie, 18, 173
Oxford Dictionary of Literary Terms, 39–40, 41

panaesthetics, 41
paraphrase, 19, 49, 51–2, 63–4, 174
  and Browning, 205
  and explication, 68
  and formalism, 232, 233
  and philosophy, 53–63
  and poetry, 225
  and Trollope, 102–3
Parfit, Derek, 143
Parker, David, 16
patterns, 42–5, 68
pedagogy, 22
Phelan, James, 66
philosophy, 6, 13–18, 26, 50–1, 52–3, 125–6, 233
  and art, 174, 175
  and Browning, 204–5, 206
  and Descartes, 190–1
  and Eliot, 147
  and generalisation, 66–7
  and literature, 53–63
  and Webster, 211–12
  see also moral philosophy
Picasso, Pablo, *Guernica*, 42–3
Pigou, A. C., *Robert Browning as a Religious Teacher*, 204–5
Plan 9 from Outer Space (film), 108–9, 234
Plato, 24, 118, 119, 124, 167
  Protagoras, 76–7
  The Republic, 219
pleasure, 48–9, 200n36
  and disinterested, 176, 177, 178–9, 235
pluralism, 176–81
PMLA, 19, 20–1
Pocock, J. G. A., 118
poetry, 8, 9, 24, 225–7
  and aesthetics, 197
  and paraphrase, 19, 49, 51–2, 60–3
  and rhyme, 45–6
  and Romanticism, 58–9
  and truth, 190
  and Whitman, 130–1
  see also Browning, Robert; Webster, Augusta

politics, 21–2, 47, 130
   and the aesthetic, 175
   and Arnold, 62
   and Eliot, 154–5, 156
   and *Hamlet*, 64
   and history, 118, 121
   and philosophy, 55
   and pluralism, 180–2
Pope, Alexander, *An Essay on Man*, 225, 226
post-structuralist criticism, 9, 10–11, 14
presentism, 108–14, 121, 124, 125, 127–8, 234
Price, Leah, *The Anthology and the Rise of the Novel*, 4
Priestley, F. E. L., 206, 208
profound, the, 186, 189–91, 197, 236
prostitution, 215–20, 230n42–4
Protestantism, 191
Proust, Marcel, 19
psychoanalysis, 115–16, 117–18, 135n41, 234
psychology, 9

Raff, Sarah, 66
Ranciére, Jacques, 50
Rand, Ayn, 2–3
rationality, 95–102, 123–4, 125, 234, 144–6
Rawls, John, 162
realism, 14, 27; *see also* high realism; social realism
relativism, 183–4
religion, 61–2, 162–3, 191
   and Browning, 204–5, 206–8
   and Webster, 211–13
rhyme, 45–6
Richards, I. A., 4, 177
Riffaterre, Michael, 65
Romanticism, 58–9
Rooney, Ellen, 28, 49
Rorty, Amelie, 76–7
Rorty, Richard, 13–14
   and history, 120, 122–4, 125, 126, 129, 133
   and rational reconstruction, 131, 132, 234
Rosenthal, Jesse, 25
Routledge Dictionary of Literary Terms, 39
Ruskin, John, 36n104–5
   Modern Painters, 23–4
Ruttenberg, Nancy, 50
Ryle, Gilbert, 185

sanity, 115–16
Sartori, Andrew, 132
Sartre, Jean-Paul, 106n36
scepticism, 176, 180–4, 194
Schelling, Friedrich, 206
Schilling, Bernard, *Human Dignity and the Great Victorians*, 18–19, 20
Schneewind, Jerome, 81, 143–4
science, 13
Searle, John, 66
Sedgwick, Eve, 45
   The Epistemology of the Closet, 12
self-control, 90
self-deception, 82–9, 91–2, 101
sensitivity, 47–8
Shakespeare, William, 109, 110, 111–12, 234
   Hamlet, 3, 56–7, 64
shame, 142, 234
   and Eliot, 152–4, 155, 156, 158, 159–62, 163–5, 167
Sibley, Frank, 186–7, 188–9, 195–6, 236
Sidgwick, Henry, 87–8, 90, 234
   The Methods of Ethics, 141, 142, 143–5
Simcox, Edith, 147
Sinclair, Upton, 3
Sinfield, Alan, 205
singularity, 48
Skinner, Quentin, 234
   'Meaning and Understanding in the History of Ideas', 118–21, 122–3, 124, 126–8, 132–3
slavery, 220–4
social realism, 65
society, 47, 148–9, 150, 193
Sontag, Susan, 189
Spenser, Edmund, 191
   The Faerie Queene, 66
Stevenson, Robert Louis, 4
Strauss, David, 206
structuralist criticism, 9, 10
surface reading, 25–9
Sussman, Matthew, 197
Suttie, Paul, 66
syllepsis, 188
sympathy, 148–9, 154, 155–7, 162–3, 165–7
symptomatic reading, 12–13, 27–8

Taft, Joshua, 210
Taylor, Charles, 13, 126–7

Thackeray, William Makepeace, *Vanity Fair*, 197
theology, 61–2
thick concepts, 185–6, 187–94, 195–8, 235, 236
thin concepts, 185–6
Thomason, Krista, 142, 153, 155, 159–60, 169
time, 19
and travel, 24, 173
Todorov, Tzvetan, 'Structural Analysis of Narrative', 10
Tolkien, J. R. R., 43–4
Trollope, Anthony, 7, 27, 102–3, 126
Can You Forgive Her?, 91–4, 96–100, 102
The Duke's Children, 84–8
The Eustace Diamonds, 77–8, 128
Framley Parsonage, 94
and judgement, 95
and marriage plot, 76, 233
and morality, 78–82, 101–2, 121
Phineas Finn, 88–91
Phineas Redux, 89
truth, 24–5, 54, 58, 190, 236
Tucker, Herbert, 205, 209
Twain, Mark, *Huckleberry Finn*, 15
tyranny, 167

utilitarianism, 80–1, 140–2, 147, 211–12, 234

value, 184–7
Velleman, David, 146, 147, 152
Vendler, Helen, 235
Poets Thinking, 225–7
Victorian studies, 132, 138n91
Viereck, Peter, 'My Kind of Poetry', 19, 20, 35n87
virtue, 140, 185–6

Wainwright, Valerie, 25

Wallace, David Foster, 24
Walton, Kendall, 53–4, 232–3
'Categories of Art', 42, 43, 44, 46
Warren, Austin, *Theory of Literature*, 9
Warren, Robert Penn, *Understanding Fiction*, 8–9
weakness of will *see* akrasia
Webster, Augusta, 204, 210–25, 227, 235
'A Castaway', 215–20, 224, 230n42–4
In A Day Set, 220–4
'Medea in Athens', 214–15
'Pilate', 211–13, 215
'Poets and Personal Pronouns', 210
Wellek, René, *Theory of Literature*, 9
Wells, H. G., 24, 173
Wells, Robin Headlam, 110
Whitman, Walt, 129–32, 234
Wiggins, David, 'A Sensible Subjectivism', 187, 188
Wilde, Oscar, 4–5, 193
The Importance of Being Earnest, 188, 195
Williams, Bernard, 186, 193, 207
Williams, Gordon, 49
Williams, Raymond, 181–2
Wilson, Edmund, 'The Ambiguity of Henry James', 115, 116, 117
Wimsatt, William, 54
Wittgenstein, Ludwig, 64
Wolfe, Thomas, 19
Wolfson, Susan, 2
Formal Changes: The Shaping of Poetry in British Romanticism, 58–9
'Reading for Form', 47
women *see* feminism; marriage
Woolf, Virginia, 6–7, 10

Zangwill, Nick, 174
zaniness, 193–4
zeugma, 188
Zola, Émile, 19
Les Rougon-Macquart, 65

EU representative:
Easy Access System Europe
Mustamäe tee 50, 10621 Tallinn, Estonia
Gpsr.requests@easproject.com